ALIEN M

UFO CRASHES—ABDUCTIONS —UNDERGROUND BASES

William F. Hamilton III

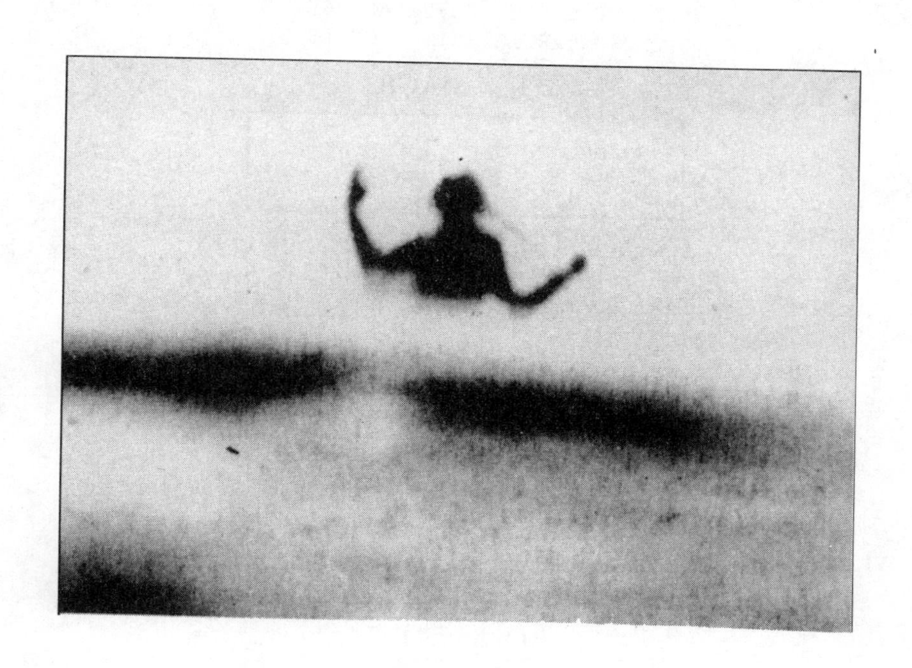

Global Communications

FRONT & BACK COVER ART BY
TUCSON ARTIST JIM NICHOLS

ALIEN MAGIC

**Dedicated to my loving wife,
Pamela, a brave woman**

Composition and Layout:
Cross-Country Consultants
P.O. Box 4127
Scottsdale, AZ 85261

For foreign and reprint rights, contact:
Rights Department
Global Communication
Box 753
New Brunswick, NJ 08903

Contents

William F. Hamilton III

PROLOGUE

I have been on an alien quest for 40 years. It has been an adventure. It has been frustrating. There have been more questions than answers. It has been a search for truth. Do other intelligent life forms exist in the universe?

Is the human the crown of creation or the pinnacle of evolutionary development in the universe?

Gazing at the night sky fills us with awe and wonder. Billions of stars form a tapestry of glowing jewels against the mysterious blackness of space. Are there others out there looking back at us?

Life took billions of years to rise from a single cell to a complex human organism. The seas and clays of earth contained the right chemical mixture. Cooked in the right proportions, the chemicals link together to eventually form a self-replicating multi-celled organism. Or so it would seem. Are we convinced that complex organisms arose from chance collisions and accidental molecular combinations?

In the Western World, we are taught that God created Man in his/her image and likeness and gave Man dominion over the Earth and all of its creatures. We have grown accustomed to our dominion. We have come to believe in our own special position in nature. What if we aren't so special, neither the crest of creation or at the top of the evolutionary ladder? Have we grown too smug to look at new evidence?

Since 1947 the world has become aware of a world-wide phenomena that refuses to go away. UFOs have been seen in the skies and on the ground all over the world for decades and have been studied by researchers from all walks of life. Those who make an open-minded study of the subject conclude that it is real, that it is physical, and that it is tremendously important.

In the fifties, certain individuals came forward to make unbelievable claims of contact with extraterrestrial visitors. Several reported meeting advanced humans from the flying disks or being taken for rides out of the atmosphere. These claims were never taken very seriously and researchers pronounced such claims as hoaxes perpetrated by charlatans who wanted to take advantage of the public's ignorance and fascination in order to make a fast buck. This is not necessarily the truth behind contactees, but it has become a widely held belief.

In the sixties and seventies, the alien abduction scenario started to emerge and researchers only took slight notice of this new unfolding drama. With the publication of *Interrupted Journey*, the capture of Betty and Barney Hill by humanoids from an unidentified craft, and their subsequent examination and loss of time, other such events began to surface. The striking similarities in separate reports appealed to the scientific researcher and challenged our attempts to explain the growing UFO phenomena that was beginning to affect people's lives in a more direct and personal way.

In the seventies and eighties, information began to emerge that our government, as suspected earlier by Donald Keyhoe, was hiding its secret studies of the UFO and Alien Life Form phenomena. The early reports that the flying disks had crashed in the Southwest deserts and that the evidence was retrieved by special military recovery teams was leaked from a number of sources and added new dimensions to the flying saucer puzzle.

In the ninties, we seem to be on the threshold of a breakthrough in our quest, yet the mystery remains, the puzzle has become as complex as ever, and we all yearn to know the truth behind the greatest secret in the world.

The aliens have shown an increasing interest in our reproductive biology. They have been reported to have taken sperm and ova to produce cross-breeds. Are they trying to develop new forms of life? For what purpose? The aliens have harvested fluids from humans and animals. How and why do they want the blood from cows and other animals?

Perhaps the aliens have been conducting their harvest for many millenia and their past efforts have brought about the genesis of modern humans. Of course all of this is hypothetical without some solid facts to support our case. Such facts are fewer than we would like.

The aliens have come into the bedrooms of America. They do not open doors to enter. They, seemingly, pass through solid material barriers, through walls, windows, and closed doors. Sometimes they just seem to materialize. Such stunts appear to us to be magic. Do the aliens use magic? Perhaps their technology looks like magic to us.

Through these pages I will review my experiences and those of others as I have pursued the elusive aliens through the decades in search of answers. I have gone through many phases and have learned a great deal about alien contacts, abductions, technologies, mathematical patterns, secret operations, and related mysteries. Hopefully, I will have lit another light in the darkness.

The Aliens use advanced technology, a technology that appears to us as television, airplanes, or computers would appear to a denizen of the seventeenth century. This technology is so advanced in some cases that its effects look like magic. I cannot rule out that aliens may be using mental magic. And with magic comes mystery. Perhaps we can begin to penetrate the fog surrounding this mystery.

CHAPTER ONE
CALIFORNIA CONTACTEES

"The Flying Saucers we see are
very likely scouting craft sent
from mother ships moored in orbit."

--T.B. Pawlicki

Some say it is the California sun or the Santa Ana winds that created the weird culture of the west coast. The inhabitants think differently. Westerners are open to new ideas. Visitors from another planet are welcome in California.

I was enthralled as a teenager to read the story of George Adamski who rode out to Desert Center, California on November 20, 1952 to meet a visitor from the planet Venus, an event attested to by six witnesses who signed a notarized statement.

In 1956, I met Daniel W. Fry who had started an organization called UNDERSTANDING. I was elected vice-president of unit 1 in El Monte. Dan Fry claimed he was taken for a ride in a flying disc at White Sands Proving Grounds in New Mexico on July 4, 1950. He documented his story in a book called, THE WHITE SANDS INCIDENT. Dan was a brilliant man. He sounded truthful. He was fond of telling how aliens broke dozens of laws just entering our atmosphere and landing their craft on earth.

Dan claimed he had taken a ride in a most unusual vehicle that he was invited to board at White Sands Proving Grounds in New Mexico on July 4, 1950. He was waiting in a small depot for a bus to town in unbearable summer heat when he decided to take a walk in the desert. During his walk he noticed that three or four stars blinked out. He quickly surmised that something dark obscured the stars and was growing in size implying an object headed on a straight-on trajectory. The object came in for a soundless soft landing on the sand. Dan noticed that it had the shape of a oblate spheroid. He had not seen any evidence of external propulsion. He thought it the strangest aircraft he had ever seen. He went close to touch the hull of the grounded craft when he was surprised by a voice thundering out in plain English idiom, "Don't touch the hull, pal, its hot!" The voice identified itself as A-Lan communicating to him from a mother ship in orbit through a speaker housed in the remotely-piloted vehicle before him. On a later meeting with A-Lan, Dan describes him as human, as a being born in space aboard an artificial planet that roamed the galaxy. A-Lan revealed that his ancestors once lived on Earth and had traveled to Mars. A-Lan informed Dan that they had been observing our society and that our lives were out-of-balance. Our material development had far outstripped our social and spiritual development, and that if we were to continue on such a course, it would lead to disaster. A-Lan emphasized that to achieve peace on Earth, we would have to promote Understanding among all the peoples of Earth.

Biologists believe that human life is a product of the long evolutionary processes that are unique to Earth. They consider it extremely unlikely that we would someday encounter human forms from another planet. This popular view has prevailed to the degree that most scientists reject the stories of the contactees. They also point out that other planets in our own solar system do not have atmospheres conducive to human life as we know it. Venus has a hot-house atmosphere and it bears down on the Venusian surface at a pressure 90 times greater than earth's atmosphere at sea level.

As a teenager I was excited by the prospect of making contact with the visitors or, at the very least, catching a glimpse of their ships over these remote desert regions. This was not a formal investigation of contactees. I had very few doubts then. I felt that the contactees were not concocting stories. Little did I know that an era was passing, that a future day would come when UFO researchers and investigators would dismiss and debunk contactees as frauds who possessed motives of greed and a need for attention and adulation. Little did I know that the contactee of the future would report a different kind of experience, that of menacing abductions and examinations conducted by humanoid, but non-human entities. Little did I know that the future would bring greater mystification rather than enlightenment.

A contactee by the name of George Hunt "Rick" Williamson had written a book in which he had detailed his experiments in telepathic and radio communication with the saucer pilots. He had started these experiments using a board with letters and numbers drawn out and using a glass tumbler as a "planchette" to allow the communicating intelligence to direct his hand to the correct symbols and spell out a message. Like the Ouija Board, others had reported success in using this device as a means of communication. Later, Rick met Lyman Streeter, a radio operator for the Santa Fe Railroad. The board had instructed his party to attempt to use radio. Often they would broadcast a message on one frequency and receive an answer in Morris Code on another frequency.

I decided I was going to try an experiment of my own.
I had made friends with a school chum, a French-Canadian, by the name of Yves Lauriault. Yves and I started a regular routine of skywatching and conducting experiments with ESP. During one of these experiments I remember hearing my name being called out, yet Yves had not spoken. On another night we heard a strange tone permeating the room, but coming from outside. Upon rushing outside to look at the sky, we saw nothing, but the strange humming sound continued.

One night in May, 1957 our experiments paid off. We were laying on the grass outside of Yves' house in Alhambra when a small disk, glowing red, traversed soundlessly overhead on a course from south to north. Yves initiated a telepathic request, hoping to communicate with the minds behind this disk when the disk maneuvered as he requested. We were under the impression that the disk was a small probe sent down to monitor our experimental activities. The instant the disk responded to our telepathic request, I had a sudden feeling that we were dealing with something unearthly. Even if I could explain this object as an unusually lighted aircraft, I could not explain its response to our silent communication. The first disk was followed by others. At one time, two flew in tandem and executed telepathically requested maneuvers. One of the maneuvers included the disk stopping its forward motion and retracing its flight path, a manuever impossible for an airplane. From that day on and for a period of three years, I had frequent sightings and the UFO became a proven reality.

Later that month I had a brief sighting while observing a forest fire in the mountains. It appeared to be a silvery, metallic disk. Clouds of smoke later covered it from view.

All during the summer of 1957 I sighted many erratic moving lights, fireballs, disks, cigar-shaped and cone-shaped craft making nocturnal appearances over the San Gabriel Valley. In most instances, I ruled out the possibility of conventional objects such as stars, planets, airplanes, clouds, or meteors. I had a growing interest in amateur astronomy and purchased my first telescope, a 50X refractor. I had become familiar with the planets along the ecliptic, various constellations, and the names and locations of some of the primary stars in these constellations. One could view the sky as a clock with various hours and minutes of azimuth and degrees of elevation for the purpose of communicating the sighting of objects to friends. Many of the unidentified objects I saw defied conventional aerodynamic behavior while exhibiting patterns of intelligently-controlled maneuvers. In some cases these objects would flash signals or return flashing signals. I felt like I was participating in a signal moment in history -- making contact with extraterrestrial intelligence's.

The first contactee I ever met was a woman who lived alone in the desert. Her name was Doris LeVesque, but she went by the nickname Teska. Teska claimed to be in contact with fourth density beings, one whom she called Deska. Supposedly, Deska was her soul mate on another plane of existence where he cruised our skies in a Master Craft. She told me that she saw this master craft on many occasions and that it was crescent-shaped and glowed with a golden light. One night I witnessed Teska call down a craft that appeared to be a transluscent disk about the size of a dime held at arm's length. There was no doubt in my mind at that time that the contactees were in contact with someone from out there.

On June 3, 1958, I saw the master craft Teska talked about. It had a characteristic golden light. It glided silently over my driveway at 9:05 P.M. Its course was from east to west and first appeared about ten degrees from zenith. It came in response to my "telepathic call." As it drifted overhead, I felt an electrical tingling travel down my back. Then I heard a mental voice in my head. It said "This is Nah-nine of the Solar Cross. You are in a deep sleep. Awake!." As the golden light disappeared over the western horizon, I wondered if I had just received my first voice communication from an Extraterrestrial Source or if I had imagined it. And what was its meaning?

I am well aware that by revealing these early experiences I had with contactee-type elements I am destroying any last vestiges of credibility that I have as a scientific investigator with other scientific researchers. I have witnessed the cavalier dismissal of these events by others who would rather guffaw at them than have the courtesy to listen and have an open mind. I have my own degree of skepticism. To superficially accept this type of contact experience and become a true believer does not satisfy my doubting mind. But, we will never get off first base or start asking probing questions until we can accept the reality of such reports.

On June 10, 1958, I was observing the four moons of Jupiter through my telescope. My neighbor, Dwayne, came over to take a peek through my new telescope. He trained it on a bright star and remarked that he could see a tiny light orbiting the position of the star in the scope. I was standing back in the drive scanning the sky to the north. Suddenly, and more swiftly than a jet, a large luminous object descended on our position coming from the north and moving south. It stopped on a dime directly overhead. Its movement halted so swiftly that my eyes tracked ahead of its hovering position. It was huge! It was totally silent! This craft was shaped like two giant cones joined at the base. The entire craft was glowing milky white through a translucent skin. Bright white lights shone from the opposite tips of the cones. I wondered how such a huge object could hover in the air. As I watched it did an incredible thing. It flipped end-over-end along its longitudinal axis, but due to its symmetry, appeared the same as before. It then instantly accelerated and climbed swiftly into the clouds south of us. Dwayne glanced up as it started to move and exclaimed: "What is that?" Its awesome, silent power climb left me with chills.

Later that summer I experimented again. I went out alone to the patio and turned the radio on, then went onto the driveway where I could view the sky. I started projecting my thoughts asking the saucers to come. I heard something like code coming over the radio. I had the urge to look southeast. Appearing out of nowhere a white glowing disk, surrounded by a glowing red corona and leaving a sparkling trail, dashed over my backyard only a few hundred feet above the ground. The disk appeared in a section of the sky and disappeared as suddenly as it had appeared. As low as it was, I heard no sound. I wondered about the ramifications of this experience. I felt that it had come in direct response to my telepathic call. I never gave a thought to the logistics of providing me with such a show.

I had one daylight sighting that year. I saw six silvery disks performing intricate maneuvers in the eastern sky. In 1959, I had more frequent daylight sightings and even photographed two disks playing in the sky above Yucca Valley in the California desert. The developed photo was disappointing. It showed two indistinct pinpoints in the noon sky. Poor evidence.

A significant experiment was conducted on February 15, 1958 in the high desert off Old Woman Springs Road about 15 miles north of Yucca Valley. An electronics technician, Carol Honey, had installed a light-beam transmitter in his car. This was basically a further development of an invention conceived by Alexander Graham Bell he called a photophone. It acted like a radio, except instead of transmitting modulation over a low-frequency radio wave, it utilized a beam of light and was only effective for line-of-sight communication. This makes it virtually impossible for the signal to be tapped by a remote listener unless he could set-up a receiver in the path of the beam. The spotlight on the car provided the light beam. This project gave me the feeling that we were conducting a citizen's SETI project. About a dozen of us gathered at this remote spot in the desert to conduct the experiment. Some contactees were present. We took turns at the mike saying somewhat silly things like, "Earth calling outer space. Come in outer space." And we waited. After a half-hour of this, I received a mental communication that said essentially, "Look for our bright blue flare in the west." That was strange. We had the receiver on and all we could hear was static. Why didn't they return our communication? Why did someone decide to respond on a telepathic channel? I was hesitant and doubtful, but nevertheless whispered to my trusted friend, John McCoy, that which I heard repeated three times. Within minutes, as if on cue, we all turned to face the west. The last glow of twilight was fading over the distant hills when, out of nowhere, a bright blue bolide appeared and traveled over the horizon. It appeared to be shaped like a dumbell and left a sparkling trail. Not only could I communicate my wishes to those magnificent men in their flying machines, but they could somehow communicate with me. It was almost unbelievable.

The next day I went to Giant Rock with John McCoy and Rick Williamson to meet with George Van Tassel. Rick and John were embarking for Phoenix on the lecture circuit and it gave me an opportunity, before they left, to converse with the contactees. Van, as his friends called him, was an impressive man with a strong personal presence. I found him exceedingly intelligent with a down-to-earth devil-may-care attitude. Van was born in Jefferson, Ohio in 1910. After leaving high school, he worked 4 years as a flight mechanic for airlines at Chicago and Cleveland. In 1930, he came to California and was employed by Douglas Aircraft at Santa Monica for eight and half years. He left Douglas and went to work with Howard Hughes in 1941. Connected with flight testing for Mr. Hughes in the desert near Barstow, he acquired a desire for the peace and quiet of the great open spaces. After two and half years with Mr. Hughes, he went to Lockheed Aircraft in Burbank for four and half years flight test work. While there he came to a decision to live in the peace of the desert, after almost 20 years of aircraft experience.

Van leased an abandoned airport at Giant Rock in 1947 and by 1951 had gathered together a small group who had a sincere interest in the greater secrets of life and the desire to understand phenomena that could not be explained by mundane science. Van found that he could go into a trance and contact beings from other life levels. A group of these beings were using a technological means of communication, a Tensor Beam of high frequency that produced audio and visual output in the brain. If this beam were not carefully focused, it would cause a burning sensation in different parts of his body. Van called this method of communication "channeling" as he said it was like tuning in a television channel to decode the electromagnetic signal. This was somewhat unlike what people call channeling today. Entities with names like Ashtar or Deska announced that they were operators of the spacecraft we saw in our skies that we called by the ridiculous appellation "flying saucers."

In 1952, it was beyond belief that someone could actually be communicating with the operators of the flying disks. Witnesses who even reported seeing one were suspect. Even today many would consider Van Tassel a little loony.

Van reports that on August 24th, 1953, during the night of a full moon, a scout ship with the same configuration as that photographed by George Adamski came to a halt eight feet off the ground out on the landing strip at around 2 AM while he was sleeping outdoors in a sleeping bag. He awoke in an instant and lit a cigarette. When he sat up, he could see a man standing about six feet away from the foot of his bed. This was not uncommon in the desert as people had car trouble frequently on the dusty desert roads. The glowing scout ship hovered about one hundred yards beyond the man.

The man addressed Van Tassel saying, "My name is Solgonda. I would be pleased to show you our craft." Van tried to wake his wife, but the man seemed to have her under some kind of mental control, a situation commonly reported years later by abductees. Solgonda escorted Van to the ship. Van stepped on a glowing spot on the sand and rose slowly into the air through an entry hatch on the bottom of the 36-foot scout craft. This lifting beam has been noted by many contactees and abductees. The lighting inside the scout had no source such as a light bulb, yet everything in the cab of the craft was evenly illuminated. Van saw three other men standing by controls and all were about five feet seven inches in height. Solgonda conducted Van on a tour of the small craft. One apparatus had transparent tubes filled with colored liquids that would continuously change levels. Van was also shown the magnetic motor and counter-revolving rotors that produced propulsion for the scout. The scout evidently carried a battery because it had to be charged periodically for its brief mission on Earth. Twenty minutes later, Van was back at his bedside. During the time Van was with Solgonda, Solgonda demonstrated the amazing ability to tune-in to his thoughts and voice replies to his mental questions. Van had a queasy sensation in his stomach after this tour and asked Solgonda if he would be okay. Solgonda replied that he would, then tapped a crystalline device around his neck and promptly vanished. A moment later the craft rose into the air and took off in a northerly direction.

Two days later Van checked the spot with a compass where the ship had hovered. When walking into the spot, the compass needle deflected 10 degrees to the east, and when walking out of the spot, it deflected 5 degrees to the west.

Van's son-in-law, Dan Boone, lived on the Giant Rock property. He was awakened at 1:55 AM that same morning by the pulsing hum of a generator, but found that he could not rise from the sleeping bag as some force seemed to prevent him from moving.

Dan Boone had many contacts of his own, but would not tell the public. He confided a few of his experiences to me, but the one I remember the most was the one where he met two men and two women at a Yucca Valley liquor store. They were asking directions to Giant Rock. Dan overheard them and offered to lead them out there. When the four arrived, Van was preparing to start one of his Saturday night meetings in the hollowed-out room under Giant Rock. The leader of the group of four was a tall, dark handsome man who called himself Venudo. Venudo sat on an ottoman near Van and Dan. The others sat on a couch across the room. About thirty others were present sitting around the room. Venudo produced a device that was hanging around his neck and tapped it just as Solgonda had done. He instantly disappeared. There was light pouring through the window from outside powered by a gasoline generator. In a minute Venudo was again visible. Dan asked him to repeat his performance. He did so, but this time Dan reached out with his hand and could feel Venudo's shoulder, but still could not see what he was touching. These witnesses had just seen a demonstration of alien magic!

During our gathering at Giant Rock, the night after our light-beam communication experiment, I climbed upon one of the large boulders adjacent to the Rock while Rick and John were having some last minute conversation with Van. Suddenly, I noticed a pulsating white light approaching from the direction of the Los Padres Copper Mines to the north. As the light came closer, I could faintly make out that it was a craft similar to the scout ship Van had gone aboard. I was excited by the prospect that it might land as it was traveling low and slow and I yelled for the others to look. Van was calm about it and told me that he could see it and I didn't have to yell. I knew from that time on that Van was used to seeing these craft.

I remember when I first met Rick and John at a lecture in El Monte in 1957 that a brilliant glowing red disk hovered above the lecture hall so that all could see it. Others told me that this frequently happened at Rick's lectures. The UFOs seemed to follow him around, and this one was no exception. It waited around the area until he and John got into the station wagon and drove away. Later, John informed me that it followed them to the outskirts of Phoenix.

During one of the meetings in El Monte, I met Harry Mayer in 1959. He said that he had an encounter with a petite blond girl from Venus at Giant Rock. The girl's name was Mary. She wore a chocolate-colored ski-type uniform under a coat. Harry had sighted globes of light hovering over the Giant Rock runway and was chasing these on foot when Mary abruptly stopped him. Mary was only 5-foot 3-inches tall and Harry was 6-foot 4-inches tall, yet she arrested him in his tracks with the strength of many men according to Harry. Harry was a no-nonsense guy who had experienced something strange and was doing his best to persuade me to go to Giant Rock and assist him in contacting Mary once more. I never passed up a chance to visit Giant Rock so I went with him. Needless to say, we never made contact.

All these human visitors were described by various contactees, those who had written books, and many who had not. Their descriptions were remarkably similar.

George Adamski had described his meeting with a man at Desert Center and remarking that the flesh of his hand was as smooth as a baby's, but firm and warm. His hands were slender with long tapering fingers. He was only five feet six inches in height and looked like he weighed about 135 pounds. Adamski estimated his age at 28. He had a round face with an extremely high forehead; large, but calm grey-green eyes, slightly aslant at the outer corners with slightly higher cheek bones than an Occidental; a finely chiseled nose...an average size mouth with beautiful white teeth that shone...skin coloring that is an even, medium-colored suntan...and it did not look like he ever had to shave for there was no more hair on his face than a child's. His hair was sandy in color and hung in beautiful waves to his shoulders. His clothing was a one-piece garment...it's color was chocolate brown...a band about eight inches in width circled his waste...it was definitely a woven material...there was a sheen about the whole garment...*saw no zippers, buttons, buckles, fasteners, or pockets of any kind...nor seams as our garments show.* He wore no ring or ornament of any kind.

Contrast Adamski's description with that given by Travis Walton when he was abducted in 1975. Travis saw a human being, a man about six feet two inches tall. He was muscular and was evenly proportioned. He wore a tight-fitting bright blue suit of material that looked like soft velour. He had course, sandy-blond hair of medium length. He had a dark complexion, like a deep, even tan. He had no beard or mustache. In fact, *a stubble or dark shadows of whiskers were not even visible.*

Contactee Orfeo Angelluci saw a beautiful man with extremely large, dark and expressive eyes and noble features. He was wearing a kind of uniform, *bluish in color, perfectly tailored and tightly fitted to the outline of his body. But it was apparently without seams, buttons, pockets, trimmings, or design of any sort.*

Howard Menger describes a beautiful woman he met sitting on a rock. She had on a uniform which had a shimmering, shiny texture...*the clothing had no buttons, fasteners, or seams that he could discern.*

Human extraterrestrials have been reported in Mexico, south America, and Europe as well. All of them have demonstrated extraordinary telepathic abilities. The uniforms they wear, first described by the contactees, are similar to those described by abductees in a later era. Some of these visitors reportedly blend in with us and could not be readily identified if they wore our clothing and make-up. This implies that they have a genetic kinship with earth humans and have evolved under similar biochemical and biophysical conditions to those found on earth. Their actual origin is unknown, but if they are from other planets or dimensions, then their existence is a challenge to our scientific dogma.

During the summer of 1959, the twins Ray and Rex Stanford paid a visit to Giant Rock. Ray and Rex claimed mental contact with the "Brothers." Ray was instructed to bring a movie camera with him as the Brothers were going to make a showing over the desert in one of their Master Craft (crescent-shaped). Ray did succeed in capturing something unusual on film. A brightly-glowing object descended from the sky that afternoon and was promptly followed by a jet interceptor. In the film, you can see the object "jump," leaving the jet crawling behind it.

Later, I drove Ray and Rex from Giant Rock to Mount Palomar to visit the famous George Adamski. Ray and Adamski argued about the function of the Master Craft. Adamski had taken us back to a small workshop where he was doing some experiments with magnets. Although Ray claims that Adamski virtually admitted that he had no need of contacts to describe what he had written in his books, I received no such impression from the man. Later, I interviewed witnesses to Adamski's contacts who described details of incidents without hesitation. Many others had described seeing the scout ships at close range. In 1957, I had seen an orange-glowing craft one night that had the same bell-shaped configuration as the one Adamski photographed. If Adamski had been constructing small models of this craft, then the large-sized original was making its appearance known in various parts of the world. After their visit with Adamski, Ray and Rex seemed to become disillusioned with contactees and even downplayed their own reported experiences.

The controversy concerning Adamski continues to this day. A few ardent supporters believe Adamski reported true experiences, and that his photographs of mother ships and scout ships are among the best UFO photos in the world. However, the majority of UFO researchers believe Adamski wove tall tales, that his earlier work of fiction, *Pioneers of Space,* foreshadowed his non-fiction tale, *Inside the Spaceships*; that he photographed small models through his telescope, models that he had constructed in his workshop. At one time it was thought that the scout ship had been identified as a chicken brooder, a lamp, or the top of a water cooler which had been made to look like a flying saucer. However, none of these explanations were ever convincingly proven. The fact that many other photos of this bell-configuration have been taken in different parts of the world, and that many independent witnesses had seen such a shape attests to its authenticity. Today, we know that photos can be easily hoaxed, but this does not mean that Adamski's photos were hoaxed.

Another contactee that I had met in the fifties was Bob Short. Bob was receiving messages via a "Tensor" Beam like Van Tassel. While Bob was out for an evening stroll in Joshua Tree one evening in 1957, he saw an orange ball of light come in to a soft landing in the sand a few yards ahead of him. It appeared to have the ubiquitous bell-shape of a scout ship. When a hatch opened in the side of the scout, and a dark form appeared, Bob got panicky and wanted to run (an emotion usually displayed by abductees), but his curiosity kept him glued to the spot. When the form got within a few feet, Bob recognized that it was a man with shoulder-length hair and penetrating eyes. The man reached out and touched the palm of his hand and Bob felt a calming, peaceful effect. The mysterious visitor, identifying himself as Sutko, said that he had landed to make a minor adjustment to his craft. Sutko continues to communicate with Bob through the Tensor Beam.

Bob's communicators have been more accommodating to him than with some of the other contactees. They have demonstrated their presence to witnesses by occasionally announcing a fly-over. Sometimes these fly-overs are precisely timed. Here is an example. Bob was receiving Tensor communication before a group of fifty or more people at a Giant Rock spacecraft convention one evening in October 1967 when the voice announced that they (the space people) were at an exact latitude and longitude north of our position and had released two reconnaissance vehicles that would overfly our position in four minutes. I remember expressing skepticism and walking away from the group grumbling about how I was beginning to think that such communications were a lot of nonsense. Exactly four minutes later, to the second, two metallic disks flew over Giant Rock heading south at about 90 to 100 mph. They each displayed a brilliant rotating light centered on the bottom hull. They were each about twenty feet in diameter and had smooth polished finishes. I estimated that they were no more than 200 feet above us as they passed over and headed down the runway. By the time they reached the end of the runway in the direction of Goat Mountain, they looked to be no more than ten feet off the ground, and executed a right-angled turn twice, then flew silently back over our heads, heading north to rendezvous with their mother ship. I was astonished by this whole display. What I saw were definitely flying machines, and their appearance was forecast in advance.

In April 1976 I attended another spacecraft convention in Tonopah, Arizona. This time Bob showed me a typed message at one o' clock in the afternoon that stated that a fly-over would take place that night at 10:30 PM. Bob started to receive his Tensor communication shortly after 10:15 and, as if on cue, an unidentified blue light appeared south of Ursa Major traveling slowly and at high altitude. A second blue light appeared traveling south and headed on a collision course with the first light. They came within kissing contact and abruptly stopped and hovered for several minutes before fading out. I could see both lights clearly attached to dark shapes through 7x50 binoculars. A faint blue cone of light appeared to descend from the objects to a point over Bob's head! Was this the Tensor Beam? There were fifty or more witnesses who saw this event including my ex- wife, her daughter, and my friend, John Maxfield.

Having witnessed such demonstrations as the one in Tonopah, I have come away convinced of the validity of some of the contactee's experiences, but this is not to obscure the fact that I and others still harbored doubts about the origins of these visitors, their motivations, and the validity of their statements to the contactees. One man who is very skeptical, yet fascinated with the contactee era is Jerome Clark who wrote a monthly column on UFOs for FATE magazine. He considers that contactees such as the well-known George Adamski were charlatans. He considers that the evidence against the early contactees was overwhelming and that Adamski and other contactees were caught telling falsehoods on more than one occasion. The remarkably clear photos that Adamski took of Venusian scout ships were fakes. Some believe that Adamski built models and others feel that he dressed up some common piece of apparatus such as a chicken brooder to look like a flying saucer, this despite eyewitness claims that craft resembling the Venusian scout ship were seen in different parts of the world. Tales of the so-called Space Brothers were no more than contrived fantasies to put one over on the unsuspecting public.

Isabel Davis who, in 1957, was an officer of Civilian Saucer Intelligence of New York, once wrote a scathing critique of the contactee's claims entitled, "Meet the Extraterrestrials." One criticism that she levels at the spacemen in the contactee's stories is that they never provide unequivocal proof. And, of course, they claim to originate from planets that scientists know harbor conditions hostile to any kind of life, much less humanoid life. The main criticism of Adamski's claims is that his visitors claimed to have come from Venus, Mars, and Saturn.

The early contactees described meeting human extraterrestrials wherever their point of origin. These human visitors had very symmetrical features; their skin was clear and translucent; their fingers were more flexible than ours; and their irises had different hues and colors than those seen on earth. They are never reported to be fat, thin, or ugly. Their hair, teeth, nails, and eyes were all without defect. I'ts as if they perfected control over their genetic breeding and produced healthier and longer living specimens than terrestrial humans.

Once in 1960, a young contactee named Paul took a photo out of his wallet allegedly showing a picture of a woman from another planet. She appeared to fit the description given by many contactees. Her eyes were the most electric blue I had ever seen.

One of the most affective of the contactees was Orfeo Angelluci. Orfeo became my friend. Van Tassel had always stimulated my mind, but Orfeo had touched a deeper level of my being. Orfeo had answers to the flying saucer mystery that embraced all of mankind within its scope. He often met with a visitor he called, "Neptune" as the name had some meaning for him. Neptune had told Orfeo that he was functioning in dimensions unknown to our world. Orfeo was astonished once to notice that Neptune's uniform looked like it wavered as if seen through rippling water and its color did not remain solid and uniform, but changed in spots. One of the precocious revelations that Orfeo revealed in his book was that the flying disks that he had seen were a product of organic technology, that they were grown in chemical baths and all systems were grown into their seamless structure. Orfeo bore a large share of ridicule from the disbelievers.

Another, little-known California contactee of the fifties was Calvin Girvin. Calvin reported many contacts with a human saucer pilot named Cryxtan. Calvin also reported going aboard one of the scout ships. Calvin was also in the Air Force and was interrogated by the AF Office of Special Investigation. Last heard from, he was living somewhere in Hollywood.

From time to time present-day abductees report an encounter with Nordic-looking alien beings that bear a resemblance to the ones described by the contactees of the fifties. Recently, a coffee shop friend found out that I was a field investigator and was eager to tell me of the odd events that had entered his life when he was a pre-teen. Like the old-timers, he claimed that a man from Mars came to visit him, and, one day, took him for a ride to the planet Mars where they entered an opening in the ground. A shaft descended five miles toward the planet's interior where he encountered the inhabitants of an ancient underground Martian civilization.

The contactee experience has its own characteristics. Some of these characteristics are shared with the abductee experience, but most are unique to a contactee scenario. Most Ufologists of the nineties have been led to believe that the contactees were charlatans out to spread religious philosophies, and this has proven a stumbling block to any proposed scientific investigation of the contactee's claims.

A typical contactee scenario usually proceeds in this fashion:

1) The contactee has an urge or impulse that he or she perceives to be coming from an outside source and this urge seems to direct them to some remote location. There is an air of expectancy.

2) The contactee is usually approached by a human being wearing a one-piece uniform that has disembarked from a flying saucer. The human can access the contactee's mind with telepathy. The visitors do not display any difficulty with English or any other spoken language.

3) Either the meeting terminates or the contactee is taken on a tour of the ship or a ride to a mothership.

4) The contactee does not experience a loss of time or lapse of memory.

5) The contactee is usually given a message or project to accomplish. One of the common themes of the messages given to the early contactees is that we are *upsetting the balance of nature.*

Many Ufologists who study abductee (or, using the newer term -- experiencer) cases generally accept that there were no legitimate contactees and that there is no precedence for the abductee scenario.

Objections to the case for the contactees are:

1) The contactee doesn't have any first-hand eye witnesses. Although true of the vast proportion of abductees as well, it was felt that the contactee should have someone else that would attest to the reality of the experience. As we have related here, George Adamski, for one, had six eye witnesses to his first contact.

2) The early contactees claimed that the visitors came from planets in our local solar system such as Mars and Venus. Space probes have proven that other planets in our system could not sustain life as we know it. It might be possible that humans with advanced technology could build protected habitats on or under the surface of neighboring planets, but they would not have originated there. Other possibilities include coming from a different frequency/density/dimension of the other planet in our system, but the visitors did not always explicitly state this as their origin. Perhaps they were deceiving the contactees or the contactees colluded with the visitors to protect their identity and origin from enemies also contacting earth humans. Otherwise, we are left with the conclusion that the contactees fabricated this part of their story or their whole story. This last conclusion is, of course, the one that wins the most votes among researchers.

3) One of the primary objections to the contactee was the apparent zeal with which they spread quasi-religious messages. This was disturbingly cult-like. The feedback of adulation and attention given the contactee may distort whatever legitimate experience he/she may have had.

4) The contactees were not very cooperative with researchers; extensively ridiculed, they were not interested in providing proof of their experiences to still another skeptical inquirer.

5) One of the biggest objections to the contactee experience is that the visitors were reported looking human and able to pass undetected amongst us if dressed in our clothing. Humans were a product of earth's evolutionary development and could not possibly arise on other worlds. Yet, reports of human entities from UFOs will not go away. We still hear of encounters with them from the new experiencers. The existence of humans originating from an extraterrestrial or extradimensional civilization is a comforting thought to our aloneness in the universe.

This chapter recounts just some of my experiences with the early California contactees. I was convinced that the flying saucer mystery had a simple solution and that the mystery would be unveiled before the next decade of the sixties had passed. Little did I know that we were facing a complex phenomena that would continue to baffle us all to the present day.

CHAPTER TWO
THE STRANGE SAGA OF BRIAN SCOTT

"Fear not --knowledge is of you. By your mind the truth --- fear not mankind --- speak this of I --- Man has cut his destiny in and on all orbits of known and unknown --- for each step forward he takes is a step backward to his end --- without control of the power he has created, the power will control him and mark his end." --The HOST

One of the most remarkable abductees that I came to know was Brian Allan Scott. Brian was born on October 12, 1943 in Philadelphia. On his 16th birthday he saw a glowing orange ball of light come down from the sky to within a foot of where he stood, then it darted skyward, leaving the youthful Brian dumbfounded. The ball of light returned on many occasions, and on one particular night it came into his house and passed in front of a dresser mirror. Its reflection could not be seen in the mirror. Brian grabbed a broom and tried to bat the ball out of the house.

Brian's first encounter with alien entities took place on the night of March 14, 1971 near Apache Junction, Arizona. Apache Junction is located near the haunting Superstition Mountains. Brian lost two hours of time the night of the first encounter.

Brian had gone out to Apache Junction that night at about 9 PM with his friend Nick Corbin to look for a good range for target shooting with a pistol. He had left the main highway and followed a dirt road for a quarter of a mile. He then parked his car to have a look around. His attention was riveted by the sound of an animal in the distance, but he could not see the animal. As his gaze wandered above the Superstition peaks, he was amazed to see a glowing oval object hovering above the mountains. He slowly realized that he was not looking at a conventional airplane or helicopter as it was too large and had a "funny kind of glow around it."

The object began to move toward Brian and, as it did, his first thought was to run back to his car and leave the area as fast as he could. Before he could move, the object positioned itself directly over his head and now appeared so large that it filled the sky above him.

The next sensation Brian felt was that of being lifted into the air. Fruitlessly, he reached out to grab something to maintain balance, but there was nothing to grab but air. A feeling of hysteria overcame him. He was being pulled upward by an invisible force through a doorway and was set down in an outer corridor of a craft. He could feel the mixing of the cool air in the craft with the warm air outside. He could look out and see the lights of Phoenix directly behind him.

When Brian turned in the doorway, he was astonished to see that his friend Nick Corbin had also been lifted aboard this craft. The two of them could only stare at each other. Brian could see bright light coming from the interior of the craft.

Suddenly, without warning, a door seemed to explode open and Brian could see four silhouettes framed in the light of the open interior hatch. Two of the creatures approached Brian and two approached Nick. Within seconds the creatures began to undress Nick and Brian. Nick started to struggle to resist the creatures' efforts. Brian, seeing any resistance as futile, cooperated with the creatures and finished undressing himself. Nick passed out as the creatures took him off in one direction, and took Brian in a separate direction.

Brian was taken for a short walk and then turned to the left where he faced another door with a symbol on it. The creature on Brian's left reached out and touched the center of the symbol on the door, and the door opened.

The creatures were described as 7-1/2 feet tall, gray in color, with skin that reminded Brian of the skin of an elephant, with large hands and a very bulky body. Their hands ended in 3 fingers and an oddly bent thumb. The creatures seemed calm and certain of what they were doing.

Brian was led to an inner room, taken to the wall where the creatures then released their hold on Brian. It was at that time that Brian thought about bolting for the door to effect his escape, yet he felt restrained to the wall by an invisible force. Brian found that he could only follow the movements of the creatures with his eyes as they stepped behind a rectangular lighted console. While this occurred, an intense beam of light was directed at him from a box attached to a pole that ran from floor to ceiling. A cable ran from the box up the pole. Another creature stood behind the box, manipulating it.

Brian noticed that the entire room was filled with a mist and an odor that smelled like dirty socks. The mist or vapor seemed to linger on the creature's skin and was absorbed by it.

The box was lowered to the floor, at which time Brian could feel the sensation of warm and cold fluids running up and down his legs. He distinctly got the feeling he had urinated, and he felt strange in the pit of his stomach as the light of the box played over his body. As the light shone in his eyes, it caused a numbing sensation and gave Brian a headache. At this point, the creature extinguished the light and departed through a doorway, at which time another creature entered the room. This new creature was taller than the others, almost nine feet tall!

The new creature approached Brian and placed his hand on top of Brian's head. Brian felt as if thousands of thoughts were rushing into his mind. Brian asked the creature who he was and what he wanted. Brian could hear the creature reply, but its speech was rapid and slurred. The creature replied again at a slower rate and in perfect English, saying, "There will be no pain of this." Saying that, all pain fled from Brian's body. He continued to ask the creature who he was, where he was from, and what he wanted. The creature then replied, "I will tell you, and I will show you." At that moment, Brian got the sensation that he was leaving the craft as if the walls

---

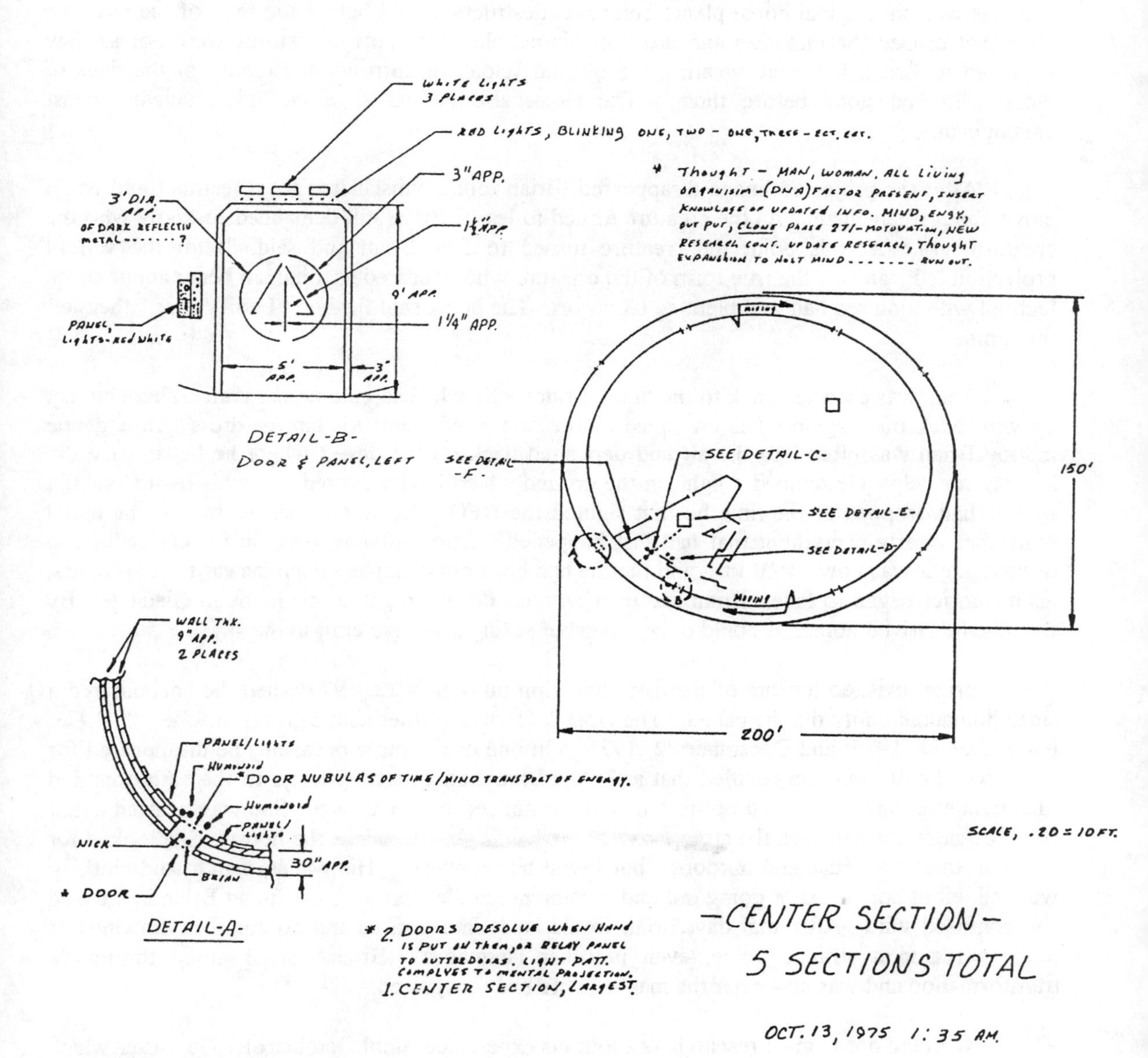

Fig. 1 Drawing by Brian Scott

---

of the craft had just melted away. Was this another demonstration of alien magic? He then saw a holographic projection of domed cities on the surface of an alien planet. The creature explained that this was his original home planet before its destruction, and before the time of the airborne virus that caused the mutation and death of his people. The hulky creatures were not as they appeared to Brian, but were wearing a projected "cloak of sorrow" in memory of the days of those who had gone before them. The cloak also served as a biological shield against contaminants.

After the projected image disappeared, Brian found himself free from restraint and could move about freely again. As the creature turned to leave, Brian still demanded to know who the creature was. At this point the creature turned to face Brian and said, "I lift the veil of projection." Brian saw the true form of the creature who appeared as a human being about seven feet tall with long red hair and piercing blue eyes. The being said further, "I am Voltar," then left the room.

Brian was escorted back to the first corridor where he had entered the craft. There he met up with Nick once again. His crumpled clothes were left there for him to dress. In a gentle motion Brian was lifted into the air and deposited back on the desert where he began to walk, looking for help. He noticed a light on the ground which he discovered to be his own flashlight that he had dropped at the time he first sighted the UFO. As he returned to his car, he could remember clearly everything that had just happened. Later, after turning on his car radio and discovering it was now 11:10 PM, and that he had been out and away from his car for two hours, his memories began to fade. Brian had over an hour's drive to get to his home in Glendale. By the time he arrived home, he could only remember seeing a strange craft in the sky.

Brian revisited the site of the first abduction on March 22, 1973 where he encountered a small humanoid entity that he called, "The Host." He was further abducted on October 25, 1973; November 21, 1975; and December 22, 1975. On one of the three occasions he disappeared for 27 hours. Scott's ex-wife testified that at 3 AM Brian had gotten up to go to the bathroom and fifteen minutes later she called out to him and did not receive an answer. She was worried about Brian because she had seen the strange orange balls of light come into the house. She looked for Brian all over the house and outdoors, but found him nowhere. His wallet, watch, and clothing were all left at home. After going out and coming home the next day, she found Brian in a dazed and confused state. After that day, Brian would lapse into trances and do complex drawings or utter words in a strange voice, even in other languages. Brian started going through a transformation and was no longer the man his wife had recognized.

Brian did not contact researchers about his experiences until October of 1975 , after which he was hypnotized by Dr. McCall at Anaheim Memorial Hospital and told to recall in detail the events of the first two abductions. A strange mechanical voice emanated from Brian during of the sessions that produced a uniform frequency of a thousand cycles per second on an oscillagraph. These sounds could not normally be produced by human or animal vocal chords. Brian also showed positive results on a psychological stress evaluation test.

Investigators from CUFOS, MUFON, and APRO came to see Brian to record the details of his reported experiences. They all had their own theories and opinions concerning what happened to Brian. Some heavily religious people wanted Brian exorcised to rid him of the bedeviling voices that emanated from him when he fell into trance. Brian was subjected to investigation and harassment for a year before he met Jim Frazier who fast became Brian's confidante and only wanted to lend him a helping hand in friendship. Jim wanted to write a book about Brian, but he first wanted a sign from those mysterious entities who were using Brian as some sort of cosmic radio or recording device.

Joyful of this, the Host sent a message through Brian at 2:10 AM on August 23, 1976 which in the peculiar style of the Host stated: OF THE HOST. OPEN RUN 1. FROM THE SKY NOW COMES A BALL OF FIRE FOR ALL MANKIND TO SEE. OF THIS 1,000 PARTICLES. OF THIS I AM, I AM. LOOK TO THE WEST, GIVEN IN TRUST, LAT 38 01' N LONG 119 50' W. OF THIS, SEEK OF I. OF THIS, HE ASKED OF I, A SIGN. GIVEN. Twenty hours after this message, a ball of fire streaked across western skies "sparkling like a thousand bright lights." According to the wire services, it "ejected particles" from Canada to Mexico and the largest fragment landed less than ten miles from the coordinates given by the Host.

There have been many witnesses to the strange phenomena that surrounds Brian Scott, and yet tangible evidence still eludes the keenest investigators. It was not only cases with the contactees which had been summarily dismissed, but the new wave of abductees, especially those abductee-contactees such as Brian were doubted time and again. Brian only helped those investigators who helped him achieve the strange mission that extraterrestrial beings had given him. The whole experience of getting involved with Brian left one charged with emotions and skewed any well-intended objective approach to the case.

One of Brian's witnesses, Lou Savage, was not available to interview. But I did interview Sue Scott, his ex-wife, Doreen (who later married Brian), and Jim Frazier. They all attested that they had witnessed paranormal phenomena in Brian's presence. Sue testified that she had seen the balls of light that flew through the Scott household, and watched Scott fall into strange trances. Doreen told the story of one day going to the bank with Brian to cash a check. She was thinking to herself that she would love to have a bouquet of roses from Brian, but did not voice these thoughts to him. They had left the car parked and locked in the parking lot of the bank. Doreen says that she never left Brian's side, yet when returning to the car and opening the still locked door, the desired bouquet of roses lay on the front seat!

Jim Frazier had seen Brian bending metal as the famous Uri Geller had done on stage, however Brian would seldom have to touch the metal utensil to have it bend. He usually lapsed into a trance when this happened. Jim also saw water materialize in droplets over Brian's head when Brian went into a trance. One time, Brian in trance, seemed to materialize an ancient Greek gold coin that was in excellent condition. We examined this coin under a 300X industrial microscope. Its antiquity was verified by numismatists. It was later identified as coming from the ancient temple of Diana. If Brian was trying to put one over on us, he was coming up with some pretty good tricks.

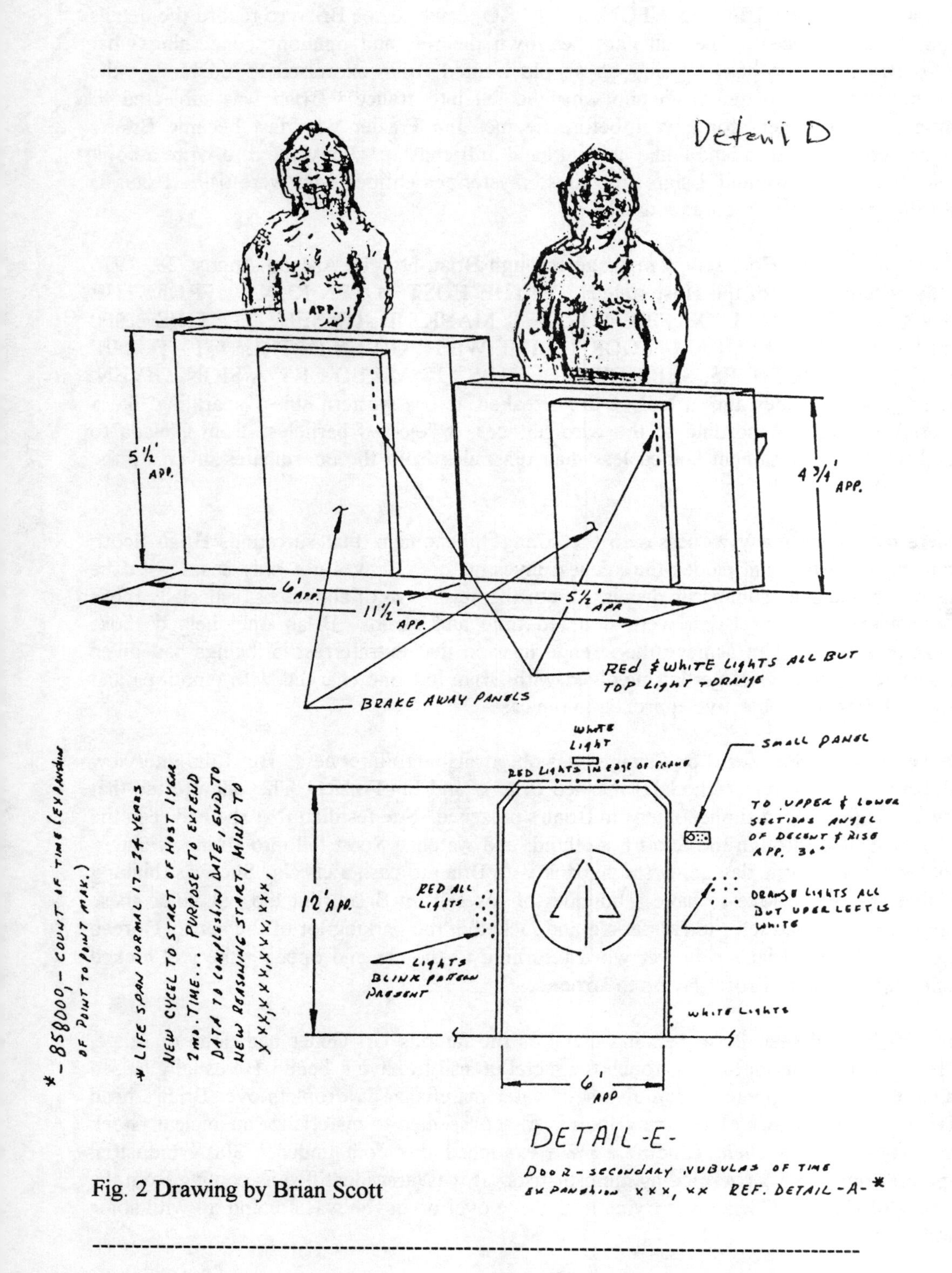

Fig. 2 Drawing by Brian Scott

Twice, I myself saw spoons bend of their own accord in Brian's hand. Both times this was witnessed by others. On many occasions we interrogated the voices that spoke through Brian in trance. Sometimes Voltar spoke, and other times a powerful voice came from Vertrex. Several times the voices would eerily reply to questions only formulated in our minds. That is some trick. Or Alien Magic. Standard electronic analysis showed that some of these voices produced a graph different from Brian's voice.

The sheer volume of automatic writings and drawings that came through Brian was staggering. Some of these related to advanced technology or science, and others related to man's past. The writings seemed to go beyond Brian's knowledge. One message came through in a dead Greek language. The writings kept pointing to an ancient link between their world and our world.

The type of evidence that can be studied in this case leads one to the belief that Brian was in contact with extraterrestrial or extradimensional beings who were involved with us in our past and who re-involved themselves with us now to prepare us for future contact and much more...the more became evident as Brian's case unfolded before us. I do not believe that Brian contrived these experiences or hallucinated them. Many abductees have now reported seeing these ubiquitous balls of light that have traveled down many American hallways.

If we view Brian's contacts as real contacts with a benevolent species of alien, then we will be open to the projects that Voltar and his people have commissioned Brian to accomplish before the end of the year 2011.

I met Scott and Frazier in early December 1976. By the end of the month they were on their way to Tiahaunaco, Bolivia where Voltar instructed Scott that he would undergo a transformation of mind enabling Voltar to share Brian's physical existence on earth and communicate with us more directly. When Scott and Frazier returned from South America, my friend John and I went to greet them at LAX. Indeed, Brian seemed like a different person. There was an a perceptible aura of psychic energy around him. He kept mentioning objects that he could see on the other side of a wall. Brian was a heavy smoker, but Brian-cum-Voltar did not smoke at all. He could discuss anything from flowers as food to black holes. This period of psychic transformation lasted a number of weeks before signs of the old Brian returned.

That night on the way home, northbound on the 405 freeway, I sighted a large object that hovered in the off-shore clouds. It had a faint orange glow on its topside. It appeared to be cylindrical and pointed away from us at a 60 degree angle. I asked John to pull of the freeway as quickly as possible so that I could get a better look at this object. When he pulled up on a side street, I hopped out of the car and looked at the object through binoculars. An intense flash of red light emanated from the side of the object and seemed to penetrate through my eyes into a deep recess of my mind. In the days ahead, I underwent my own transformation and experienced a state of cosmic consciousness that lasted weeks. That event had a big impact on my life, but is the subject of a book in itself.

ALIEN MAGIC by William Hamilton

Have extraterrestrial entities influenced our own growth and development in science and technology now and in the past? Were the remarkable constructions at Stonehenge, Giza, Tiahuanaco, and other places throughout the world inspired by visitors to our world? Authorities do not think so, but the possibility cannot be eliminated. Were the mathematics of the Hindus and Mayans developed by these ancient people without any outside assistance, or were the fundamentals of these systems taught by other-worldly teachers? Were the ancient priests of Amun in Egypt early-day contactees who became custodians of a science from the stars? Is there any evidence that we, today, are receiving information from alien sources?

The genius behind alternating current electricity, Nikola Tesla, believed he had received signals from space. An old newspaper article from 1899 reads: "Mr. Nikola Tesla has announced that he is confident that certain disturbances of his apparatus are electrical signals received from a source beyond the Earth. They do not come from the sun, he says, hence must be of planetary origin; probably from Mars; he guesses."

Tesla believed in life on other planets and believed he could communicate by radio with this life. Were Tesla's later experiments and concepts of force fields, death rays, and resonant thought-control devices the result of knowledge he had received from an extraterrestrial source? Most would think such an idea is absurd, that Tesla possessed a brilliant and creative mind and did not need help from outside minds.

Our sciences and technologies have experienced a tremendous growth, seemingly growing exponentially since 1890. Since that period of time more of our thoughts have turned to life on other planets, space travel, and advances in all frontiers of knowledge.

My first encounter with an inventor and contactee who claimed to have received knowledge from an extraterrestrial source was Mr. George Van Tassel in 1957. George said that he was shown the gravity motor on a flying saucer back in 1953 and was given the principles of an electro-static magneto-gravitic generator which he was to incorporate into a structure he called the Integratron. George planned the Integratron as a domed non metallic building 38 feet high and 58 feet in diameter. The work was begun in the desert near Landers, California. The dome is an electro-static generator with armatures over four times larger in diameter that any other in existence. The fields generated by the machine were to encompass the entire structure. The dome does not contain any nails, bolts, or metal in its assembly. George was going to initially use the Integratron to charge biological cells with energy in order to rejuvenate humans and animals. He spent over 20 years working on the project using money solicited by donations. George had many detractors, and debunkers said the whole project was a magnificent monument to pseudo-science. Sadly, George never finished his project and died of a heart attack in February 1978, his dreams now getting buried by desert sands, the dome withering in the sun.

In 1959, George Adamski showed us a small laboratory in back of his home at Palomar Gardens, California. He was experimenting with magnetic fields and gravity. He had a number of metal discs that were radioactive on the bench. Nowhere in evidence were small models of the scout ships he photographed as debunkers so often repeat. Something drove Adamski to learn the secrets of the saucers.

In 1959, I heard a magnetic tape recording of an interview with Dr. Wilbur Smith of Canadian Project Magnet. Smith claimed to have made contact with human beings from flying saucers. He even claimed that they sent him information on how to design a coil that could receive their signals when attached to a television receiver. When he attached this coil to a television set, he said he received clear pictures in color from orbiting spacecraft. He could see both uniformed men and women on the spacecraft.

By 1975, Brian Scott was receiving voluminous information from his abductors. My friend, John Maxfield, who had a background in computer programming as I had, and I set ourselves the task of attempting to decipher the volume of data Brian had recorded. Brian had been receiving information and drawings on:

1) Binary and trinary computer mathematics
2) Data on genetics and cloning
3) Orbital mechanics and astronomy
4) Equations on electromagnetics
5) and Quantum Displacement Physics (teleportation)

Scott said that some of the data was transmitted by a computer inside a probe that had become a satellite of the moon. A lot of the data on the satellite's position and orbit was forwarded to Duncan Lunan, an astronomer in Scotland, in an attempt to encourage Mr. Lunan to transmit a radotelescopic signal to the satellite and receive a response. Brian referred to this satellite as the "Selene Orbital." Scott claimed that the satellite was the same that was responsible for the long-delayed echoes received by Stormer and Van der Pol in 1929. At one point in time, Scott had recorded the satellite's signals, an electronic sonar-type beep, on a tape recorder without any radio attached. In fact, several times when the voices came through Brian and were recorded on tape, a playback of the tape would reveal the additional sounds of beeps.

Could the ETs be taking tissue samples for the purpose of precipitating a genetic transformation of our species, or, as frightening as it seems, are they cloning individual members of our race to see if the clones could adapt to a new world? Are they looking for their own cross-bred descendants? Whatever line of speculation we wish to pursue, the abductees describe on board body exams that imply that we are objects of a biological survey.

In a transmission to Brian dated December 1, 1975, the Host indicated that their original world was in the constellation of Bootes and that the first descent to Earth from the Secondary World happened in 40,500 B.C. when there occurred "SEXUAL IMPLANTATION OF KNOWN LIFE --- KNOUS 1350 -- 1450cc," these figures given refer to skull capacity in cubic centimeters. Another transmission indicates that the place of their first descent was in the Andes.

In a frightening prophecy the Host describes destruction on the Earth: "MOUNTAINS DASH TOGETHER -- AND HEAVEN IS SPLIT IN TWO -- THE SUN GROWS DEAD --

THE EARTH SINKS INTO THE SEA -- THE BRIGHT STARS VANISH -- FIRE RAGES AND RAISES FLAMES AS HIGH AS HEAVEN." This is, evidently, a quoted piece that predicts coming cataclysms. Messages like these have been given to other abductees. Sometimes abductees are shown a movie show of coming destructive events on board craft. Brian saw such a show projected on the wall of his apartment. Either these messages are given as a warning, or they are meant to test our reactions to loss and catastrophe.

Brian was told about ten gifts to bestow on mankind, gifts of extraterrestrial science and technology, yet not beyond our means to engineer and construct. Brian was to design four solar pyramids to be placed in specific locations throughout the world to help stabilize planetary balance. Brian completed the blueprints for one solar pyramid which will serve as a solar energy converter and power plant. Within the base of the pyramids are magnetic generators that will help balance irregularities in the geomagnetic field. Also the pyramids act as storage containers for human cells, a clone cell bank to preserve human genomes until the year 14,000 A.D.

The second project given to Brian was to write the history of the people "from beyond the stars" who first contacted him on that March night of 1971. This book is to reveal their relationship to the people of Earth.

The third project was the design of machines which will function on mental commands. These machines will help man raise his level of consciousness and increase his mental functioning.

The fourth project involves placing time capsules in orbiting satellites so that we may preserve the events and information regarding UFOs and their purposes in coming to Earth.

The fifth, and one of the more fascinating projects, is the design of a **Biological Monitoring Belt**, an electronic, mind-activated device that has four phases of development. In the first phase, the belt is worn around the mid-section and monitors and displays the body's weather conditions and will alert the wearer to any critical malfunctions. If any of the body's readings go into abnormal ranges, this will alert the wearer. In phase two, the belt will be linked to a computer and could trigger the release of specific nutrients to the body to bring metabolism and functioning into balance. In phases three and four, the belt will be upgraded to accomplish **Quantum Displacement,** the teleportation of the wearer from terminal to terminal.

The remaining five projects have not been disclosed to Brian.

When the Host communicated orbital factors in the transmissions to Scott, three formulas for magnetic interaction and magnetic flux were given. One of the equations, found in our own textbooks in relation to gravitation force was: F=Kmm'/r2 and was used more than once to describe "RAPOR" (rapport). One equation turned out to be used for magnetic flux variations in a toroidal coil as given in the *Handbook for Chemistry and Physics.* It was surprising to find this kind of data in the transmissions if we assume that the data came from Brian's own mind as we could find no evidence that Brian read any scientific books or journals. A spacefaring race would and should be concerned with magnetics and gravitics. Our own sun has a huge magnetic field that extends past the orbit of Pluto.

Biologists are now realizing that organisms develop weak magnetic fields and are sensitive to changes in magnetic flux and polarity. In fact, it is becoming increasingly apparent that a magnetic field is necessary for the sustenance of life. Geologists now realize that there have been 171 magnetic polarity reversals of the geomagnetic field in the past 76 million years, and coincident with such reversals, entire species have vanished.

We also know that UFOs exhibit electromagnetic effects and that these space-time craft develop powerful magnetic and gravitational fields which can disable electric motors and generators and cause radio and television interference. From indications given by the Host, he is concerned with changes in magnetic flux. For him, it might be a life-or-death situation in spacecraft navigation.

All of the transmitted astronomical drawings received by Brian contain strange and familiar symbols. One of the drawings shows a diagram of an orbital path from their world to Earth. Their original world was described as orbiting two artificial suns. During a tragedy that occurred many thousands of our years ago, their world was evacuated. They searched space for a new home. Brian said they found that new home on the fourth planet orbiting the star we call Epsilon Eridani.

One of the diagrams shows 36 stars, together with their catalog numbers and light-year distances to Earth. Voltar's home world of Epsilon Eridani 4 is shown as 10.8 light-years from Earth. Tau Ceti and Epsilon Eridani were sun-like stars that were the objects of a search for extraterrestrial life made in 1960 by Dr. Frank Drake at the Radio Astronomy Observatory at Green Bank, West Virginia.

Stars have been classified according to their light or spectral emissions as detected by spectrophotometer. Those stars classed as spectral types F, G, and K are most likely candidates for supporting habitable planets. Our sun is a type G star. Tau Ceti is a type G star and could be similar to our sun, supporting at least one habitable planet in orbit.

Another of Brian's diagrams shows the size and distance of planets in our own solar system. All figures given in the drawings agree with standard textbook astronomy. We do not know the purpose of these diagrams.

At one point in the messages, the Host refers to his first descent on Earth dated to our year 3113 B.C., and says: "DNA CODING NOT COMPLETE -- ENVIRONMENTAL DAMAGE." There are repeated indications by the Host that his mission to Earth is *biological.* He refers to "SEXUAL RAPOR," "SEXUAL IMPLANTATION," and "GENETIC TRANSFORMATION" by the Secondary World at the dawn of our known world. These messages were transmitted to Brian before there was any wide-spread talk of aliens and genetics. Perhaps Brian was given a key to abduction cases that have occurred throughout the world. Repeatedly, as with Brian, the abductors have performed some type of medical or biological examinations of humans.

Most of these drawings and writings received by Brian in a state of trance were identified as coming from a single source, the Host. In biology, a "host" is classified as an organism which, temporarily or permanently, supports another organism (a parasite) at its own expense. Brian contends the Host to be a vital force which transcends physical death. In that analogy, the parasite dies, but the Host lives on.

In an a transmission given in October 1975, the Host states: "ONE CELL HAS LIFE, AND THROUGH IT MAN WILL STRIVE. CLONING BY OF YOU, FROM MIND, AND LIFE." A clone, according to the language of zoology, constitutes the descendants of a single individual; a pure line; an asexually produced individual. Cloning is mentioned many times by the Host. Today we have experimented with cloning plants and animals in our laboratories, yet the Host is talking about the cloning of man, his mind, and his life. Extracting a gene from the nucleus of a cell and reproducing a clone of the host cell, produces an exact copy of the original. If we wanted to save an endangered species, we could clone members of that species and produce replicas for continued survival. Perhaps an entire planetary population could be cloned and transplanted to a colony world. The biological technology of cloning would be a definite asset to a spacefaring race. Even now the first chapter of Genesis comes to mind when God said, "Let us make Man in *our image."* Were the first men on Earth clones of the Gods?

There are many hints of early genetic experimenting given by the Host. In one message the Host states, "DNA TRANSFERS AT ORIGIN OF TIME, I, THE HOST WILL RETURN -- 2011 AD December 24." The Host promises to return to the point of DNA transfer in our past at an exact time in our future.

In many instances, the Host uses a form of Logic and "Inverted Logic" with a numerical superscript that is subject to interpretation. Here is an example: "EXPANSION OF THOUGHT/ENERGY4 = TIME." Is Energy4 a level of energy? We don't know.

The Host states again and again that "TIME IS OF THE MIND." The concept of time as a mental phenomenon has been argued in philosophy. To a spacefaring race who are able to travel the immense distances between stars at relativistic velocities, or bore through space using wormholes, the statement by the Host is perfectly understandable. In other statements concerning time, the Host refers to the conversion of energy from mass, nuclear transformation, producing or being related to time transformation. Accelerating particles to near light-speed causes time dilation. Those mathematical laws which define the relationships of magnitudes in one system to another are known as laws of transformation.

Einstein has said of time: "The experiences of an individual appear to us arranged in a series of events; in this series the single events which we remember appear to be ordered according to the criterion of 'earlier' and 'later'. There exists, therefore, for the individual, an I-time, or subjective time. This in itself is not measurable."

The Brian Scott case is a complex case with many fascinating facets, not the least of which is the study of knowledge. Like many other experiencers who cannot present proof of their experience, Brian has had to suffer through ridicule and denial. Psychologists want to approach

Brian as if he were experiencing psychological abnormalities, falling into trances, speaking in strange voices, compelled to visit remote locations, and all as if this was all occurring deep inside the recesses of Brian's mind. But the physical manifestations that have occurred around Brian spill outside of the perimeters of his mind into the consensual physical world we all inhabit. Materialization of water or coins could be construed to be psychic phenomena only and not implying the influence of alien entities. The knowledge, the drawings, the witnesses all comprise parts of a larger whole that begs for a new description of reality, one that might include the people from beyond the stars.

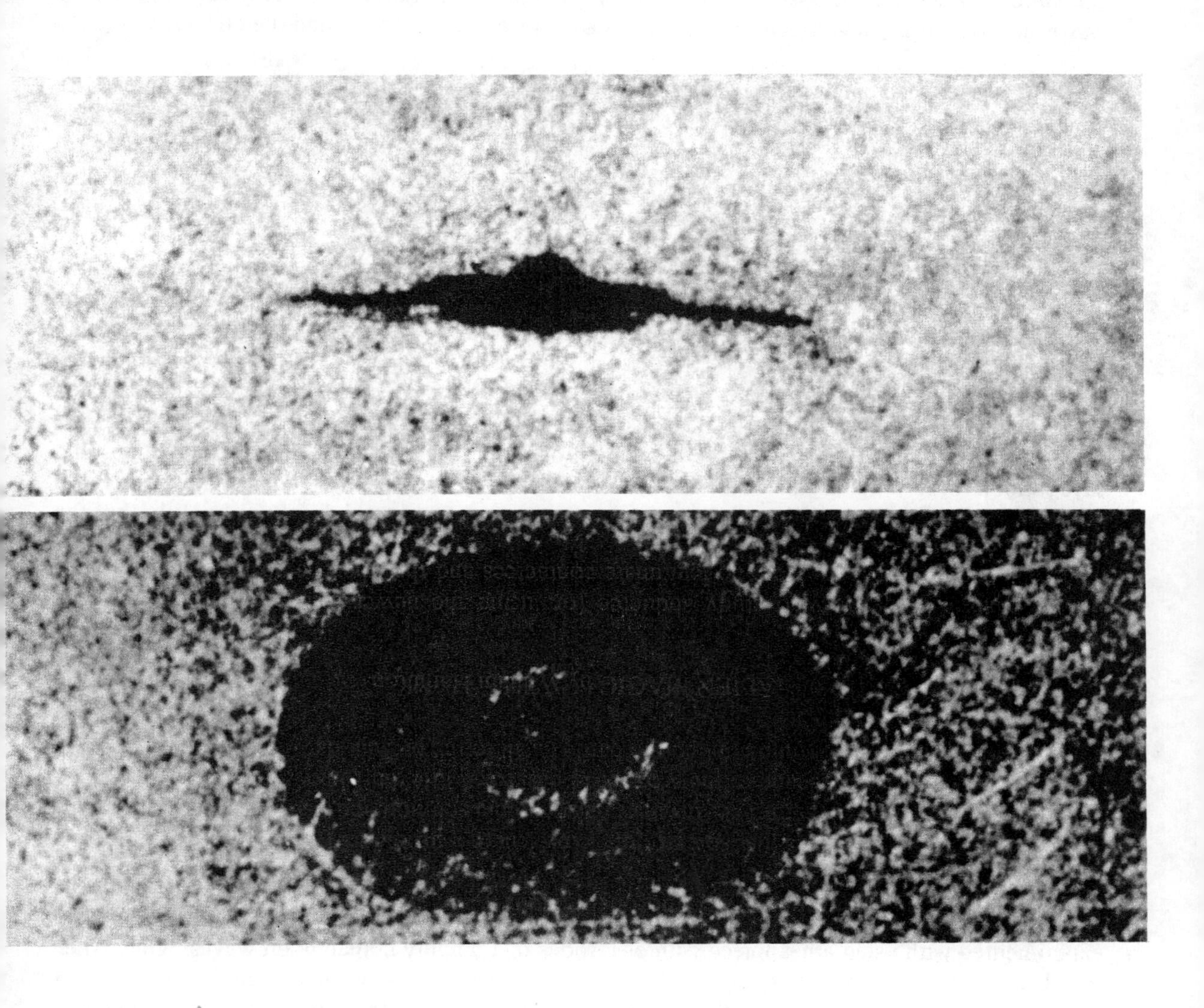

CHAPTER THREE
ARIZONA SKYWAYS

I moved from the smoggy skies of southern California to the Valley of the Sun in 1980. I stayed for most of four years. There are many UFO hotspots in northern and southern Arizona. I moved to Glendale, the same city Brian had lived in when he had his Superstition Mountain encounters. I became an Assistant State Section Director for Maricopa County for MUFON. I was eager to start my investigation of sightings and close encounters around the county.

I became acquainted with a man named Michael, a local Mormon who had an interest in close encounters. He was the friend of a man named Daniel from Las Vegas who had taken photos of a UFO on the ground. Daniel was a contactee. Later I met Daniel. Daniel had been on board saucers, but also received strange writings in trance. The messages he received were like those Brian had received.

One message was sent from Quantella. Daniel's contacts were with a group he called "Nordanians". They would sometimes signal him when they were coming in overflights. The message from Quantella reads: "Essence thru water and fire -- the capabilities of man lies within his mind, his endeavors, his thoughts of mind, and thoughts of water are man's destiny; waters of the lake pertaining to the essence of this old one; the clearness of space, his endeavors, his value to humanity, his dreams of mountains, his dreams of peace, the people of the sky..".. The remainder of the message predicts the movement of his craft in the west over the mountains and says to look for it in the handle of the Dipper. I found the messages have a quality similar to those sent by the Host to Brian. The grammar and prose are not equal to high school English, but the rhythm and the words seem to touch deeper parts of our minds.

Michael also knew a young man named Russell who had an encounter on the night of the full moon on August 25, 1980 in Paradise Valley off of Bell Road heading west. The full moon theme seems to pop up again and again in close encounters of the fourth kind. Russell saw an orange ball of light coming from the southwest. When it got closer, he could see a domed flying saucer that had three hemispherical appendages on the bottom side of the craft. Russell then lost a short period of time.

I remember Russell telling me that the beings who came for him were humanoid. They brought him inside the craft where he sat at a table with a metallic plate positioned in front of him. The aliens used this touch-plate to control the craft, it was evidently their interface to propulsion and navigation, a kind of mental avionics. Mental avionics is something the U.S. Air Force has experimented with using a headpiece with electrodes that amplify human brain waves. Only when the alien was in contact with the touch-plate would the ship's systems be activated. At one point the domed ceiling darkened, and Russell could see stars projected against the inky ceiling. It appeared that lines connected one star to another indicating a route traveled by these visitors.

Others have mentioned this type of alien avionics, a piece of alien magic enhanced by psychotronic amplifications of orders from the mind.

I called Wendelle Stevens one day asking him for a hotspot to investigate around the Phoenix area. He indicated his belief that most hotspot activity was happening around the Verde Valley in northern Arizona, especially a small place called Childs, and, of course, Sedona. However, he thought that I should check out a place about twenty-two miles to the west called the White Tank Mountains. I started organizing some trips into the White Tanks with some new friends to interview witnesses and skywatch. We found a person in a local bar that had seen a UFO in the area of these mountains and had heard of a close encounter between a police patrol car and a blue ball of light.

On the night of June 28, 1980 I had organized a field trip with cameras and binoculars into the White Tank Regional Park zone. I was disappointed that I could not contact Lu or Carol who wanted to go on the field trip with our group. Our group went to the park and stayed until 11:30 PM before we decided to seek out a restaurant for coffee. A *full moon* had been rising in the east behind scattered clouds. It was Monday before I found out that Lu and Carol had gone out that night looking for our skywatch party. We had gone out looking. They went out and encountered that which we were looking for. It was not an event they were expecting.

Lu, Carol, and Carol's daughter, as well as their two dogs were packed tightly into Carol's little Honda Civic looking for the road to the White Tank Regional Park on the night of the 28th. They had not followed previous directions and ended up at the extreme end of northern Avenue where the paved road changes into a dirt and gravel road. They decided to continue driving over the dirt road as the White Tank Mountains appeared to be a short distance away in the moonlit darkness. They suddenly came upon a dead-end sign so decided to park their car at an oblique angle on the road with the car facing southeast.

It was a hot night and Lu, Carol, and Laura (the daughter) were all very alert and in good spirits. They rolled down all the windows on the Honda to aerate the car and Laura had crawled up between Lu and Carol. Lu had a full view of the White Tanks on the passenger side of the car. The two dogs were hunched down in the back seat. Lu called Laura's attention to unusual lights that appeared at the base of the mountains. At that moment Carol felt uncontrollably drowsy, although feeling alert and awake up to that moment. She asked Lu for the time. Lu replied that it was 1:44 AM, then all of them fell into a deep sleep. The next thing Carol was aware of was hearing a voice she thought was Lu's voice saying, "Oh, there is a car". Lu heard the voice, thinking it was Carol talking. Lu glanced at her watch which now read 2:01 AM At that moment, Carol was glancing out the front window of the car and saw a beige-colored Hearse of 1930 vintage drive by, but could not see a driver. Her mother, Lu, also watched the Hearse as she saw the bright red taillights of the vehicle head down the road westward in the direction of a gate marked "No Trespassing". They simultaneously realized that they had not heard the sound of a car motor, nor had they seen any dust that would normally be kicked up by the passage of a vehicle on a dirt and gravel surface. Carol started to have a creepy feeling and turned the key to start the Honda, but the Honda failed to start. They tried again. This time the Honda started, and Carol drove hurriedly, leaving that forebidding area.

Later that same morning, Carol and Lu both felt that something strange had occurred to them on that dark deserted road and decided to drive back in the daylight to look for the tracks of the mystery car. Something else was noticed. The horn on the Honda no longer worked. When they returned to the site, they found nothing to indicate anything had ever happened. When they returned home, Carol decided to try a meditation technique used to bring up suppressed memories. Carol started getting images of helmeted men who surrounded her. Laura also remembered something, but fell asleep during the meditation exercise.

On June 31st, Lu called me up and asked me to investigate the incident. I asked if Carol was willing to try hypnotic regression and she was. On July 2nd, I regressed Carol to the time of the incident. Lu had a block on this technique and Laura had already been impressed with her mother's story. Carol turned out to be a good subject and suggested that she would be able to remember every detail of the incident clearly. Here was a case of multiple abduction in three generations of one family. This one held a few surprises for me.

Carol recounted the incident in clear detail, but as she went deeper into the events that transpired on the morning of the 29th, her emotions started to swell. She had drifted off to sleep that morning, but was awakened by three small beings who were wearing what looked like sea-diving suits with heavy helmets. The heavy helmets appeared to be more suited to ocean diving than special gear used for breathing and protection from our atmosphere. The helmets had two-inch holes dotting the surface. A ring-like lip surrounded each aperture. Glistening inside of the holes was a gel-like substance.

Carol got out of the car as did Lu and Laura. Lu said something like, "this is it, Carol" and all three of them bounced or floated over a two-foot irrigation canal that is always filled with flowing water. I went back to inspect this canal later and could not find a way that little Laura could have jumped clear over the canal. They all moved off in the direction of a silvery dome that was some hundred yards to the south of the road.

When a group of us went back to inspect the abduction site to make a determination of locations and distances, we found the area heavily thicketed and figured that the actual physical transportation of the three females would have to be accomplished by levitation or chances are that they would have gotten themselves quickly entangled in the brush. We found another abandoned dirt road about 100 feet from and parallel to northern Avenue that could serve as the landing field for the grounded UFO, however no landing tracks were found.

Upon approaching the silvery dome, Carol could see another little man standing on a rim or lip that protruded approximately three feet from the bottom edge of the dome. The dome had a silvery-white sheen in the full moonlight. The little man pointed something resembling a flashlight at Carol and a beam of light spread over her body. She felt this was a purification or decontamination process. A rectangular opening appeared in the side of the dome and Carol entered the craft. Her mother and daughter were close behind accompanied by one of the little helmeted men.

Carol spotted at least five of the little men inside the first room she entered that she describes as a control room. This room was filled with buttons and screen and varicolored lights, especially yellow lights. From this main control room, she was directed up a ramp and toward a wall. She had the sensation that she was floating up the ramp. Wherever she placed her hands or feet, she could feel an electrical tingle and that area glowed as if responding to pressure-actuated plates. When she nears the end of the ramp, she hears a sound and a door opens in the wall to another room filled with bright blue lights.

In the second room she encounters a very tall man whose face is covered with a veil of sorts that has intricate designs or symbols embossed on it. She estimates that this man stands over seven feet tall. She receives a telepathic urge to shed her clothing and then recline on an L-shaped table that is fastened to the ceiling. Carol describes a plate where she inserts her feet when lying on the table top. As she places her feet, she again feels a tingle and the foot plate begins to glow. The tall man speaks to her inside her mind. He tells her that he is adjusting her energy centers and that this adjustment is necessary for the critical functioning of her faculties. He seems to chide her for eating chicken that night which has disrupted her energy pattern. Normally, she is a strict vegetarian. Carol feels an ache within her ear during this process, but soon the pain subsides and he requests that she get off the table, get dressed, and sit in a chair that is situated in the center of the room.

Carol sits in the chair and resumes a dialogue with the tall man. She believes that the tall man is in someway her "father". He scolds her for not being intent on her mission and that she will not be able to assist them in her present condition. He causes an instantaneous appearance of a shelf of books. He tells her to pick one book off the shelf. She selects one and opens it. It is full of charts and diagrams. He tells her to read books such as the one she holds to assist her in her mission. He tells her that time is short and the people of Earth must be told the truth about the coming of UFOs and their mission to Earth. She feels impelled to stay with the man, to go back with him wherever he came from, but he tells her that she must leave and wait for further instructions. Carol leaves with tears in her eyes, and the little men escort all three of them back to the car. When they enter the car, the little men just vanish!

Carol had her feet dangling out the window when she had abruptly fallen asleep, yet upon awakening her feet were planted on the floor of the car. It was upon the second awakening that she had heard the voice and had seen the mystery Hearse.

This was a case of real Alien Magic. Others have reported similar phenomena. How did the tall man materialize a shelf of books? Did Carol really pick a book out of thin air? Someone speculated that the aliens could produce a holographic image that looks real, but would it feel real? An image is just a play of light, not a solid object. Is it possible that a tangible object can be produced by stimulating the brain? If so, then the aliens can produce simulacrums of reality. Others have referred to this type of alien magic as virtual reality scenarios (sans headpiece and gloves). The mystery car that Carol and Lu saw was similar to the scenario Pam and I would experience near Area 51 in 1993.

About a week after this occurrence on northern Avenue, Carol and Lu were on a trip to northern Arizona and they experienced trouble with their car lights. When they pulled off the highway, they could see an arc of white light, a sort of midnight rainbow in shape appear in the clouds just above the road at a time close to midnight. They could not determine the source of this light. Both Lu and Carol experienced weight loss after this event and continued to experience changes in their lives.

The White Tank Mountains may not have been a hotspot, maybe just a warmspot for UFO activity, but hot things were happening in the Verde Valley in the north and around Tucson in the south.

In 1980 I flew to Houston for a MUFON conference. I was presenting a paper at the Advanced Propulsion Workshop sponsored by NASA scientist Alan Holt. At the conference I met Gary Lambert and mentioned the Brian Scott case and the frequent occurrence of specific numbers. Gary understood the significance of these numbers and tried to make sense out of them. One of the frequently occurring numbers was the number 22. Gary was abducted in Lincoln, Nebraska on December 25, 1967 just 22 days after the abduction of patrolman Herb Shirmer near Ashland. Gary had discovered that UFO waves occur in five and half year cycles, but smaller cycles occurred just about every 22 days. The numbers that most frequently occurred in UFO events were the number 13, 31, 14, 41 , 5, and 22. To Gary they all related to a 4:1 ratio. These numbers would appear as highway numbers, day of the month, age of witness, or some other synchronicity.

Four of Brian's six abductions by UFOs took place on the 22nd day of the month. His two visits to Tiahuanaco took place on December 22, 1976 and June 22, 1977, the summer and winter solstice days for the southern hemisphere and days of celebration for magicians. This type of number coincidence is termed "synchronistic", a term coined by psychologist Carl Jung who interpreted these sychronicities as meaningful messages from the collective unconscious. Alan Vaughn in his book on sychronicities, *Incredible Coincidence* cites case number 22, a sychronicity that involved UFOs in the movie *Close Encounters of the Third Kind.*

Gary had a drawing made illustrating the pertinent dimensions and angles on the broken windshield of highway patrolman Val Johnson's car that was shattered when he collided with a UFO. One particular triangle stood out and has appeared in other cases. It was an isosceles triangle with proportional dimensions of 22-41-22. Gary also showed me a photo of the rear end of a car that was lifted off the ground on a highway in Missouri when it had a close encounter with a UFO. It had two indentations in the trunk that, together with the ornament on the trunk, formed an isosceles triangle of the same proportions. When you inscribe this triangle inside a circle with the apex at the circle's center, it produces a golden cut of the circle, or golden sector which contains the ratio PHI (1.1618:1). Are these numbers and symbols a clue to Alien Magic?

When I started to study the geometry of the relationships that evolved from the various numbers Gary worked with, I began to perceive a universal pattern that altered my consciousness.

One night I was discussing some of these concepts with my friend Christy. She was having some unusual dream experiences. She had dreams of continuity. In one of these dreams, she believed she spent two weeks on another world. In some dreams, the dream would break off one night only to continue on the next night. This particular night, on May 8, 1981, she was discussing an energy converter that had the shape of a pyramid. I was revved up that night and when I got home I had a hard time falling asleep. I wanted to make contact and learn the secrets of power conversion from the aliens, but nothing was happening. Then I drifted into a hypnogogic state. Though my eyes were closed, I could see my bedroom. It was a hot night and the window above my bed was open. The curtains were blowing in a light breeze.

Suddenly, three figures appeared at the foot of my bed. I was startled by this, but found I could not move. Psychologists, such as Robert Baker, would attribute this experience to a hypnogogic hallucination, but I am not so sure. These three little figures were marshmallow white and wore helmets with visors. The one at the apex of their triangular formation removed his helmet and stared straight through me with large, bright eyes. It was after midnight. The leader must have been about 4 feet tall. He made himself known as Yamatrix. I mentally asked him how he got in the room and where he came from. His mental reply was that he had come from the south near Casa Grande. I thought that was ridiculous. Aliens don't come from Casa Grande. I rephrased my question to indicate that I meant from what solar system? Yamatrix replied, "The Pleiades". I thought this was ridiculous as well. I felt the powerful presence of his mind or the combined presence of their triad mind-link so I asked him what gave him the mental force that I was feeling. He turned in sideways profile to show me the bulge at the back of his head and indicated that it was due to evolved brain functions. Then, he turned and looked at me with a penetrating gaze and I heard a buzzing sound go through my head. As this happened, the three of them vanished, and I came instantly alert and jumped to my feet!

As I did, I took a big gulp of air and was overcome by the pungent smell of ozone. I felt chilled by a presence. I looked all over the house for any burning insulation. Then I realized that there must have been a real presence in the house.

The next day Christy reported to me that she had been out walking her dog when she saw a light high in the sky approach Phoenix from the south. The light hovered over Phoenix for an hour after the midnight hour. A week later a friend of mine who lived in Casa Grande reported to me that he had seen a light that same night inside his trailer and when he went to investigate, he could detect the pungent odor of ozone!

At the time this dream-like visitation occurred in my bedroom in Glendale, I had never heard of alien bedroom visitations. I believe that the physical traces left in such events suggest that they are more than night dreams or hypnogogic hallucinations.

I started to visit Sedona in 1981 and 1982 and heard reports of UFO sightings in that area. On one visit while dining at the Oaxhaca restaurant, a group of us met Nancy. Nancy noticed a UFO book that one of us put on the table and blurted out that she had seen a large UFO over Sedona around May of 1981. She stated that the craft seemed to be several football fields in length, larger than our aircraft carriers. It was a dull metallic color, flat on the bottom, shaped like a shark with a turret or dome filled with lights. The UFO first attracted her attention by the vibration she felt in her house.

On another occasion Nancy had seen three black triangles flying at low altitude while out hiking near Sunset Crater. Nancy and her daughter go out hiking a lot. Her daughter was 18. In April, 1982 she was on a camping trip in Fey Canyon near Sedona. She had erected a tent for the night. Her daughter and baby granddaughter were with her. That night she saw a lighted disk and a small entity entered the tent and grabbed her arm. All three were abducted. This was another three-generational abduction. She recalled that the entity spoke "inside her head" and that they were rearranging her molecular structure for the purpose of facilitating communication and travel. She does not recall what happened between the time she left the tent and returned. She mentioned a memory of having seen seven beings from the sky when she was only six years old. They told her that she had a purpose in life and that she was not a bad girl. She had another sighting on July 4, 1982. Nancy was typical of other cases in the Sedona area involving campers and abductions, especially in the Boynton Canyon area.

Residents of Sedona have reported black helicopters seen in the canyon areas. There is a belief that the government or military has a secure installation in Secret Canyon. I traveled to Sedona on May 6, 1990 to check out the rumors. A man named Gardner Sullivan acted as my guide in the area. We drove around Long Canyon and stopped to look at a defunct housing tract. I heard the sound of a rotor in the distance to the north. Gardner assured me that was in the direction of Secret Mountain. Soon the helicopter became visible rising above the canyon mountains and passing directly overhead headed south. It was an unmarked olive drab helicopter usually flown by the National Guard. I wondered what it was doing coming out of the canyon.

Later that day I met John A. who was a resident caretaker of another defunct housing project in Long Canyon. He had not only seen the helicopters in the canyon, but had seen UFOs. One of these was a large boomerang flying on its side and trailing a sparkling plume. John also claimed he could hear sounds like moving trucks at night. The trucks sounded like they were moving through underground tunnels!

In early June, a friend named Robert went to check on my reports and drove up Boynton Canyon at 2 AM As the jeep trail ended, he got out and hiked in the direction of Secret Mountain. He could hear helicopter motors ahead of him. When he got close, a loudspeaker or bullhorn voice notified him that he was trespassing in a restricted area. The voice said that it was not warning him, but ordering him to turn back. He then noticed a red laser targeting light on his chest and turned around knowing that the voice meant business. The next day a black helicopter followed him for about 30 miles along highway 40 going toward Williams.

In 1992, I was in the Cottonwood area with a gathering who were skywatching. I was looking off toward Secret Mountain. I saw a strobing light dancing around above Sedona. I recognized this object as identical to the ones I had seen over the Antelope Valley and nicknamed them "jumpers" as they performed erratic jumping motions unlike any aircraft I have ever seen.

CHAPTER FOUR
CRASHES IN THE DESERT

"Crashed and retrieved UFOs, I believe,
are the only source of potential proof."
-Leonard Stringfield

My first interest in crashed saucers came to me in 1953 when I read Frank Scully's book, *Behind the Flying Saucers.* When the primary sources of information for Scully, Silas M. Newton and Leo A. Gebauer were brought up on charges of land and oil fraud in Colorado in November of 1953, it seemed all but the end of the case for the UFO crash at Aztec or research into other reports of crashed disks. The little known Roswell case had died a quick public death in 1947 when it was purported that the Air Force had retrieved the debris of a mere balloon and rawinsonde. After all, if flying saucers were real, and were extraterrestrial spacecraft of advanced design, why would they be prone to failure and crash?

To reiterate what I wrote in my book, *Cosmic Top Secret* a simple review of our own history of air crashes involving technically sophisticated aircraft such as the F-16 or B-1B bomber refutes the idea that advanced technology is immune from failure. Highly complex electronic systems are prone to malfunction when subjected to radio, radar, or microwave emissions. Electromagnetic Pulse (EMP) from a nuclear explosion can wreck havoc on electronic devices. Random noise can occur in transistors and other semiconductor devices. Any electric device which must receive electromagnetic radiation will pick up radiated random noise as well as signals. Filters must be included in such circuits to limit bandwidth detection and reduce noise that can overwhelm signal strength.

In a Los Angeles Times news article of November 9, 1987, it states that routine radio waves can knock the Army's most advanced battle transport helicopters out of the sky. Transmissions from radio antennas, radar, and microwave towers can interfere with the wiring and electrical components of the Army's UH-60 Black Hawk helicopters and generate potentially devastating false commands. One senior Army aviator said "EMI (electromagnetic interference) is causing these aircraft to flip upside down and crash and kill everybody aboard.". The article goes on to say that the Soviets were perfecting a radio-wave weapon to exploit this vulnerability.

It doesn't take much imagination to conceive why the U.S. pursued directed-energy weapons in its SDI program. Lasers were tested that could knock out an aircraft's control systems. Actually, a high-energy pulsed microwave MASER could knock airplanes out of the sky.

A memo written to the Director of the FBI from Guy Hottel of SAC, Washington dated March 22, 1950 states that an investigator for the Air Force describes three so-called flying saucers and their pilots which had been recovered in New Mexico. The memo also states that a high powered radar set-up in that area interfered with the controlling mechanism of the saucers. How did they learn this interesting tidbit of information? Were C-band radar waves beamed at saucers to deliberately bring one out of the skies so we could retrieve and examine it? Saucers are known to generate powerful electromagnetic fields and the technology used to generate these fields could be susceptible to EMI. Electronic countermeasures are deliberately used by our military to jam signals and introduce noise into the enemy's electronic circuits. If the flying saucers were considered intruders, then there may have been a plan to develop a means to bring them down to earth.

The most famous of the UFO crashes is receiving a lot of publicity and the case for a UFO crash at Roswell and the recovery of crash debris and alien bodies is the strongest of cases, but does not stand alone. An investigation of the Roswell crash has been launched by Congressman Steven Schiff of Albuquerque, New Mexico who solicited the aide of the General Accounting Office (GAO) in ferreting out any documents found in the vast mound of paper archives. Nine months after this search for evidence began, the Air Force released its own report on the Roswell Incident suggesting that the debris found was the remains of a highly secret Mogul balloon.

It couldn't have been a flying saucer. It was just a balloon, a favorite Air Force explanation that has haunted UFO watchers since 1947. General Roger Ramey announced that the wreckage found on the Foster Ranch wasn't the wreckage of a flying disk as announced earlier in the Roswell Daily Record, but the metallic remains of a radar reflector from a rawinsonde weather balloon. Major Jesse Marcel, the Air Force Intelligence Officer who was sent out to inspect the debris, had said that it was definitely not a balloon. The material was like nothing he had ever seen.

A little research on weather balloons, not found in the aviation section of the library, but in the meteorological section, revealed that rawinsonde balloons lofted a radar reflector for the purpose of reflecting radar signals from a weather station to determine variations in wind speed. The Air Force was saying that the debris field was composed of the remains of the reflector, not the balloon. What happened to the balloon? A little thought questions why a weather station would try to send a rawinsonde aloft during or before a lightning storm. Surely the metallic reflector would be susceptible to lightning strikes. Of course, one has to ask what kind of material was used in this reflector. If aluminum foil, what kind of aluminum foil would not dent or mar, and then, when folded, unfold back to its original shape?

The balloon explanation was used to cover the debris field, not the crash site of the wreckage of a downed spacecraft.

Other weather balloons carry radio instruments aboard and are known as radiosonde balloons. Back in the forties, the National Meteorological Center received 980 radiosonde and 500 rawinsonde reports every 24 hours. There was nothing secret about these balloons. They were doing their job of sensing weather conditions before weather satellites were used.

ALIEN MAGIC by William Hamilton

John Keel, a critic of Ufology and Ufologists, who has expressed a negative opinion of Ufologists, advanced the idea that wreckage found on the Foster Ranch was the remains of a Japanese Fugo balloon, a device used by the Japanese toward the end of the war to carry incendiary bombs to distant targets. I guess it was hoped that prevailing winds would carry the balloons to their intended destination. These gas-filled balloons were made of laminated paper or rubberized silk, hardly fitting the description of the debris material handled by witnesses.

Balloons always popped up as an easy explanation for UFO sightings. The Air Force once declared that it was a weather balloon that Captain Mantell was chasing in his P51 above Godman tower in Kentucky in 1948. When it was found that no weather balloons were released in that vicinity on the day in question, then the official explanation for the large metallic object chased by Mantell was given as the planet Venus. Since these absurd explanations foreshadowed those contrived by Phil Klass, we might come to think that he received a grounding in Air Force methods of contriving explanations for the gullible public.

One would think that the balloon controversy would have been settled by now, using a careful analysis of reported facts just as one might expect in a court of law. But the outcry by Ufologists demanding an official release of documents on the Roswell Incident has caused the Air Force Department of Official Explanations to delve deeply into it's file of best cover stories and out popped another balloon. After all, if there were no crashes of alien spacecraft, and no secret autopsies of alien entities, perhaps the public's belief in UFO sightings and alien abductions would erode. After all, the authority of my grandmother was sufficient to convince me that ghosts did not exist!

The GAO prying started by Rep. Steven Schiff, R-N.M., opened the door on a long-locked stale-aired room that the Air Force surely wanted shut forever. The Air Force spokesman this time, a Col. Richard Weaver concluded in a 25-page report that the debris found on the Foster Ranch *probably* came from a once top-secret balloon designed to monitor the atmosphere for evidence of Soviet nuclear tests. This was known as Project Mogul. The sensing device (a generic blurry term) was most likely a Geiger Counter, an instrument that would have landed with the balloon. I'm sure Maj. Marcell would have recognized a Geiger Counter if he had found one in the debris field.

The breaking story now is that the 20-page GAO report of a records audit of events surrounding the Roswell crash indicate that many important records, such as the outgoing messages from Roswell Army Air Field, were **destroyed without proper authority!**

Note: This says that a balloon crashed, not a reflector. Do balloons crash? Big gas-filled balloons were made of rubber or plastic materials that are pliable. What happens to one when it crashlands on earth? Would it fragment into thousands of little metallic-like fragments strewn over hundreds of yards? Does this mean that Col. Weaver is ignorant of balloons or ignorant of the descriptions given by witnesses. And what if some of that material is still in the hands of witnesses? And Weaver declares that our facts are undocumented, taken out of context, self-serving, or dubious. Where are the documents that prove it was nothing more than a balloon? Or is this a self-serving explanation for the Air Force? It certainly is a dubious explanation.

A little further research revealed that the first Soviet atomic test was detected in the South Pacific on September 3, 1949. This took America by surprise as the Finletter Commission had estimated this event would not take place until 1953. A B-29 detected the higher than normal radiation count, not a balloon. Why would we be sending up balloons in 1947 to detect such Soviet tests before any such test took place?

Just to add a little spice to all this speculation I will mention a document published by Len Stringfield that he believes has validity. It is dated 9 July 1947 and states that a preliminary investigation of a recovered "Flying Disc" and remains of a possible second disc concludes that they was not manufactured by another country on earth and goes on to say that the propulsion system was believed to be a bladeless turbine similar to a then current development at AMC (Air Material Command) and the Mogul Project.

Was the Mogul Project bigger than balloons? Was it also trying to develop a new and revolutionary type of propulsion system? Was it determined that national security required that such propulsion systems were to be kept a permanent secret?

I was taught cover stories when I served in Air Force Security Service. These are true lies. It is the way you word your story. There are some things that the public should never know. That's policy. The Air Force certainly has generated enough hot air to raise another one of those balloons.

Kent Jeffrey, a Roswell researcher, has authored the Roswell Declaration in an attempt to get an Executive Order to declassify any existing U.S. government-held information concerning UFOs or extraterrestrial intelligence. A copy of this declaration is available from the MUFON HQ in Sequin, Texas. Any member of the public who has an interest in seeing the declassification of UFO information should sign this declaration and send it to their representative in Washington.

To complicate the Roswell controversy even further, word got out that a producer by the name of Ray Santilli had obtained old 16-mm film footage from a retired military photographer by the name of Jack Barnett. This black-and-white footage allegedly shows an autopsy performed on alien life forms. When this film was viewed, in part, on May 5, 1995 in England, Roswell researchers were convinced that the film was a hoax. Santilli is not a UFO researcher, but is convinced the film is authentic. There is no doubt that supposed evidence of this nature should be subjected to the most critical analysis before a conclusion is reached. By the time the reader has read these words, a great deal of additional information will be made public.

I was quite content investigating close encounter cases, but something about the UFO crash cases beckoned to me. I wanted to find out for myself if witnesses told incredible stories that correlated in the same way that abductee cases correlate. There are specific details about military operations that are mentioned by independent witnesses. There are also specific details about the craft that are reiterated by independent witnesses. In other words, there's a good case for crash-retrievals.

ALIEN MAGIC by William Hamilton

In 1980 I talked to ex-Navy seaman Wayne Henthorne about his strange encounter on a road just outside of Globe, Arizona in January 1947. He was driving a jeep. An unnamed friend was with him. On the road in front of him was a military blockade. Beyond a cordoned-off perimeter they saw a large flying saucer with a transparent dome. It was sitting on tripod legs. It did not look as if it crashed. They were told to leave the area and say nothing about what they had seen. Unless Wayne was telling me a tall tale, he had encountered a retrieval before the Roswell incident if his recollection of the date is correct. No other witnesses have ever recalled a retrieval near Globe. This is a single witness case as are most of the ones I have had an opportunity to interview. This does not mean these cases are hoaxed. They are inconclusive. Others could come forward someday and confirm some of the events described by these witnesses. If documents are ever released, these events should appear in such documents if they are valid military retrieval incidents. The interesting aspect of these incidents are the bits and pieces of the technical puzzle they fill.

Also in 1980, a woman named Mary had told me of her contact with a producer who claimed to be in possession of a 17-minute segment of film showing a retrieved saucer and 5 alien bodies. Somehow, this segment was taken out of Air Force archives. He wanted to show it to some interested researcher, but feared being caught with stolen property. Supposedly, this person was associated with the production of the movie, "Hangar 18." At first, I tried to make a connection with researcher Wendelle Stevens to see if he could help, but later I made contact with Leonard Stringfield at the 1980 MUFON Symposium and asked for his help. I put him in contact with Mary and Mary put him in contact with the mysterious producer by phone. He talked long enough with Leonard for Len to be convinced that the man might be telling the truth. He was too frightened about negotiating with Len to show him the film. In the end, the man simply dropped out of sight and we will never know whether he had an authentic document.

Not directly related to UFO crashes, I interviewed a Captain Creighton when I lived in Arizona in 1981. Captain Creighton was a radar officer with the Air Force and told me about a radar sighting at his station in Wisconsin. A UFO appeared on the screen and hovered some 50 miles north of the station for a period of time. Then within one sweep of the scope, the blip representing an unknown object disappeared from its initial stationary position and reappeared 20 miles closer. As this unknown was hopping all over the radar scope, Captain Creighton wanted to film it. After filming the antics of this UFO, he took the film to his superior officer who accepted the film, then threw it in the round file saying that he did not want to get involved with UFO redtape.

In 1982 I interviewed a Ms. Sylvia whose daughter-in-law was stationed at Luke AFB near Glendale, Arizona. A formation of unknown objects flew over Phoenix one night and were tracked by radar at the base. Her daughter-in-law reported that communications were received by radio at the base from the UFOs and recorded on magnetic tapes. These tapes were immediately demounted from their drives and stored in a time-locked vault. The next day, a General arrived from the Pentagon, picked up the tapes and flew out.

My interest was increasing in military UFO stories. I knew the military could keep secrets. I kept a few of those secrets myself when I was a member of the Air Force Security Service reporting to NSA. Maybe the General staff at the Pentagon had some of the answers to the UFO mystery, but they sure were not sharing their knowledge with the public or civilian UFO organizations.

In April 1988, I took a vacation trip to New Mexico and intended to visit Aztec, Dulce, Albuquerque, and Alamagordo. New Mexico was indeed a land of mystery and beauty. While making all of these stops along the way, I encountered a man who had once been stationed in San Antonio, Texas while in the Army in 1948. One night, he said, a number of troops had been loaded on trucks and were driven to a remote site in the darkness of night. He had no idea where they were when they disembarked from the back of the covered trucks. They had been driving for hours. It is even possible that he had the date wrong, and the year was 1947 and the site was Roswell, but none of that was confirmed. He was assigned to pick up fragments of metallic material that was extremely light weight. Later when he picked up a piece of titanium, he thought that it resembled the material they had picked up in the desert. The site of the crash was over 10 hours drive from San Antonio.

In 1988 I also talked with a psychologist who had been attending UFO meetings and support group meetings by the name of Perry. He revealed that he had participated in a retrieval of a "Class 3" vehicle from Great Falls, Montana in 1947. This unknown designation apparently referred to some early classification system. He flew the recovered craft in a transport plane to Wright field. He was not very forthcoming with additional information and I have not talked to him since.

On September 23, 1990 I was introduced to a man named Ozzie who related a detailed story of his participation in two crash-retrievals while he was in the Army stationed at Roswell in 1948 and 1949. This is a single-witness story that has not been corroborated by other witnesses. He doesn't know the exact dates of the crashes, but believes the first one occurred in the desert near Socorro, New Mexico. His recounting of this incident took place inside of a locked car with rolled-up windows which seemed a little paranoid to me. There was no doubt that he came across as sincere, answering all my questions without hesitation and to the best of his knowledge. His attitude was one of not caring whether he was believed or not as he claimed he had already been the butt of much ridicule. He currently held a job at a large aerospace company and did not want to publicly divulge his background. I found this to be the case with other witnesses I have interviewed.

One night in 1948 he was called out of his barracks to climb aboard a bus that looked like an old school bus with darkened windows. After hours of riding through the desert on a generally westward course, the bus came to a stop during the very early hours of the morning and he could see a disk standing on the desert sands illuminated by floodlights. It was like a movie set, but there were no movie cameras or directors barking orders. The disk was silvery and about 30 feet in diameter. He learned that two aliens were recovered from the disk. One was alive. White-coated doctors walked the live alien around the site. It lived for 12 hours. The disk had one compartment with a shaft running up the center of the compartment. The exterior hull of the craft felt smooth and slippery to the touch. Ozzie said that only 3 men lifted the lightweight craft onto a flat bed truck. Men went ahead and scouted a backroads transport of the truck away from the site. Ozzie accompanied a scientist who caravaned along the backroads until they reached their ultimate destination at a little auxiliary airfield on the edge of Groom Lake in Nevada. There were only five buildings at this airfield and they arrived at night. The truck drove up to one of the buildings and Ozzie saw two living aliens standing by this building. One of the doors of the building opened, he could see that six other disks had already been retrieved and placed inside the building.

The whole recovery team was taken into a room in another one of the buildings and debriefed. Ozzie saw pictures on the wall of the room that depicted six different types of aliens. He remembers that one of the aliens looked human. Short grays were also in one of the pictures. He did not say whether these were photos or drawings, but he called them pictures so I assume they were photos. At one point during the debriefing, a small alien appeared to pass through one of the walls of the room. He was holding a small black box that Ozzie called an "augmenter."

Ozzie made some interesting detailed observations, but it is admitted that his story has bizarre elements to it. But, when we compare some of these bizarre elements to stories told by abductees they seem less bizarre by far. We find it hard to believe that the military had such a high degree of involvement with aliens as early as 1948.

Ozzie claims that he was called out on a second retrieval in 1949 at close to the same site as the first retrieval. The second disk was 100 feet in diameter and ten dead crew were found at the site. Their skin had turned a purplish color. These beings were about 5' 8" in height. Ozzie had to carry one of the aliens and estimated its weight at only 55 pounds. He was very emotional about this incident. The aliens were dressed in one-piece coveralls that have a velcro-type fastener at the back. Of course, velcro-type fasteners did not exist in 1949 and Ozzie is only comparing what he saw to what we know today. The big disk had a conveyor on the floor that transported the crew from one control center to another. There was also an instrument that contained colored fluids. A central column ran through the center of the craft which had multiple rectangular compartments. When inside the control room of the craft, Ozzie said you could plainly see through the sidewall of the craft and the desert was plainly visible even at night. The metal of the craft could not be marred with any of our tools. This disk was also transported to the site at Groom Lake.

That ended Ozzie's involvement in crash-retrievals though he has kept in contact with others he had met during his involvement. He also claims that he has a photo of the second retrieval locked in a vault for safekeeping. He does not know when it might become safe enough to bring out this photo as evidence. So we are left with another story and no corroborating evidence, but a pattern begins to emerge from the details as we talk to other witnesses.

A man named Frenchie was stationed at Edwards AFB in 1951 when he was called out of his barracks along with others because something had crashed just south of the air base. When he got to the site, he was not allowed to get any closer than an outer established security perimeter, but could see men lifting up large chunks of metal. Sheets of metal were all over the crash site, but no engine or fuselage was visible. Frenchie said they had to cut out a piece of a C-47 to enlarge its door to fit a large piece of the retrieved material into the plane for transport. The large piece was light weight and was lifted by two men. Frenchie never found out what the object was.

A lot of this crash debris was supposedly transported to the Air Material Command at Wright Field. However, craft recovered in one piece were probably shipped elsewhere, perhaps Groom Lake. The engineering division at Wright Field called T-3 had already concluded that the UFOs were advanced aircraft or spacecraft which used nonconventional methods of propulsion and were constructed from composite layers of light-weight material. It was the opinion of the General staff that the unidentified objects were interplanetary spacecraft.

William Steinman had discovered that Dr. Robert I. Sarbacher of the Washington Institute of Technology had some involvement in the scientific study of crashed disks. He wrote a letter to Sarbacher in 1983 asking for verification of the involvement of individuals in a list that he enclosed in his letter. Sarbacher replied that John von Neumann was definitely involved as was Dr. Vannever Bush and Robert Oppenheimer, the scientific leader of the Manhattan project. Sarbacher also mentioned Dr. von Braun.

Consider the involvement of top scientists in the investigation of the recovered saucers when we read the contents of a document, faded with age, given to Leonard Stringfield by a credible source. The document is a report on the preliminary investigation of a flying disk and indicates there was a presidential directive dated 9 July 1947 to carry out such an investigation. It also mentions the remains of a possible second disk. The data in the report is said to be furnished by the engineering staff of T-2 and Aircraft Laboratory, Engineering Division T-3. Additional data was furnished by the scientific personnel of the Jet Propulsion Laboratory, CIT, and the Army Air Forces Scientific Advisory Group headed by Dr. Theodore von Karmen. Von Karmen was an expert in aerodynamics and founder of Aerojet General Corporation.

The report mentions that the disk was circular and did not resemble anything in the design stages or under known military development. No external propulsion system, power plant, intake, or exhaust ports were found on the craft. German scientists from Fort Bliss and White Sands could not identify it. A compartment containing a possible atomic engine was discovered. Dr. Oppenheimer and Dr. von Karmen were consulted regarding this engine.

A description of the power room follows: "A doughnut shaped tube approximately thirty-five feet in diameter, made of what appears to be plastic material, surrounding a central core. This tube appeared to be filled with a clear substance, possibly a heavy water. A large rod centered inside the tube, was wrapped in a coil of what appears to be of copper material, ran through the circumference of the tube. This may be the reactor control mechanism or a storage battery. There were no moving parts in the spaces examined."

The report goes on to say, "The activation of an electrical potential is believed to be the primary power to the reactor, though it's only a theory at present."

The report also describes a ball turret underneath the power plant. This turret was about ten feet in diameter. It was believed that the air outside the craft was ionized, propelling the craft forward. Coupled with the circular air foil for lift, the craft would presumably have an unlimited range and airspeed. This may account for the reported absence of any noise. There is a flight deck located inside the copula section atop the craft. The absence of a canopy, observation windows, or any optical projection led to the belief that the craft was guided by remote control. The craft had no weld marks, rivets or soldered joints. It appeared as if the components were molded and pressed into a perfect fit.

The reference to ionized air refers to a principle in electroaerodynamics where electric charges are applied to high-speed vehicles such as supersonic aircraft or B-2 bombers to reduce air drag or eliminate sonic booms. High-speed ions are projected forward from the leading edges of the craft. This coronal discharge repels air molecules away from the aircraft's leading surfaces.

Researcher Clifford Stone has compiled stacks of government documents in his search of verifying the government's continuing interest and involvement in UFO incidents. One of these documents refers to Project Moondust. Moondust may have been the code name for retrieval operations that not only involved U.S. or foreign satellites or space debris returning to Earth, but also the recovery of remains or debris of alien spacecraft.

There have been reports of many alleged UFO crashes. Most of these reports have never been thoroughly investigated and, as Kevin Randle has suggested in his book, *A History of UFO Crashes* many will turn out to be false reports. I am still not absolutely positive that the Aztec crash was a complete hoax. We may still find out that there was something to this story, but I do not think it was some kind of distortion of the Roswell Incident. In August 1952 a disk purportedly crashed near Ely, Nevada and 16 bodies were recovered. There are no further details or listed sources of this report. A cursory check could be made to see if such a report is worth pursuing. There are more such reports. This includes a crash near Holloman AFB, New Mexico on June 12, 1962. I did talk to a man who saw light-weight metallic fragments inside a building at Holloman. No more is known about this.

There have been recent crashes reported in Canada, South Africa, and other places. All of these reports are of dubious origin. Several of these have been denounced by UFO investigators. No one has yet come up with a smoking saucer.

I met Sergeant Charlie S. in 1994. Charlie was a member of a special operations group in the U.S. Marines during the early Vietnam era. He was stationed on the aircraft carriers U.S.S. Oriskany and the Valley Forge. Their team went in to recover a landed disc in the hills of Vietnam just east of Hue. Charlie says the craft landed and two aliens emerged and walked away from the craft. Some native farmers saw the aliens and took up pitchforks in fear. They stabbed the aliens to death. The disc was about 30 feet in diameter. Charlie calls it an IRC-10 which translates into Interplanetary Reconnaissance Craft of 10 meters. In retrospect, Charlie says that the IRC-10 was an old model. It did not have the electromagnetic mind-link panel used to control the craft, but a touch-control panel by the seats. This touch-control panel is similar to that described by Russell. The craft was lighter than a VW bug and could be lifted easily by a few men. This is what Ozzie said concerning the disc in New Mexico. Charlie said the disc was transported to the flight deck of the aircraft carrier. Ultimately, it was stored on the flight deck cushioned between mattresses and covered by a tarpaulin.

Examining the craft, Charlie says the entrance hatch was found on the bottom of the craft. The craft was supported by three landing legs. When the hatch was closed, it fit into the hole so tightly that no seam could be detected. Between the three landing gears there were three drive amplifier pods that fit flush against the undersurface. Charlie felt that this craft descended from an orbiting mothership. He did not say how he obtained this impression. The control cables from the flight deck to the avionics on the top deck were composed of fiber-optics embedded in the hull. These fiber-optics signals could not be affected by the electromagnetic flux of the ship. He feels that when openings closed, such as the hatch, they molecularly bonded with the shell of the craft.

The craft was transported on the carrier back to San Francisco where it was unloaded. The captain of the carrier used the cover story that the tarpaulin covered saucer was a new watertank they were bringing into port for maintenance and it was covered to protect it from storms at sea.

Charlie mentioned tidbits he had heard about the Roswell craft that were shared with members of the inner circle of involved people. Charlie continually networks with some of these people. He said that the metal fragments were found to be a strange alloy of beryllium (Atomic Number 4/Atomic Weight 9.013). This was different from ordinary beryllium in it's atomic structure which was in a very tight matrix giving extraordinary strength to the material; it could bend but not break. He said the ceiling of the craft had another metal, that when energized, lit up and glowed. It used a wave guide operating in the microwave S-band which confirms contactee Calvin Girvin's information that the central column is a magnetron. The Aeroshell was only .75 to 1.25" in thickness and was put together in compressed laminations. Perhaps our advanced technology stealth aircraft that use composite skin structures with compressed laminations derived their inspiration from interstellar or interspatial craft. Charlie went on to say that all the discs he had knowledge of, the IRC-10 and IRC-16 (referred to as the Sports Model by Bob Lazar) seem to have six wedge-shaped side support members bonded to the aeroshell itself. The instrument used to study the metal fragments was a spectrochromatograph.

As I have not seen exactly this type of structure analysis in print, I am reproducing parts of Charlie's conversations with me to elicit further corroboration. Charlie has had technical training in electronic engineering and is very precise in his speech. He also freely admits when he doesn't know anything about a particular topic.

I had first heard of Charlie from a friend and heard that he was writing a letter to OMNI magazine concerning their articles on UFO cover-up. I obtained his address and wrote him a letter. Within days I received a letter in return, but not from Charlie. Someone intercepts Charlie's mail and after testing this a few times, I am convinced he receives little in the way of mail at his home address and circumvents this by using another address. The letter I received was from someone in a veteran's association who stated that material in OMNI was peppered with deliberate disinformation, and that those who had hands-on experience with alien technology were stupid for breaking their oaths as loyal Americans. It was stated that the high level of security involved at the UFO level is not under a 30-year minimum expiration limit, but is *permanent.* I was warned to not try to contact Charlie again. It was stated that, "Any unauthorized individuals who break into this security mutually protecting our visitors and our governments, would likely be terminated, along with their associates." It goes on to say that by interfering in matters beyond my understanding and none of my business, would only make things more difficult. One cryptic sentence reads, "We need the assistance of one of their Federations to protect us from the expansionism of another." It was signed: R. Quinlen (almost indecipherable).

Was this letter a hoax? If it is, it uses serious language to deter me from visiting with Charlie. I really do not think that Charlie has told me enough to be a threat to our national security or the security of the visitors. Charlie never knew I received this letter and I had to provide him with a copy. He fears interrogation and threats, but they also anger him. Since we have openly shared information, he has received one direct threat. Charlie is not the only person that I know who has been threatened by mysterious agents. I do not think that we can just shrug off these incidents as a practical joke. There is more substance to these threats than I will go into in this work.

As for the philosophy behind the sentiment expressed in the letter, we are at odds. Researchers intend to make discoveries and report those discoveries to others. Security is in place to thwart our making discoveries. Security is antipathetic to the scientific process. If the security oath regarding the alien presence is permanent, then we are battling against an implacable barrier in trying to penetrate the security shielding that is meant to keep us in the dark. The philosophical problem contained in this dilemma is one that has confronted many leaders involved in making decisions that will affect populations. Is the threat to our existence and welfare on this planet of such a nature that just revealing the truth would be enough to bring down retribution so secrecy protects the people. The problem with secrecy is it divides us from one another. Ultimately, it is communication that makes a people a civilized society and a breakdown in free communication ultimately leads to a disintegration of society. If the cells in your body started to erect security barriers and ceased to communicate among one another, the body would die. Though individuals are more autonomous than cells, the cohesion of a group is fundamentally based on communication and consensus. Would the truth make us free or bring down the sky on our collective heads?

What do we have to gain by learning advanced alien technology and would we understand it to the degree that we could duplicate it after a fashion?

We could learn:

1) New Physics -- Energy sources such as antimatter; solar; zero-point; etc. and methods of electro-gravitational propulsion.

2) Materials Science -- New composites; new atomic and molecular matrices; sandwich or laminated construction; organic growth technology; use of new kinds of metals and plastics.

3) Weapons -- Beam weapons; neutral particle beam; antiproton beams; microwave beams; and ultrasonic beams. Also stealth technology including optical invisibility.

4) Electronics -- Transistors; ICs; Organic molecular; superconducting; etc.
5) Optical -- Enhanced laser; diffuse lighting; bending light beams; etc.
6) Communication -- Gravitational wave; neutrino; spacetime; telepathy
7) Computing -- Electro-optical; holographic; parallel processing; artificial intelligence; intelligent machines; etc.
8) Biological -- Genetic engineering; cloning; evolutionary development; terraforming; etc.
9) Psychic -- Telepathy; out-of-body; remote viewing; telekinesis; precognition
10) Exotic -- Time-travel; teleportation; Reality Engineering; Dimensional shifting

This list is just an estimate of some of the technologies that could be used by aliens, and from which we could benefit, but there may be more that we could not even guess at, technologies that do not even fit our frame of reference.

The February 1987 issue of *Gung-Ho* magazine had a very interesting article discussing projects called "Unfunded Opportunities" (UFO). It said that these programs were dealing with technology levels so advanced that one Air Force officer involved in SR-71 development said: "We are flight testing vehicles that defy description. To compare them conceptually to the SR-71 would be like comparing Leonardo da Vinci's parachute design to the space shuttle."

"We have things that are so far beyond the comprehension of the average aviation authority as to be really alien to our way of thinking," says one retired colonel. Rumor has it some of these systems involve force-field technology, gravity-drive systems, and "flying saucer" designs. Rumor further has it that these designs are not necessarily of Earth human origin. "Lets just put it this way," explained one retired Lockheed engineer, "We have things flying around in the Nevada desert that would make George Lucas drool."

The latter statement seems to be a veiled reference to the Groom Lake or Papoose Lake locations at the famed Nevada Test Site designated Area 51. Do we have deep black projects based on past studies of alien technology? Have we developed our own flying saucers? That is a possibility I will explore further in a later chapter.

CHAPTER FIVE
Bogies

The pilot and crew of a Japan Airlines Boeing 747 spotted a spectacular UFO on Nov. 17, 1986 in the skies over Alaska. The Captain, Kenju Terauchi, a pilot of 29 years' experience, saw a gigantic walnut-shaped aerial object that he estimated was larger than an aircraft carrier. This large "mothership" was accompanied by two smaller lighted craft. According to the pilot, the objects appeared on the aircraft's weather radar.

This case received so much notoriety that the FAA made the results of its investigation of the incident available to the public.

Despite the pilot's graphic description of a huge UFO, the press rushed into print with a Klassic explanation. Klass's explanation for the sighting: the pilot misperceived either the planet Mars or Jupiter. And the radar return? Inconclusive.

The Air Force has been offering canned explanations for UFOs ever since the first dribble of reports signaled that something very strange was invading our air space. When Captain Thomas Mantell was chasing a large disk over Godman Field in Kentucky in 1948, the Air Force concluded that he had been pursuing the Planet Venus! Planets, planes, balloons, clouds, and swamp gas were some of the clever explanations used to dismiss thoughts of space visitors from the public's mind.

When the Air Force released its Project Bluebook Special Report 14, a statisical analysis of UFO sightings, it had concluded that at least 20% of those analyzed could not be explained. An additional 2% had insufficient data to reach a conclusion. What were these unexplained objects? The answer certainly wasn't forthcoming from the Air Force.

A new twist on explaining UFO sightings has emerged in recent years. That new twist is: Advanced Technology Aircraft. Based on the public's increased awareness of black programs such as the development of the B-2 Stealth Bomber, and on rumors of back-engineering alien technology, some UFO sightings in recent years are explained as products of our own secret research and development.

On October 1, 1990 an article in *Aviation Week and Space Technology* reported that well-qualified observers had sighted strange advanced aircraft flying over Southern California and Central Nevada deserts. Several articles followed this initial article reporting more sightings and speculating on the new engine and materials technology developed by Aerospace companies that went beyond the known white-world technology employed by our standard run-of-the-mill jet aircraft. In a subsequent May 1992 issue of *Aviation Week* sightings of a high-speed "pulser" vechicle were reported. Photos of knotted-rope contrails that were left by an unknown aircraft flying over Amarillo, Texas were reprinted in the article. Aviation experts speculated on the type of propulsion system that would cause a pulsing roar and leave a knotted contrail in its wake. Their conclusion - the aircraft uses a pulsed detonation engine.

The situation gets more complicated by December 1991 when *Popular Mechanics* features a story about America's New Secret Aircraft. The author of this article begins by telling us that skywatchers have gathered off Highway 138 just west of Lancaster, California and just south of the Tehachapi Mountains hoping to catch a glimpse of mysterious aircraft that officially don't exist. That is not what we were doing at all! Having organized some of these first skywatches myself, I know damn well what we were doing out there. Looking for UFOs -- the alien kind. But that does not fare well with those authorities who never admit such a thing. That's just not an acceptable, logical explanation for what many were seeing over desert skies.

One of the dark black shapes that has been seen cruising between Wrightwood and Lancaster is described as triangular with bright white lights at each of the apices and a pulsing red light under the center of the body. It moves slowly and silently and has been estimated to be larger than a sprawling two-story house. Boys playing near an aquaduct in Hesperia sighted one of these mysterious triangles divide into two parts and the two parts fly off in different directions. Ah, but triangular planes are not unknown.

According to Aviation Week, one of these triangular objects could be the highly secret Northrop TR-3A, a classified tactical reconnaisance vehicle. This plane is about 42 feet long and about 60 feet wide. Thats bigger than a house. Its engines run more quietly than the muffled GE jet engines on the Stealth fighter. But jets move fast. With the exception of the Harrier, which is loud enough to break a window, jets don't hover or lollygag along at a runner's pace. They also don't just stop and ascend straight up as one of our mysterious triangles was seen to do. Oh yes, did I mention flying on end - you know with the normally flat surface upended vertically to the ground. How do these amazing jets do that? Without crashing or controlling the inexorable force of gravity?

It wasn't difficult explaining the vast black flying wings seen over the Antelope Valley. These 600 - 900 foot monsters amble their way over the desert at bicycle speeds sporting dozens of lights just to terrify jackrabbits and country bumpkins who gaze at them in awe. How do they suspend themselves without tremendous volumes and velocities of airflow? *Popular Mechanics* had no lack of imagination here. It could have been a new-fangled lighter-than-air craft. Like a blimp with quiet propellers. Forgotten here are eyewitness reports of instantaneous accelerations or the complete winking out of one of these monstrous wingships like the disappearance of a magician's rabbit. More high tech? Whose? Is anyone getting confused yet?

Let us add to the mystery. According to an article in the *L.A. Times* on Sept. 17, 1992, mysterious tremors have boomed throughout Southern California from Los Angeles to San Diego. The experts at Cal Tech's seismic station said that the booms were not caused by earthquakes. More rumors said that they stemmed from an exotic spy plane that has reportedly been flying out of a secret Air Force base in Neveda, but these rumors could not be confirmed.

Of course, the Air Force denied it. The Air Force is not only denying any knowledge of UFOs, **but is also denying any knowledge of secret aircraft!**

Interestingly, the *L.A. Times* said that (unnamed) sources had told the *Times* that the Air Force was using a secret base called S-4 near the dry Groom Lake in Nevada and that the Air Force was attempting to duplicate flying saucer aerodynamics. At Edwards AFB, spokesman Dennis Shoffner said, "When it comes to confirming any kind of plane like that, I just don't have anything for you."

All the denials may be about to backfire on the Air Force. In the Business section of the *L.A. Times* for Dec. 5, 1992 an article stated that the Air Force may have to scale back on its National Aero Space Plane program. Under its new plan, the craft will fly at much lower speeds, only between Mach 12 to 15, instead of the Mach 25 necessary to fly into orbit. The article went on to say that the new Air Force plan raised questions about long-standing reports that it is already flying a craft at speeds of Mach 8 which can only be achieved using an advanced supersonic ramjet. The Air Force spokesman, of course, denied knowing of any such craft, again. Experts want to know why the Pentagon would be proceeding with it's new plan when some Aerospace company has already developed a secret craft that can achieve the necessary high velocities, this, based on numerous sightings around the world.

According to Bill Sweetman, writing for the March issue of *Popular Science*, the Aurora replaced the retired SR-71 and is most likely powered by a combined-cycle ramjet engine. *Jane's Weekly* says that this wedge-shaped spy plane flys up to 5,280 miles per hour - eight times the speed of sound. This would make it 2-1/2 times faster than the SR-71 Blackbird. A trained aircraft observer spotted this plane flying over the North Sea in formation with two U.S.-built F-111 bombers and a KC-135 tanker. Please note that these other two planes are Air Force craft.

What a monumental embarassment! The Air Force wants to develop supersonic ramjets, yet a secret aircraft it denies having any knowledge of, is already performing what is only planned. Oh what a tangled web. Now the *Aerotech News and Review* reports that the follow-on contract for a replacement to the SR-71 was cancelled sometime in 1986 and that sightings of the hypersonic phantom aircraft should be "debunked." This sounds similar to the recommendations of the 1953 Robertson panel with respect to UFO sightings. One news report said that the Aurora had landed at Lockheed's Helendale facility which has a short 4,000-ft runway. The Air Force responded that this would be "amazing." Of course, the Air Force also does not bother to explain the strange glowing golden orbs seen floating around the Lockheed Helendale facility and other such facilities.

Not only is the Air Force embarrassed by reports of secret planes, but NASA is embarassed to explain bogies filmed from orbit as "ice crystals" from a urine dump. Richard Hoagland believes that the anamolous objects seen on the NASA video that aired on *Sightings* are truly extraordinary electrogravitational craft that can travel outside the earth's atmosphere. The one object that makes a hard right turn and accelerates is first seen coming up from beyond the horizon, glowing in the earth's atmosphere, then dimming as it leaves the airglow behind and shoots off into space. Some type of energy beam is fired in the direction of the departing craft. A

Star Wars test? Ron Mattley investigated the shuttle footage at the NASA film library in Houston and discovered a missing segment from the missing STS 48 film. Is someone hiding something here?

The UFOs started to appear in numbers in the forties. By the fifties visionaries were conceptualizing new anti-gravity propulsion technologies. A coincidence? I think not. As early as 1949 Dr. Eric H. Wang went to work at Wright-Patterson's Foreign Technology Division as a mechanical engineer to begin reverse engineering the saucer's energy and propulsion systems in an attempt to duplicate the technology (or, at least, simulate it).

In 1957 G. Harry Stine thought there was a good chance that the rocket would be obsolete by the year 2000. By 1957 several important things had been discovered about gravity propulsion. This was not just a new idea that Bob Lazar dreamed up. Scientists and engineers had already determined that the flying disks were employing field propulsion and generating or altering gravity. Gravity propulsion doesn't act on only one part of the ship it is pushing; it acts on all parts simultaneously. They can accelerate rapidly, abruptly change direction, and stop instantly without producing heavy stress on airframe structures or crew. The directional control is done by changing the direction, intensity, and polarity of charges in capacitors. Just as the electrical coil is the link between electricity and magnetism, the capacitor is the link between electricity and gravity.

Many aircraft companies were researching the problems of anti-gravity in the fifties -- the Glen L. Martin Company, now Martin-Murietta which has just acquired G.E. Aerospace; Bell Aircraft; General Electric; and Sperry-Rand. In fact, the Martin Company, who was prime contractor on the project Vanguard satellite, had established a subsidiary, RIAS, which had as its chief mission the investigation of gravity.

The Gravity Research Group out of England published a paper on Electrogravitic Systems in 1956 based, in part, on the results of Project Winterhaven in 1952, a project testing Townsend Brown's ideas on electrogravitational propulsion. A Whitehall-Rand report dated 1967 describes using an electrohydrodynamic field propulsion system for use in space vehicles, a radical departure from rocket propulsion. This system would employ a flame-jet generator to produce a plasma vortex to create lift.

What happened with all this research started in the fifties? Have we given up on saucers and gone back to rockets? I don't think so.

Saucers are still seen, photographed, and video taped from Highway 375 near Groom Lake. The numerous visitors to the area have not discouraged ongoing test flying. In some instances the objects have come right up to the highway. It is then apparent that these are not just RPVs as some have suggested. Even a large cigar-shaped craft was witnessed by a physician/pilot who made the trek to see these exciting displays. Another man witnessed a disk fly in from over the Jumbled Hills to his position off Highway 375. The disk projected a beam of light over the top of his pickup truck. This last November a number of skywatchers from a UFO Conference being held in Las Vegas visited the Mail Box Road along with a camera crew from a Las Vegas television station. The TV cameras caught a multi-colored ring of lights on video -- it looked like a classic flying saucer.

In the deserts of Southern California Secret Aerospace research facilities have some very strange-looking aeroforms mounted on stingers (pylons) for electromagnetic and radar testing. These scale-model aeroforms do not have airfoils or wings of any kind. One afternoon in June of 1992 we witnessed bay doors opening on the strip at one of these facilities owned by Lockheed (the aforementioned Helendale facility). It is called the RCS (Radar Cross Section) test range. It is located next to the site of the Helendale auxiliary airport six miles north of Helendale, California, and two miles south of the southern edge of the Edwards AFB restricted airspace. The main buildings and large antenna array are near the south fence. The primary underground entrance can be seen at the north end. Construction of the first mile-long, 400-foot-wide testing range was completed in 1983. It was lengthened in 1985 to 1.5 miles and additional underground facilities were built, including a 40-foot-high building situated 21 feet below ground level at the north end of the range. That building sits atop a concrete-lined equipment silo that is 33 feet wide and extends an additional 217 feet deep.

The model aircraft is mounted on the stinger underground, then the stinger is raised through the trapezoidal doors to come in line with the antenna array at the end of the strip. The aeroform mounted on the stinger looked roughly ellipsoidal and appeared a bright metallic white (see photo section). Was this a model of a secret gravity craft? The model is rotated rapidly to reflect directed radar beams off of various shaped surfaces. The range was designed to test low-frequency radar signals. The sight is highly classified. Openings in the test range that appear diamond-shaped from the air allow the stingers to emerge with mounted model aircraft, wings, submarines or other objects(saucers?). The models are housed in 20-foot deep, 60x94 foot bays that use hydraulic rams to elevate the models.

The bogies will not go away and neither will the public's interest as long as they continue to appear all over the world. The videocam has given us a new investigative tool with which we can document and analyze the mysterious behavior of these craft. Hundreds of videos of UFOs over Mexico have now been taken since the July eclipse of 1991. Videos of strange lights over Gulf Breeze are numerous as well as those taken by the Mail Box Road in Nevada. The volume of this mounting evidence cannot be ignored.

Some of these bogies may now be classified as Advanced Technology Aircraft. Some of these aircraft may be classified as using highly unconventional modes of propulsion. Other bogies, such as the flying saucers, flying triangles, and flying boomerangs, may be flown by alien visitors. Thus, we now have sightings of both aircraft and spacecraft. The bottom line is that a craft that flies on gravity, and not air, is a spacecraft.

In my book, *Cosmic Top Secret*, I mentioned an announcement by the DOD in July 1989 of the development of a pilotless saucer called the SHADOW. This six-foot pilotless disk uses a ducted fan engine and is capable of vertical take-off and hovering. Sikorsky also built a pilotless saucer-shaped vehicle. The mission of these vehicles involves carrying out surveillance operations. They can fly-in at low altitudes and hover while cameras and infra-red sensors look for targets.

The latest from Lockheed-Martin skunk works is a pilotless reconnaissance plane nicknamed "Dark Star", a UAV (Unmanned Air Vehicle) which looks like a flying saucer with wings. It flies at speeds of 345 mph at altitudes above 45,000 feet. If anyone witnesses the Dark Star in flight and reports a UFO, the Air Force won't deny it because it has already been unveiled. It will not fly like a conventional field-propelled flying saucer, but that does not prevent sceptics from using UAVs as an explanation for UFO sightings.

An article from the *N.Y. Times* News Service on February 1, 1993 states that "Rumors and reported sightings of a secret U.S. superplane have been proliferating lately almost as abundantly as yarns about *unidentified flying objects."* The article goes on to say that the rumors are based partly on sighting of large and unusually shaped airplanes, peculiar looking condensation trails left by high-flying aircraft, and strange rumbling sounds near Edwards AFB and other places around the world. Some experts believe that a hypersonic reconnaissance plane referred to as project "Aurora" may be a source of some of these sightings. The belief is that "Aurora" was intended to produce a new spy plane that would succeed the SR-71 "Blackbird", which was retired in 1990. Donald B. Rice, Secretary of the Air Force, called all reports of such aircraft "fantasy." An Air Force spokesman said that "we have looked into all such sightings, as we have for *UFO reports,* and we cannot explain them. No Air Force aircraft were operating at the times and places of the alleged sightings."

Reviewing Air Force statements in these paragraphs is enlightening. We would think that the mission of air defense alone would be sufficient cause to thoroughly investigate any UFO sightings in U.S. air spaces. After all, we could be under surveillance by a foreign power that is poised to strike at our heartland. Funny stories about alien spaceships may be readily laughed off, but when we are talking about unusual airplanes flying through our air spaces, and the Air Force treating these reports in the same light as UFO sightings, illustrating a total lack of concern, or debunking credible witnesses, that is when I think we need to bring these attitudes to the attention of our elected and representative government. We are footing the bill for the defense of our nation. We are shown films that depict interceptors on mission to identify friends and foes that fly through our air spaces or no-fly zones. Yet, we find foreign objects fly through these same air spaces with impunity and we are offered no explanations or ridiculous explanations.

Aviation writer Bill Sweetman has stated that "many of these sightings were from highly qualified and credible observers, and even if the Air Force is not directly involved, the plane might be operated by some other organization, such as the National Reconnaissance Office." The NRO has coordinated intelligence from satellites and aircraft for decades, but its very existence was consistently denied by the government until recently.

Researcher Dr. Paul A LaViolette has written a paper that argues that the B-2 Stealth Bomber is using T.T. Brown electro-gravitic technology. Basing this, in part, on an article in the March 9, 1992 *Aviation Week*, he discloses that the B-2 charges both its wing leading edge and exhaust stream to a high voltage. Positive ions are emitted from wing leading edge and negative ions are injected into the exhaust stream with a potential difference in excess of 15 million volts. In effect, the B-2 can become one of Brown's flying capacitors. This would give the B-2 capability of enormous accelerations and produce an atmospheric envelope around the bomber that would reduce any sonic booms or noisy shock waves. The B-2 may not be the only aircraft employing this technology. Some of the mysterious black triangular craft may be using this technology as well as scramjet technology.

One little clue that Northrop may be involved in electromagnetic aircraft propulsion comes from the company's Newsbriefs in which a scheduled lecture was announced for September 17, 1993 on the use of wavelet transforms and 3-D modeling and this technology as a new capability for automatic target recognition could be used in *advanced electromagnetic vehicle design.* If this refers to electromagnetic propulsion technology, then we are developing aircraft that simulate alien technology.

Air Force pilots may report a **bogie** in the sky, but now they may just be attempting to intercept a secret aircraft. They will probably be told: "You saw nothing. The nothing you saw does not exist. Tell no one about it."

CHAPTER SIX
MAGIC CAVERNS

> "What secrets perchance are about us? We do not know as we lie there, our bodies resting, our souls filled with peace, nor do we know until many years passed out through the back door of time that tall basalt cliffs conceal a doorway. We do not suspect this, nor that a long tunnel stretches away, far into the interior of majestic Shasta." **- Phylos**

Mount Shasta, in the northernmost part of California, has been a center of mystery for many who study mysteries. The mountain is an extinct volcano that rises over 14,000 feet above forest pines. I was once told of a secret entrance, a swinging rock doorway that lay hidden just above Panther Meadows. This *gate*, as it was called, led into a tunnel that penetrated the deepest secrets of this mystery mountain. Witnesses have seen strange tall men come down from the mountain and trade with Gold in the nearby town of Shasta. Other witnesses have seen light beams penetrating the night from the forest slopes of Shasta. Others even report encounters with UFOs near the snow-capped mountain. Even lenticular clouds hover above its serene apex as if covering up the landing of a spaceship from another world. Are there tunnels in Shasta? Does Shasta hide a secret saucer base? Rumors have abounded for years.

There are many legends and stories of flying saucers from the underground world. UFOs have been seen going into and coming out of mountains in the wilderness. Some believe that vast unexplored caverns exist beneath our feet and that some of these caverns house ancient cities peopled by ancient dwellers. The Paiutes have a legend that the Hav-Musuvs came to the region known as Death Valley in prehistoric times. When the land changed, they built cities in underground caverns in the Panamint Mountains. They built flying canoes which had the appearance of silvery ships with wings. They moved with a slight whirring sound, and a dipping movement, like an eagle.

The passing centuries brought other changes. Tribe after tribe swept across the land, fighting to possess it for awhile and passing like a sandstorm. In their mountain city inside the caverns, the Hav-musuvs dwelt in peace. Sometimes they were seen in the distance, in their flying ships or riding on the snowy-white animals. The Hav-musuvs were described as a beautiful people with a golden skin, a head band holding back their long hair, and always dressed in white fine-spun garments.

At first, only a few abductees told of being taken by aliens to underground bases. None of the popular books on the subject of UFO abduction mentioned the underground experience. What was especially disconcerting was the fact that abductees recalled seeing military personnel alongside of alien beings working in these secret bases. Skeptics find it hard enough to believe that abductions have a basis in physical reality. The presence of human civilian and military personnel inhabiting the same underground physical spaces exceeds the skeptic's mindset by several orders of magnitude. The skeptic would rather believe that stories of aliens and humans in underground bases are fabrications designed to elicit attention from gullible believers. This is hardly what one would call an objective approach to these stories. An open-minded skeptical attitude is desirable, but a close-minded debunker mindset is of little value.

One of the earliest cases I heard about was the case of Judy Doraty. In May 1980, Judy Doraty was driving with her son on a rural highway near Cimarron, New Mexico. While driving, they observed at least two discoid craft in the process of abducting a young calf from a field. Both Judy and her son were abducted and taken aboard one of the craft to be taken to an underground installation. Judy observed a vat in the underground installation that contained various cattle body parts floating in a liquid. A few researchers have concluded that Judy was taken to an underground base in Dulce, New Mexico. This alleged facility received a lot of notoriety in the 1980s and more than one researcher, including myself, trekked off looking for evidence that such a place existed. Since no testable evidence was ever discovered, skeptics have had a good belly laugh over our gullibility. What the skeptics don't understand is that the issue of alien underground bases isn't one of blind belief. It is not an issue of gullibility. It is a report, that like other UFO reports, deserves an investigation. The fact that independent witnesses have described similar details about underground facilities is a factor also present in so-called abduction scenarios. The search for proof or disproof must involve research and investigation, not derision and ridicule.

The first case of subterranean abduction that I investigated occurred in 1988. I never reached a firm conclusion regarding the information that resulted from this investigation, but did receive corroborating reports from other abductees. The incident occurred in the Rosamond area of the Antelope Valley in California up on the sides of the Tehachapi Mountains. The Tehachapi mountains rise on the north side of the valley. There is a saddle in the mountains and a secret Northrop electromagnetic testing facility in the area just below the saddle. The Northrop facility has been dubbed the "Anthill" or the "Black Hole" by some of the locals who refer to it as a multi-level underground facility.

Ray and Nancy worked at the Northrop B-2 assembly facility in Palmdale. Ray is a Native American. Ray was an aircraft inspector and worked the swing shift. One June night he decided to take a midnight ride with Nancy up to the cut in the Tehachapi mountains. This cut appears as an inclined whitish mark on the side of the foothills. It actually marks the site of a road that winds up around the mountains. On the backside is an entrance to an artificial plateau that had been blasted out of the rocks. Ray parked his truck on this plateau. They got out to look at the stars and the city lights of Lancaster and Palmdale in the valley far below. While looking at the stars, Nancy noticed that some of them were moving around and brought it to Ray's attention. Ray got his flashlight out of the truck and started signaling the lights. At some point, Nancy noticed a bright basketball-sized orb hovering just above a nearby knoll. They both walked closer to get a better look at the orb. Ray thought it had just risen out of some invisible opening in the ground. It seemed to be flashing and sparking. Some sort of line dangled from its underside. It rose a little higher and Nancy tried to speak to it, having an intuitive feeling that some intelligence had guided the orb to that plateau for their benefit. As they watched this strange phenomenon around one o'clock in the morning, they next observed the morning dawn light over the far distant eastern hills. Something had just snatched four hours of time out of their lives. The orb was gone. They were terrified and drove quickly home. The next day, they felt a vibration going through their apartment. When they went outdoors, they saw two orbs hovering above their apartment. This scared them badly.

I took Ray and Nancy to a local hypnotist and she regressed Ray. Nancy refused to be regressed, expressing fear over what she might discover about those four hours of missing time. Ray was an excellent subject. When in trance, with little prompting, he fell backwards nearly to the floor before we caught him. The regression brought out some amazing revelations. Ray and Nancy had been abducted and taken underground!

Under hypnosis he kept mentioning the Kern River to the north. "There is an area near the Tehachapi Mountains called the Kern River Project. The upper river is being used by the government for hydroelectric power to power the underground facility at Tehachapi Ranch (actually, the Tejon Ranch). The mountain next to the power facility is being hollowed out...there is mud all around and it's so obvious, but apparently people aren't looking. All the power is being used for the Ranch, which is the site of underground 'skunk works' where highly technical aircraft, spacecraft and all kinds of stuff are being dealt with. It is a huge underground base, probably close to the size of one under 29 Palms Marine Base. It has huge hangars and very large elevators as well as technical laboratories. There is a whole city under there, large passageways...the whole valley is full of tunnels. You can drive from one end to the other underground. You can drive from Palmdale, site of the Northrop, Lockheed and "black project" areas, to California City...all underground. There are tunnels all the way to George AFB. Aliens apparently have access...they've been seen all over the place. The government lets them do whatever they want. They're probing the human brain, trying to find out weaknesses and learning how to control us. They dissect humans...can't describe the dissections because they are not humane. Really morbid. The government knows it...they just turn their heads. Some people in the government want to stop this but they don't know how to stop it."

Ray was disconcerted that Greys had Nancy strapped to a table in this facility. He could see instruments all around. During hypnosis he would freeze up when recalling this scene. He yelled and became very emotional. He was convinced they would rape her and violate her, yet he was helpless to prevent it. He and Nancy also felt they had contact with a benevolent race of aliens who had observed their capture. After a few months, Ray and Nancy announced to me that they wanted little more to do with reporting further events. They felt exposed and monitored and feared retribution if they continued talking. They last told me they intended to go to Bible classes to find refuge from this enormous evil that encroached upon their lives.

Many witnesses have observed unusual phenomenon over the Tejon Ranch. One night on March 3, 1991 Pearl Schultz and Aric Leavitt sighted 5 or 6 UFOs moving in pairs at various speeds and sometimes switching directions over the Tehachapi Mountains. Each had a pulsating light that alternated from bright white to heavy red. Mrs. Schultz noticed orange and yellow colors. Some of the UFOs seemed to come from the saddle area.

A man named Stan saw a bright flash of orange light which seemed to have a cigar-shape. He saw this from Avenue I looking northwest over the Tehachapis.

Three witnesses went up to the plateau near the Anthill on January 31, 1991. They saw a green-glowing disk take-off from this facility without any apparent acceleration and climb at a 45 degree angle to the south. They also heard a tone when they sighted the object. When traveling back down the road (170th Street West), they saw two black vans and two black helicopters.

In the morning dawn, a pilot was flying out of Fox Field on Avenue G headed for Merced. His flight path would take him over the Tehachapis. When passing over the saddle where the Anthill is located on February 23, 1991, he observed four white rectangular objects hovering over the facility. He described them as being four times the size of a typical highway billboard. They were each separated by about 200 yards. Another observer, who was called on the phone, drove his car out to the highway and observed these same objects before they winked out!

One local man who has property on 170th Street West reported seeing the ground open up like a missile silo within the fenced perimeter surrounding the Northrop installation. He saw a flying saucer emerge from this "silo" and take off. He also claimed that someone from Edwards had come to talk to him about his story and told him to shut up. I further found out that the man's name is Chuck and he was a contractor who worked on the underground tunnels in the Anthill facility. He said the tunnels have round doorways with panels that have red and green lights for ID and entry. There are no doors covering these doorways, but some kind of field is projected from cylinders embedded in the door wall. Tiny globes hovered in the tunnels and followed Chuck and his crew around. He thought they were being used by the Air Force as sensors. But where did the Air Force get the technology to levitate these orbs?

Joe told me a lot of stories. He attended many of my Uforum meetings in Lancaster. He claims to have had a close encounter and missing time when traveling a road through the southside of Edwards AFB one night. Joe was in construction and held clearances for working in military operation areas. He said that he had worked on an underground tunnel project below Haystack Butte on the Eastern boundary of Edwards near the NASA Rocket Test Site. He also claimed that he saw orbs roving around these tunnels. He painted numbers inside a box located on a stripe that ran horizontally midway along the tunnel walls. I asked him how far this tunnel ran below the earth's surface. He said that he and fellow employees used to count as the elevator descended to the tunnel level. From the count and from the elevator speed, I estimated that the tunnel must have been around 3,000 feet deep. One time he saw a door open to a room in one of these tunnels and he could see a very tall alien standing next to two men in white lab coats. He thought this alien was all of nine feet tall. He claims that he saw two grey aliens inside a hangar at China Lake one day when he went back inside the hangar after finishing his work to retrieve a tool that he had left behind. Joe was always telling me fantastic stories, yet he seemed very sincere. I never knew whether to believe him.

One day Joe told me about two old school buddies he had run across. They both held jobs in underground facilities and had worked at the Anthill, he said. They would work underground for two weeks at a stint. They lived in condos when working underground. These condos were also built into the underground facility. The government even picked up the tab on one guy's alimony. One was known as a computer genius. He said that he had seen both grey and reptilian life forms in various underground facilities. One of the underground projects was Project Startalk. The work involved lasers. The informer, a guy named Paul, said that he worked in a big underground building (350 feet across). Project Startalk utilized a powerful laser which strikes a mirror and is sent into space. The laser is modulated with a signal and acts as a beacon to bring in UFOs. Apparently, the beacon is directed at friendly forces from other star systems. He also worked at the Douglas facility near LLano. He once saw a saucer land and go into an underground hangar. Inside the underground building is a huge computer complex. The workers wear white clothing and white socks (no shoes). The computers use an alien symbolic language. Manuals indicate codes that can be entered. There is a large lexon plastic screen in this complex that displays various star systems and galaxies. A wax pencil is used to indicate targets for the laser. The technology used is so far advanced that it is beyond known engineering technology. The laser is also capable of interdimensional communication. Security workers accompany all workers, even to the bathroom. Phones are tapped, even workers home phones. It took Paul and Gopher (the second guy) two years to get a security clearance.

Gopher also worked at the Anthill as a computer specialist. He has also worked at Lockheed's Helendale facility and at the Nevada Test Site. Gopher says that we are working with aliens and alien technology and it scares the hell out of him. He gets paid well. He makes $145 thousand a year and the government pays his alimony. He says he has also worked at Section D, better known as the Dulce facility. He has seen reptoids and Greys in these underground facilities. He doesn't have a life of his own. He worked with white-skinned reptoids. He has also seen members of the Orange race. He has not seen any benefit to humanity. He is trying to find out what is going to happen. He is worried about what the future holds. He foresees an alien war. He has a good lifestyle underground. Besides the condo, he has swimming pools, saunas, and a gym at his disposal. They have an underground parking lot. He works 14 to 16 days on a shift. He is not allowed to leave the country and must obtain permission to leave the state. He says the main control center in the valley is at Haystack Butte. A tunnel runs from Haystack Butte to the Anthill. Gopher believes there are benevolent aliens and says he saw one once. They are from a Federation. The one he saw was human looking, a tall blonde (Nordic) that wore a white jump suit and had a green coat on over it. He believes that we are trying to enlist the aid of such friendly beings. This is a very similar scenario to what I received in that letter from a veteran.

My friend's stepson obtained a job in an underground facility at Los Alamos. He says there is a tube shuttle that runs from that underground facility to Section D. He worked in Level 1 which runs under Main Street. One block from the PAN AM building is the old high school, now used as an engineering facility by MAKEN & HANGAR (Originally ZIA Corp). Inside the facility is an elevator that descends to the computer room. From the computer room a side tunnel intersects the main tunnel transit tube that runs from Los Alamos to Albuquerque. These levels are protected by PROFORCE Security. At deeper, more secure levels exist automatic devices that kill intruders. A security guard accidentally tripped an alarm and was killed by one of these. These tunnels are a minor part of a vast network of such tunnels. One other thing mentioned by this source is an underground city which housed a population of thousands who occupied *condos*. Many of these people lived permanently underground. Some of the advanced technological research going on involves genetic labs and laser fusion. The budget for the surface facility is over a billion dollars a year, but the underground research projects get many times this amount.

Pam and I were introduced to an abductee named Diane a few years ago. Diane lives over in the Apple Valley area. She had ongoing alien encounters since she was a child. As she grew older, she started experiencing abductions by humans that took her to underground facilities. One of these underground facilities she believed was located at China Lake Naval Weapons test center. She was taken down to lower levels in an elevator. Her description of this elevator matched the description given by a man named Thomas of an elevator in use at the Dulce facility. Thomas' description of this and other details were never published so that we could check out corroborating eyewitness reports. Evidently these elevators have an unusual shape and operate on magnetic forces in the elevator shaft rather than using cable systems to run the elevator up and down the shaft. Diane also reports that she was taken on a tour of one part of the facility by a man in a white coat. He showed her humans that had been biologically altered. These humans were housed in cages set about a foot above the floor. She also saw altered animals. Her story was just as bizarre as Thomas' story of Level 7 at Dulce.

The story of an underground base on Jicarilla Apache Indian Reservation first came to light around 1980 when Albuquerque physicist Paul Bennewitz reported the crash of an alien ship on the slopes of Archuleta Mountain. Paul wrote a letter to Senator Pete Domenici and Paul Gilman in Washington D. C. This letter was accompanied by a report. He said, "Atomic ship originally outlined in my report ...copy to you...several years ago had crashed approximately two miles northwest of Dulce, NM near Archeleta Peak on Archeleta Mesa." He believed there was a concern because gamma and neutron radiation could be emitted from the crash site if there had been a nuclear meltdown. Paul's Thunder Scientific Corporation manufactured various detection instruments.

In his Project Beta report, Bennewitz stated that humanoid aliens had a base near Archuleta Mesa and that he had established direct computer communication with aliens at that base. He did not believe the aliens to be trustworthy. Paul became paranoid about the government, the aliens, and admitted abductees whom he believed were being controlled by the aliens. At a MUFON conference held in Las Vegas in 1989, featured speaker Bill Moore made the statement that Paul Bennewitz was fed disinformation by intelligence agents, that he contributed to this effort, and the whole story concerning the Dulce facility was constructed around these bits of disinformation that were fed to Paul. However, testimony from Walter Baumgartner and state police officer Gabe Valdez indicates otherwise. According to them, they had seen video images of aliens that Paul had made contact with using his special equipment. These aliens would send messages that would output on Paul's computer printer. Some of the sentence structure was disjointed. Were intelligent agents taking extreme measure by hoaxing computer communications with Paul? For what purpose? Apparently Bennewitz was using special transmitter coils to send and receive electromagnetic signal to and from the alien base.

Then along came Thomas. Thomas E. Castello was born in Glen Ellan, Illinois on April 23, 1941. Thomas was the man who released the Dulce papers. His good friend, Ann West, tells his story as Thomas has not been heard from since 1991.

Thomas had a passion for antique cars, any antique car, but especially Packards, and especially the big-nosed cars of the forties and early fifties. A lot of his spare time was spent modifying his 1949 Packard, and he needed special parts. His friends told him about an older man in town that had a machine shop that could rebuild antique cars. This old man was Ed West, Ann's father. He found Ed easy to talk to, not just about cars, but anything. The two spent endless hours discussing cars, planes, and the space program. Tom and Ed found they were both fascinated with flying saucers.

After a few months, Ed introduced Tom to "The Organization", a group that did deep research on flying saucers and contactees. Tom completed initiation into the group and was soon on several assignments.

At that time in 1961, Tom was in the Air Force, stationed at Nellis AFB in Las Vegas. He was schooled in photography, and had received a top secret clearance. He was given the opportunity of receiving additional training in Virginia. There, he had his first experience of working in an underground base. When he left that facility, his top secret clearance was upgraded to TS-IV.

His duties as an Air Force sergeant included photographing a runway exercise in Florida. He would meet with Ann during his off-duty time in Orlando. Tom was pleased to discover that Ann drove a classic 1950 Packard straight-eight with a beautiful swan as a hood ornament.

The next year, 1963, Ann moved to Las Vegas to be near her folks.

When she was in Florida, she had a close encounter with a glowing flying saucer and was actually taken on board. The haunting dreams and memories of this incident bothered Ann. Tom introduced her to "The Organization." After a few visits, Ann became initiated into the group and started certain assignments. She and Tom began to collect books, articles, and magazines about UFOs. They would spend nights doing research.

Over the years, Tom became like a brother to Ann. His parents were killed in a car accident so he adopted Ann's parents into his heart.

Tom stayed in high security photography for seven years, then left the Air Force in 1971. He began working for Rand Corp. in California as a security technician. Within a year, his clearance was upgraded to ULTRA-3.

Tom met Cathy in 1972 and got married. In November, 1974, Cathy gave birth to Eric Scott Castello. They moved to Santa Fe, New Mexico in 1977. Tom had been transferred and his clearance upgraded to ULTRA-7. He found his new position financially rewarding, but more stressful. He told Ann that he worked in an underground facility that had incredible security for the photography department. His job touched on all aspects of photography from large format cameras to mini cameras. It was his responsibility to check, align, and calibrate all the security video cameras, from the doors to exit tunnels. His position required that he be armed at all times. It was also his job to escort visitors to certain areas of the base. This facility came to be known as the Dulce Base. When Tom finally left his job, he had earned the security rank of Major.

Tom and Cathy, TAL and Mary Levesque, all lived in Sante Fe, New Mexico in 1979 when Ann went to visit them. Tom seemed more intense than usual. He said that he wished that he could talk to Ann about his concerns, but his high security clearance prevented him from saying much. The day Ann left New Mexico, Tom pressed a folded piece of paper into her hand and whispered quietly, "don't let anyone see this." She slipped it into her pocket. That night, alone at a motel in Durango, she opened the paper. There were three things on its yellow page: a sketch of an alien; an inverted triangle; and the name Dulce. She stared at the mysterious drawing and tried to figure out what it all meant. The alien in the drawing had a large head, big black eyes, no nose and no hair. The triangle was shaded black. After looking at it, she flushed the paper down the toilet. That night, she had nightmares about aliens.

The next morning, over coffee, she was looking at a map for a route back to Vegas when she noticed the name of a small town near the New Mexico state line called "Dulce." Were there aliens in Dulce? What was Tom trying to tell her? Then she remembered where she had seen the black triangle before. The symbol was on a hat on Tom's coffee table. It was burnt orange with a black inverted triangle with gold bands cutting it in three sections. She decided to drive through Dulce looking for something suspicious, but found nothing. She went back to Durango and drove to Cortez. She fell in love with it, and moved to Colorado.

Early in December of that year, Tom paid Ann a surprise visit. He told her that he had walked out on his job some months ago after a major dispute broke out between the security workers and a military group. Tom said that the security force used "flash guns," but the military group was armed with machine guns. He said it was like a war with screaming and panic in all the tunnels. A lot of people died in the conflict. He wondered what story the government would use to cover-up the deaths. In February, 1980, the media reported a prison riot near Los Alamos and that many prisoners died. Was this the cover-up?

Tom admitted that he was in trouble. He went back to the base and took photos, papers, and other items. He had entered and left through a ventilation shaft inside an ice cave. After leaving the cave, he returned to a prepared box, put everything in the box, and buried it. He went back to his car, but security was waiting for him. They questioned him about his purpose for being there, but allowed him to leave. He was on his way to Colorado Springs, and now he was "on the run." He asked Ann to have faith in him and that he was still the same man she had always known as a friend.

The next day, after he had left, three men from O.S.I. showed up and questioned Ann about Tom's where-abouts. On four other visits in December other men questioned her and she told them she knew nothing about where he had gone. In January, the CIA came to her door. They insisted that she was withholding information.

Ann had been in a car accident in 1978 and had recurring headaches. In January, 1980 she checked into a hospital in Farmington, New Mexico. She went in for an angiogram, but woke up to find that she had had a stroke. She had to re-learn everything again. At that time the OSI and CIA stopped bothering her.

It was June of 1982 before she heard from Thomas again. He called from her dad's house. They talked for hours. He had been running for his life and had been in twenty states and four countries. He showed her medical papers and scientific diagrams, but Ann could not make sense of it all. Tom told her that the government had a treaty with an alien nation and that aliens had been on this earth for countless centuries. He showed Ann pages of alien written material and translated papers. It was horrifying. He told her that Cathy and Eric had been kidnapped and were being held captive in a subterranean base. He needed a safe place to hide all the original papers that he took from the Dulce Base and other things of a substantial nature to prove the alien conspiracy. Tom and Ann buried the box of materials on a mountain. Years have changed the terrain, and Ann has not been able to relocate the exact burial site.

Sound like a tall tale? Many think it is. Ann has photos of Thomas and details of his life in her files. TAL met with him once. He is a real person. He answered some of my questions by mail. He fully believes what he says and has answered the questions when he knows the answers. Some of this information has been published in hopes of eliciting further witness testimony. So far, I only know of three others who claim they have been to this underground facility. One man is known to a friend of mine and was trained as a nuclear physicist.

The Dulce Facility is a seven-level underground research base, run by the D.O.E. and connected to the Los Alamos labs. Level 1 has garages, street maintenance equipment, photo labs, hydroponic gardens to grow fresh vegetables, fruits, legumes, etc., human housing, a mess hall, VIP housing, a kitchen, and a security vehicles garage. Each of the levels has color-coded electric carts that are used for short-distance transport. Level 6 houses the infamous "Nightmare Hall"; a security arsenal; a military arsenal; military security; and a generator/impulsor. The generator is 200-feet in diameter, and has a two-level Electromagnetic impulse device that can create a perfect clone of a person.

Science-Fiction? Abductees have described being taken to similar facilities.

There is no proof unless someone can find the box. If it is there!

However, these stories have prompted researchers, including myself, to find documented evidence of underground facilities, and we have found plenty. That such an underground empire exists in almost total secrecy is absolutely amazing. Few question its existence, its purpose, or the tremendous expenditure of monies that must have gone into the design, construction, maintenance, and operations of these facilities. More on this in a moment, but first one more intriguing story.

John Metas graduated with a PhD in Pharmacology from the University of Michigan in Ann Arbor. He played football. He went to work at UCLA, becoming part of a federally funded research program looking for cancer cures. He was frustrated by redtape and bureaucratic delays. He took a change of course and entered the entertainment industry and lived in Las Vegas. In 1989 he started his own company - Celebrity Entertainment, involved in Pay-for-View TV. He started a UFO project about July 1992. I met John at the Whole Life Expo on Sept. 13.

FIRST INCIDENT: John gets a call from Callahan (FBI), a business friend. He is asked if he will attend a meeting with the "Company." He is given the address of a four-story building on Atlantic in Long Beach. Upon arriving there on Labor Day (Sept. 7), he is greeted at the door by a man introducing himself as "Tom." He asks Tom for credentials. Tom shows him ID with a picture, no name, a letter-number series, and the word Langley on it. The ID also has a computer bar-code on it. They take him through several rooms (these rooms are rounded) and he is placed in one room that has a conference table and a TV in it. They (there were 3 men altogether) invited him to sit. Later they ordered a steak and lobster meal. They chatted about his background. They knew a lot about John. When they got down to business, they asked about four names: his partner's; Fred Bell; Cooper; and Watkins. They did not like Cooper. At some point they mentioned a new 7-level facility in Arizona(!). John fell asleep on the couch. When he awoke, it was later than he thought. His watch had stopped and he felt he was missing time. He was there from 2 PM to 6:02 AM the next day. Before he left, one of the men asked him if he was going to continue with the project, and when he said "yes", the man replied, "good." A regression was done on this episode on Sept. 14 - the tape did not record. During the regression, John mentioned 13 other people present in the room who were Nordic and dressed in green jump suits. He mentioned the numbers 18; 800; and 2003.

SECOND INCIDENT: (brief synopsis) John has a second meeting on Friday Sept. 18, 1992. He is told to be out in front of the Century Plaza Hotel in Century City at 5:30. When he does, a dark blue Chrysler LeBaron pulls up with a driver and a man in the back seat who identifies himself as "Vincent." He is dressed in civilian coat and tie. He asks John to retrieve his car and follow them. They go through traffic to the Hawthorne exit in Torrance (to right) to a private airfield. There he and car are taken aboard a huge transport plane. He is seated in a plush cabin with no windows. A woman in a gray suit attends him and identifies herself only as "Karen." He refused drink and food. The flight takes about 45 minutes. At one point the driver addresses Vincent as Colonel. Vincent tells him they are going to Arizona. When they land, it is night. He deplanes down a long ladder. He and Vince get in a jeep driven by a man in military Khakis who wears a red beret and has shiny boots. They drive down a smooth road between hills for about 2 miles. Then they arrive at what appears to be a DWP pumping station, a building surrounded by a chain-link fence. They drive up to the building and exit the jeep. Vince uses an entry card to enter door. They go through a door into a small anteroom to an elevator door. They enter the elevator (keycard controlled) and proceed downward at a slow, quiet pace. He exits underground into another anteroom, then into a large warehouse-sized room. About 90 feet across this room there are about 20 people in blue-and-white lab coats milling around a metallic object that is half-covered. Vince takes John to a room on his immediate left. In this room is a chair and a TV monitor (blue screen on). He is told to sit and watch. He is given a slide show - various craft planforms (front/side/top views). There is a disk and a jello-mold shape. One stands out. It looks elongated with pontoons. These are seamless and shiny metallic-looking craft. After the show, he is taken out another exit, up a cylindrical elevator controlled by a black button on the floor and outdoors into a huge courtyard surrounded by a thirty-foot wall with mounted flood-lights. There are two captain chairs for him and Vince to sit in. Predominating the center stage in the courtyard is the pontoon craft of huge dimensions (larger than a 747 Jumbo Jet). Vince takes out a slender pen-mike and says "We are ready" and John hears a tremendous whirring noise that echoes around the courtyard. In the blink of an eye, the pontoon craft is gone and appears in the sky overhead and instantly starts circling maneuvers. Then it does slicing turns (like cutting a piece of pie). Then it jumps from one part of the sky to another for a number of minutes. Then, without sound or warning, reappears in its original ground position in the courtyard. This astounded John. Vince returns him to another slide show. No questions are answered. The second slide show has pictures of craft, labs, creatures (one encased in a blue cube), and a diagram of the 7-level facility in a wedding cake layer design followed by 11 encoded lines of text. End of slide show. He is returned to plane. He is taken to Luke AFB, by request, for disembarkation. The trip takes 15 minutes. He takes his car, drives to Mesa, and a few minutes later I meet him in the hotel lobby at the Holiday Inn.

ANALYSIS: John is truthful. He remembered a lot of details. He was not asked to keep silent about this experience. He was not requested to sign a security oath. He may be being used to get out a story or for spin control purposes. Other meetings to follow. We will go with the flow. From analyzing the airtime and other factors, it has been determined that John was flown approx. 222 air miles east and was most likely taken to a facility within the borders of the Yuma Proving Grounds, south of Blyth and north of Yuma. Description of terrain/heat lightning/smell of night air and dress of military; color of plane (olive green) all indicate an Army facility. From the YPG to Luke is about 80-85 airmiles and would take 15 to 17 minutes flight time which is in accord with John's estimates.

Conclusion: John reported having another experience and reported being taken to an underground research facility at Wright-Patterson AFB. After this last experience, he ceased all further contact with us. He still had plans, at that point, to do a UFO documentary, but this time he indicated that the information would be supplied by the government and they would arrange the airing of a program that would present indisputable proof. Such a program has not been forthcoming and, I believe, someone wanted John diverted from his project. I have since talked to other ex-military personnel who have worked in underground facilities. All of them have told me that the entrance is usually through a small fenced-in building which conceals card-controlled elevators. One of my fellow workers told me that he worked in such a facility in Iran and he only had access to one level. At this time my conclusion is still inconclusive regarding Tom's story, John's story, and others, but the fact remains that underground bases exist and there are more of them than anyone realizes.

One of the earliest American underground facilities was built at Raven Rock in Pennsylvania. The military refer to it as "Site R." Sounds like "Section D." Raven Rock was picked because it is made of greenstone, a type of granite that is the fourth hardest rock on earth. Construction started in 1950, and engineers had completed a series of tunnels and a three-story building by 1953. Two more three-story buildings were completed by 1963. The complex lies 650 feet beneath the 1,529-foot-high summit of Raven Rock and can be entered through four portals. The mountain has everything needed to survive a catastrophe: cars, some of the best dining in the Army, chemical suits, a fitness center, a medical facility, a barbershop, legal services, a chapel, designated smoking areas and a convenience store. It has six 1,000 kilowatt generators and 35 miles of cable on 180 telephone poles. Remember, this is one of the early underground sites, and probably does not compare with some of the new underground cities that have been constructed in more recent years.

One of the first of nearly 100 Federal Relocation Centers was built in rural Virginia's Mount Weather. It took years to complete, but when complete resembled a city more than an emergency installation. Mount Weather was equipped with such amenities as private apartments and dormitories, streets and sidewalks, cafeterias and hospitals, a water purification system, power plant, and general office buildings. The site includes a small lake fed by fresh water from underground springs. It even has its own mass transit system--small *electric cars* that run on rechargeable batteries and make regular shuttle runs throughout the city.

As recently as 1992, the papers reported the existence of a Cold War secret, the government had built a $14 million underground bunker in West Virginia and maintained it for more than three decades for Congress to use in the event of a nuclear attack. The hideaway Capitol was built under the fashionable Greenbrier resort in White Sulphur Springs, about 250 miles from Washington. Its location was known only to a relative handful of the nation's highest-ranking officials. From 1958 on, the very existence of this facility was a closely guarded secret. Very *few in Congress or the executive branch knew of the program.* The rumors that an underground city exists under the Enchantment Resort in Boynton Canyon in Sedona, Arizona may not be so far fetched after all. Eggs cannot be put in one basket. The Greenbrier bunker has living quarters and work space for 800 people as well as separate meeting halls for the House and Senate.

We are always willing to release more about the other side's secrets than our own. We find that the Kremlin and other buildings in Moscow are still linked by underground *rail tunnels* to an area about six miles outside the city center called Ramenki, site of a vast subterranean bunker designed for the country's leaders and their families. It was described as an underground city about 500 acres in size, built at several levels from 230 feet to 395 feet. This bunker could shelter as many as 120,000 people! That is the size of a moderate American city.

According to the Napa Sentinel, a secret underground installation is under construction near the Oakville Grade in Napa County, California, and is being used by the Government for direct satellite communication, the Continuity of Government (COG) program in case of nuclear attack or other disasters, and secure communication links with the outside world in case of disaster. Mysterious helicopter flights have been seen going into and out of the area. Supposedly, the secret government site is replacing other installations and combining them into one underground center.

Not all underground sites are shelters. The Yucca Mountain Site Characterization Project took a first step in November, 1993 when it started construction on the entrance pad for its Exploratory Studies Facility (ESF). This pad is the launching point for 14 miles of tunnels that will be drilled directly under Yucca Mountain. The tunnels will measure 24-30 feet in diameter for some and 16-18 feet in diameter for others. This project will eventually cover some 70 acres of surface and underground facilities. This DOE project will contain alcoves for experiments located along the tunnels.

Skeptics have expressed doubts about the existence of extensive underground tunneling and cavitation. They always ask, "Where is all the dirt?" This method of asking a question to disprove an allegation is misleading and faulty logic at best. Skeptics favorite question about the alien presence is "Why don't they land on the White House Lawn?" Of course, the rejoinder should be "Keep off the Grass signs prevent them." One of the new methods of tunneling that have been under study is "nuclear tunnel boring." U.S. Patent No. 3,693,731 dated Sept. 26, 1972 describes a method and apparatus for tunneling by melting. It says, "a machine and method for drilling bore holes and tunnels by melting in which a housing is provided for supporting a heat source and a heated end portion and in which the necessary melting heat is delivered to the walls of the end portion at a rate sufficient to melt rock and during operation of which the molten material may be disposed adjacent the boring zone in cracks in the rock and as a vitreous wall lining of the tunnel so formed. The heat source can be electrical or nuclear, but for deep drilling is preferably a nuclear reactor." The melted rock is forced into cracks wherein heat is given up to the crack surfaces and freezes as a glass at some distance from the penetrator. This amazing boring device is capable of drilling at depths totally inaccessible with previous drilling techniques, even, according to the patent claims, down to 30,000 meters.

The nuclear tunnel boring machines were invented by scientists and engineers at Los Alamos. They called their new machine, the "Subterrene." In 1975, a cost comparison was done between the Subterrene and other tunneling methods by A. A. Mathews, Inc. This report reveals that the initial experiments utilizing this technology were done in the early 1960s. This study reveals that the Subterrene performs its job rapidly and economically. The report states that the economy comes from "the formation of a glass lining bonded to the ground and capable of providing initial and final ground support without the delay and cost of separate installations. The use of a nuclear reactor and heat pipes to provide power for kerf penetration within the tunneling machine itself contributes to the overall economy of the system and is considered exclusively in this study. Nuclear power is not, however, a requirement for Subterrene tunneling." In fact a Los Alamos symposium held in Atlantic City in 1986 proposed the construction of a Subselene for tunnel melting for high-speed lunar subsurface transportation tunnels.

Thomas spoke about a subterranean highway through America just like our own Interstate highway system, except its underground. The underground highway uses trucks, cars, and buses driven by electric motors. You wouldn't want gasoline fumes polluting tunnels. He mentioned another style of transport for freight and passengers that is linked together in a world-wide network called the "Sub-Global System." It has check points at each country entry. There are shuttle tubes that "shoot" the trains at incredible speed using a mag-lev and vacuum method. They travel in excess of the speed of sound. Did Thomas concoct this from a science-fiction scenario or does such a system have a basis in fact, and, if so, how much more of what Thomas has told us exists in reality?

Engineers Robert Salter and Frank P. Davidson of MIT have both discussed and given papers on the Planetran concept for moving people rapidly underground. Salter describes the Planetran as an ultraspeed, electromagnetically propelled and levitated transportation system of the future. Such a system could carry passengers across the United States in less than an hour in a quiet, economical, fuel-conservative, and nonpolluting manner. Planetran would require a tunnel over 2,500 miles in length, perhaps assembled from 100 25-mile long segments.

Skeptics have scoffed at claims that 100-mile long tunnels ran from one military operations area to another. Yet, engineers have planned for tunnels to span the nation. Of course, skeptics are somewhat deficient in imagination when it comes to accomplishments. There were skeptics that never believed we would reach the moon, and certainly not by rocket. Skeptics do not believe in alien visitations. It is even more difficult for them to accept the idea that aliens have inhabited the earth for a long time and like to live underground and out of sight.

Huge structures discovered in close-up photos of lunar features indicate that ancient alien artifacts have graced the surface of our satellite. It is only a small step for aliens to have come to earth and built habitats.

We cannot prove that aliens or alien technology exists in secret underground facilities constructed by the government. We have not been able to prove the existence of Section D. There are an increasing number of abductees who report being taken to underground bases. Some of these abductees have described seeing things that really exist in documented underground facilities. Perhaps ancient underground facilities will eventually reveal the truth. The magic and mystery of these dark places continues.

Northrop facility in Tehachapi Mountains

The pentagon house where Pamela had numerous encounters.

Lockheed's underground facility at Helendale.

Lockheed facility showing pylon with elliptical aeroform mounted.

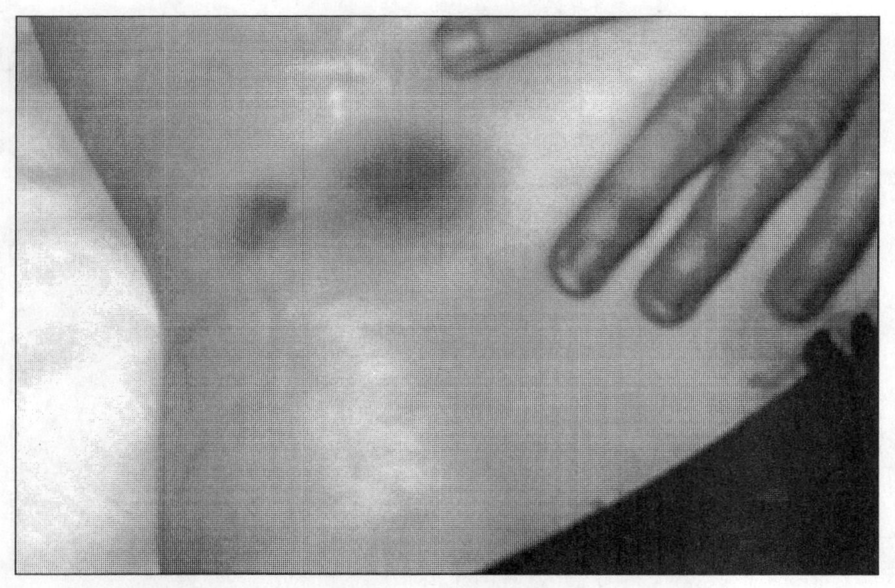

Mysterious bruise that appeared on Pamela's body in 1993.

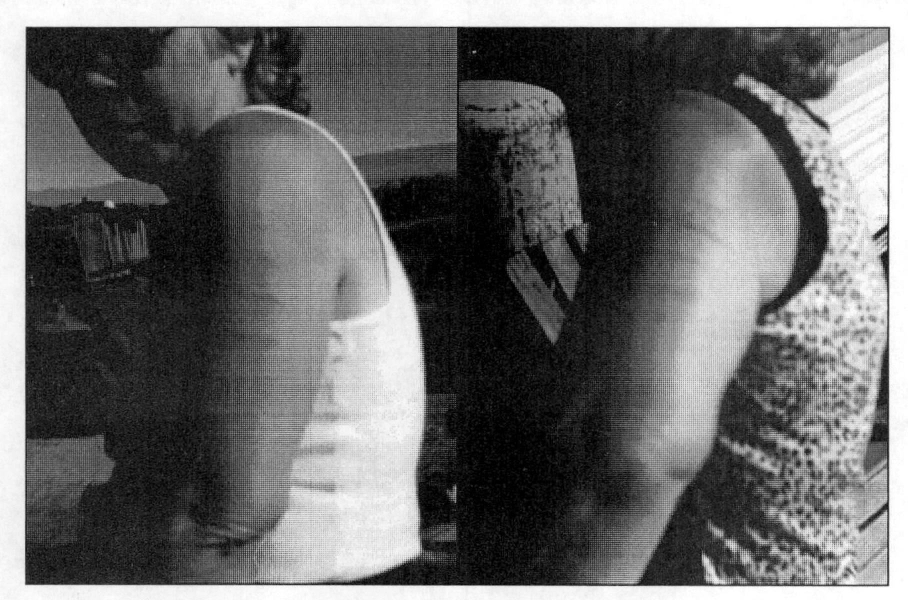

Mysterious scratches that appeared on Pamela's arm in 1991.

Bill Hamilton, Jordan Maxwell, and Pamela at the Little A'Le'Inn at the UFO friendship campout on Memorial Day weekend, 1995.

Bill Hamilton and Bill Uhouse at the friendship campout.

The author and his wife, Pamela, at the Black Mail Box off the Extra-terrestrial Alien Highway—Highway 375 in Nevada in May 1995

The bright orbs in picture approached my truck on the night of March 16, 1993 off the alien highway.

CHAPTER SEVEN
THE PERILS OF PAMELA

Pamela was and is an experiencer, an abductee, and a contactee. She has experienced most if not all of the major indicators of this type of experience: missing time; waking up during the night and having feelings of paralysis; nightmares or vivid dreams of aliens and/or their technology; sleep disorders, also waking up consistently at a specific time (usually 3 A.M.); physical marks on her body; repeated sightings of alien craft; clear remembrance of alien contact and interaction; and numerous other indicators and events that correlate with others' incidents.

I first met Pamela in 1991 when she was married to Al. Al had witnessed some of the phenomena that Pamela had, but was totally non-committal and not supportive. After Pamela finally obtained a divorce after long proceedings, I married her in September 1994. Her experiences have not stopped since I married her, but they have lessened in intensity.

Pamela's remembrances go back to her crib years between 20 and 24 months of age. At that time she would see a tall man appear in her room. He was always wearing a top hat, a long coat, and a ruffled shirt. Later when she saw pictures of Abraham Lincoln, it always reminded her of her mysterious tall visitor. He would stand waving something with his arms. He would never say anything. She did not fear this man. He gave her the feeling of watching and protecting her.

Then the Greys came. They would only come occasionally. They would put their long arms through the bars of her crib. Of course, at that age, she did not know who or what they were. They always seemed to come from the closet. For that reason, to this day, she does not like to see the closet doors left open. She thought they were little monsters that came out of the dark recesses of the closet. This was around 1949 when she lived in Indianapolis, Indiana.

At the age of 3, a very tall nordic male with perfect features came to her when she was playing with her toy blocks in a cute little sundress and high-top shoes. She recalls that he told her that she would be on a mission involving leading people through mountains in the year 2011.

When she was in the second grade of school (1953), she would often sail little toy boats in the water of a fountain near where she lived. One day, a beautiful blonde-haired woman appeared standing beside her. She had perfect features and beautiful blue eyes. Pamela describes her as angelic-looking. She wore a white gossamer gown. She would say things to Pamela telepathically. Pamela does not recall all that she said, but one thing did stand out. She remembers the blonde saying, "you are protected," then she would just fade out or vanish. She has seen this woman several times. The last time she saw this woman was when she was living with me in Reseda in 1993. One other thing she remembers being told when a little girl is that she had something to do in the future, some sort of mission to accomplish.

Pamela's mother was a housewife and was afraid of talking about paranormal happenings. One time there was a strange creature, maybe from some other dimension, leaving tracks on the carpet on the stairway, but her mom did not want to discuss it. When she heard Pamela talk about these experiences, she attributed it to Pamela's imagination.

Pamela's father was in electronics and worked under contract for Naval Ordinance. It was possible that her father was a contactee as he spoke of people from other planets and even took photographs of UFOs. Some of these were day shots and some were colorful lights taken at night. He told Pamela about life on other planets and warned Pamela not to talk openly about it and to be careful who she talked to about her experiences. He told Pamela that there was intelligent life on the moon, Venus, and Mars contrary to what was being told to the public via the press. Raymond was a man who worked on the instrumentation for Gemini V and also worked on avionics for the Boeing 707 jetliner. He was also a tech writer. When he was in the Navy, his occupation was radioman second class. He worked for Rockwell when they moved to Kansas City. Pamela remembers strange men in suits always coming to the house to talk with her father.

When she was 9 years old, sometime during the summer of 1957, her parents went out. She saw a flash of light in the picture window. Two Greys with big heads and black eyes came into the house and stuck a needle at the base of her skull when she was sitting on the couch. There was probably some missing time with this episode. When her parents came home, they could seen the mark on her neck and found dried blood. She then started having headaches, but nothing physical would show up when tests were run. She also experienced fainting spells and black outs, but no physical cause was found.

After the incident, she was standing in the driveway one night near their old green Ford when she saw a large cigar-shaped craft hanging low in the sky. Its surface was reflecting moonlight. She estimates that if she had held her thumb and forefinger out at arm's length, that it would have spanned two inches. It was a dark cylinder and showed no lights and no windows. It made no sound.

Starting at age 11 and lasting for a year-and-a-half she would see the wall "open up" and life-like scenes would play out. In some of these scenes she could see dinosaurs munching on vegetation. Other scenes showed cave dwellers, or erupting volcanoes and molten rivers of lava. In some she could see planets exploding. She could even smell scents and hear sounds. She distinctly remembers hearing a Brontosaurus making a loud trumpeting sound. Some dinosaurs roared. Most of these scenes showed natural catastrophes. They were somewhat like holographic movies.

From age 13 through 16 she saw many flying discs in daytime and at night. The night discs showed counter-clockwise rotating lights. Two of these discs made a definite whirring sound. One had pulsating lights. This one came over a lake in Brown County in Indiana. From the shore she could see red and white fluorescent pulsating lights..

Many times she felt followed by a man dressed in black. Many times she would see him standing by the street light at the corner. He never approached her.

Sometimes she would go to bed with night clothing on and wake up without clothing. One time she found grass in the bed and on the floor. Sometimes she would go to bed in her room, then find herself in another part of the house, usually the family room and found she had dirty feet even though she bathed the previous night. On occasion she would hear her name called from outside, then wake up outside blocks from her home on the sidewalk.

She would have vivid and lucid dreams from the age of 16. She would find herself inside of craft and receiving instructions on how to fly the craft. She remembers seeing symbols on panels. She saw a huge crystal in the center of the craft. When she first got married at age 17, she still went on having the dreams. Her first husband was a skeptic and thought the dreams were just dreams.

In 1982, Pamela had married Al and Al brought her to his handbuilt home at the foothills of the Tehachapis in California. The incidents started to step up as soon as she moved into Al's five-sided house on two-and-half acres of desert property.

One of Pamela's new visitors was a Reptilian Humanoid (Reptoid) that stood at least seven feet tall. I remember when my friend TAL told me about his initial experience of seeing a reptoid in his house in Santa Fe, New Mexico in 1979. TAL had a map placed on the hallway wall showing sites of UFO landings, underground caverns, and animal mutilations. One night, he saw a seven-tall reptoid staring intently at his map. The reptoid looked solid, but translucent in that he could also see through him. At the moment of confrontation, the Reptoid turned to look at TAL, and TAL hurled a stuffed animal at him from the bed. The stuffed animal went sailing through the Reptoid, who looked a little astonished at the foolish human act, then hit the wall behind the creature. The Reptoids eyes seem to reveal a great deal of intelligence. The Reptoid proceeded to touch a point on his belt and disappeared.

Pamela's Reptoid had luminous amber-colored eyes like a cat's and skin that was charcoal, green and grey in color. His massive chest sported a breast plate, much like that worn by Roman soldiers. He had sharp claws on his four fingers. When he would appear in the room, the air would thicken, Pamela would hear a high-pitched sound in her ears as well as buzzing and clicking. In seconds, she found it difficult to breath. Her chest would feel as if it were crushed. She was paralyzed and immobilized and the Reptoid would literally flip her on her stomach. Then he would proceed with a type of tantric sexual intercourse that would leave her absolutely exhausted. She never feared him. She sensed he was extremely powerful and very aggressive as if a member of a warrior caste. She even felt protected by him. She could not smell the Reptoid. Greys were different. She could smell them. They had the smell of decaying bodies, putrid.

Pamela often awoke with scoop marks on her legs or holes in her hips, or triangular marks on her back as well as bruises and scratches and puncture marks. These began appearing in childhood. One time she had five distinct scratches across her left upper arm. We believe that the Reptoid left his claw marks on her in this one particular incident. The scars from these scratches are still visible to this day.

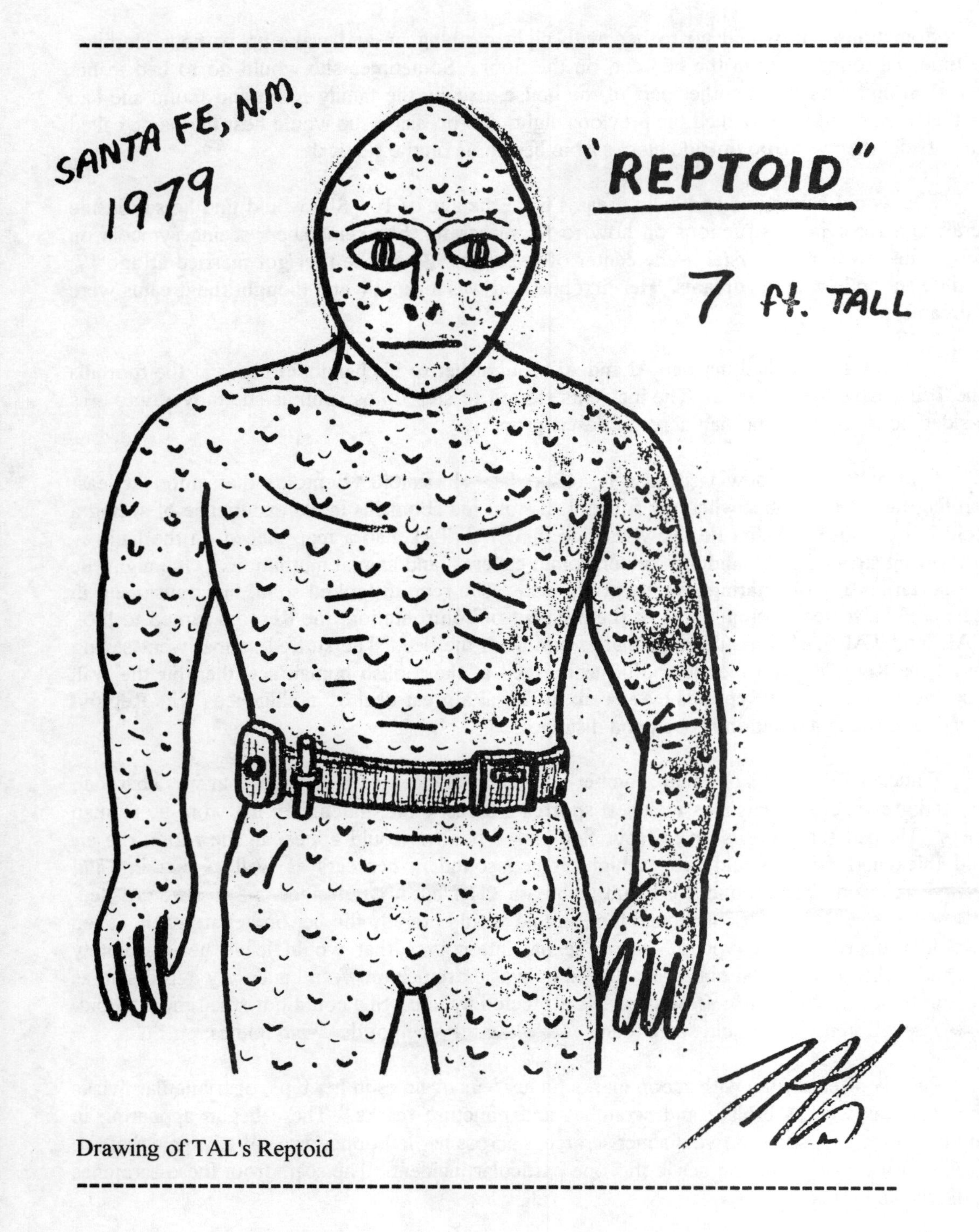

Drawing of TAL's Reptoid

The Greys have taken her blood, inserted needles in her neck and fooled with her eyes and ears.

From 1983 through 1991, she would have orbs appear in the pentagonal house. These balls of light ranged from the size of tennis balls to basket balls. Some were white, some were orange, and some were blue. All were silent. They could burst into view with a flash, and float through the house. Sometimes they would come right through a wall and out a closed screen door. Al would remark that he could see them, but he didn't know what to think about them. He would just shrug his shoulders.

In June of 1990, a little tan-colored alien dressed in a black flight suit would abduct her. On one particular night, she saw an orange fireball descending to the east of the property. During the summer months, she would sleep outside up on the deck near the summer bedroom on the second story of the house. There was an old bus stairwell that was used to get up onto the deck. She remembers being on the stairwell, fully awake, arguing with the little tan guy. She kept saying to him that he had to stop doing what he was doing -- taking her. She had a postal route to start in the morning, and he was interrupting her sleep and might awake Al. His expressionless demeanor conveyed the impression that he wasn't accepting any of what she was saying.

Once, while traveling in 1991, Al and Pamela had stopped in Jerry's restaurant in Blythe, California. A mysterious man deliberately looked at her through the window, then came into the restaurant. He was dressed solidly in black, had a very pale face, silver hair, and was over six feet tall. He sat at the counter and ordered coffee and water, but never touched either one. He just continued to stare at Pamela. No one else in the restaurant paid any attention to him.

Once during that same year, she remembers an incident where she was taken to an underground base in the Tehachapi Mountains. The only recall that is clear to her is a landing pad with a large circled number 38 painted on the surface. Inside the underground area were two older men with grey hair and white lab coats on. They wore glasses and pens and pencils in their coat pockets. There was a lot of equipment, including video screens, up against the walls. She was positive that she was in the mountains north of her home. Later, a pilot friend flew her above the region looking for some tell-tale sign of an opening or landing pad, but she could find nothing that gave away the location of this secret hideaway.

All of this seems like a prelude to a terrifying encounter that occurred on the night of May 14, 1991 when three Greys attempted to remove Pamela from her bed. She had just gone to bed and turned off the television to read. She was awake reading, and not asleep when this occurred. She sensed something and looked up to see the three Greys in their black flight suits standing in a triangle. One was at the foot of the bed, and the other two were on either side of her bed. That was not all. Standing in the room next to her bookshelves was a man dressed in black clothing, holding a black box with a cord dangling from it. Pamela struggled with the Greys to free herself from their control. The man in black stood there and told her she had no electricity. She attempted to turn on the lights that were powered by the generator in the backyard, but the lights failed to come on. She managed to grab a flashlight and rush over to the kitchen window where she could see numerous lights circling in the sky and illuminating her yard. A deck that projects

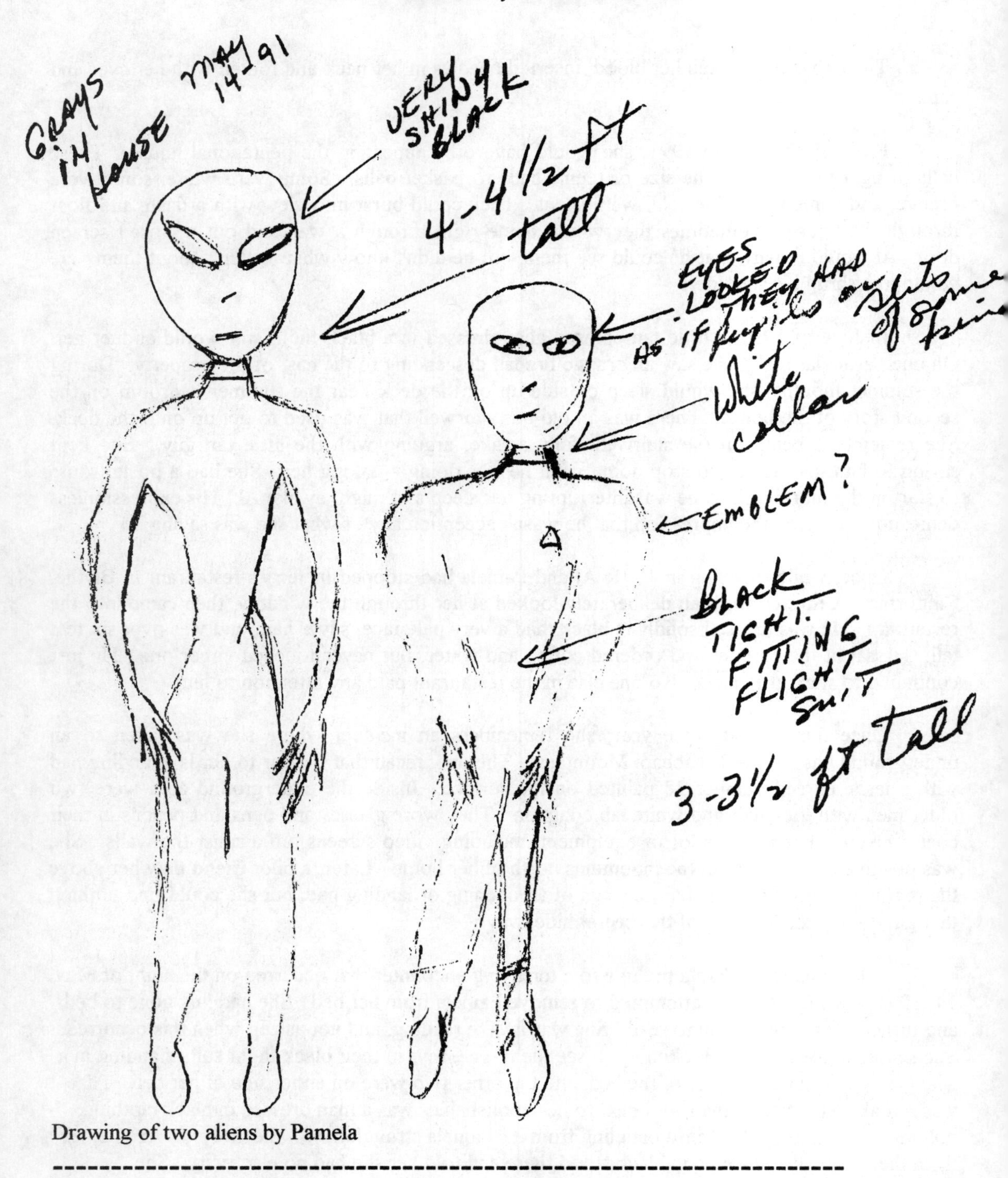

Drawing of two aliens by Pamela

---

off the roof to her right was occupied by an oriental-looking man dressed in Air Force blues and a dark beret. He was laying prone on the deck and gazing down at a K-9 sentry dog that was in the yard with Pamela's own 100-pound Labrador who was barking at the strange German Shepherd. She yelled at the man not to kill her dog. The three Greys she had seen before were now in the yard and the man on the deck was yelling at them to get Pamela "out of the GD house."

The next thing Pamela knew, she was standing in the yard behind the Generator shack. She remembered that her husband had come from the back room to the kitchen window after she had yelled for him, but now she was alone. Her husband was gone, the dogs were gone, the Air Force Officer was gone, and the Grays were not in sight. All she could see was above her. A huge disk rotated. It had bright red lights and was emitting a fog or vapor from portals along the underside rim of the craft. Her next conscious memory was awaking on the bed at about 3:50 AM. Over four hours of missing time had elapsed in one of the strangest and most terrifying encounters that she had ever experienced. It left her with more questions than answers. Later, under hypnosis, a portion of her missing time aboard the hovering ship, was recalled. All of this was on her mind when I drove up to her gate the following morning around 10 AM. She was hysterical and crying. She could not believe all that had just happened. We found out later from her girl friend and neighbor, that her girl friend had noticed a vibration that night, and when looking northward at Pamela's place, saw it enshrouded with a fog. Her trailer was shaking violently and the dogs were going berserk. After she ran out into the desert and saw the fog around Pamela's place, the commotion stopped.

Pamela had a number of other encounters that year, but none as dramatic as the one that happened in May. Throughout the summer, Pamela, I, and others had several sightings of strange moving night lights over the Antelope Valley. Some of these I have nicknamed "Jumpers" because the light-strobing objects seem to jump from position to position in the valley skies instead of moving on a continuous course. Aircraft with strobes could be seen moving on a continuous course for comparison. We also witnessed a train of lights coming in from the west late one evening in July. The individual lights in the procession were glowing with a beautiful golden glow and were surrounded by plasma coronas.

On November 4, 1991, on her birthday, Pamela had a spectacular sighting of an arrow-head shaped object moving above the Antelope Valley Freeway at 7:18 AM. on her way to work under clear daylight conditions. The object was charcoal black, had no vertical stabilizers, emitted no sound, had some sort of tiling on its bottomside, and was about the length of a football field.

Pamela had helicopters flying over her property. On one occasion one came down to within 100 feet of the ground with the side door open and the men inside very visible. She also feels that men in a low-flying highway patrol plane buzzed her place and took her picture when she was standing in the yard. With my prompting, she started to photograph these helicopter overflights. Another abductee in Southern California, Licia Davidson, had taken numerous photos of various helicopters that had buzzed her house. On many occasions, helicopter personnel were seen pointing cameras at the witnesses. Some of the copters carried sound booms that could amplify conversations and sounds emanating from the ground.

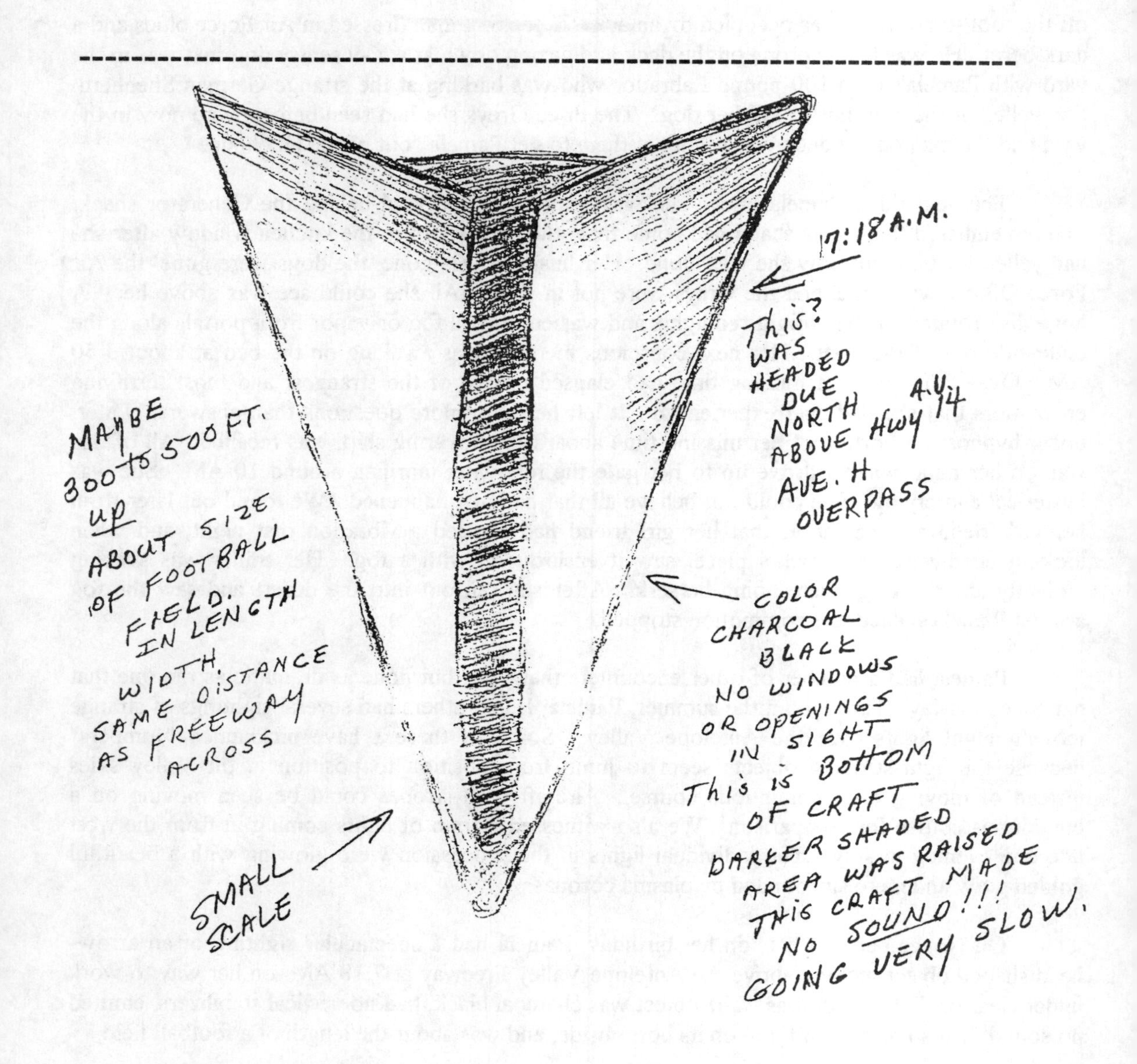

Drawing of Arrowhead Craft by Pamela

A surprising incident occurred to Pamela in late October prior to her November 4th sighting. She was looking out her kitchen window and saw seven strange objects form symbolic patterns in the sky over the saddle of the Tehachapi Mountains. She went outside and yelled to Al to follow her. At that time a brilliant ball of light came rushing out of the center of the formation as she watched. It came at great speed straight toward her and she ducked as it circled and came within two feet of her face. Then it slowly circled her and Al and shot straight up, vanishing along with the formation of symbols. This is one of the few incidents that Al fully admitted to when I queried him about the matter. Almost immediately following this extraordinary event an old 1959 Chevrolet came tearing in through the south gate of her property and two men and one woman emerged from the car when it came to a stop. One man, a good-looking blonde, was wearing blue jeans and a white shirt while the other two wore military Khakis. They all appeared to be in the their early thirties.

Ignoring her husband, the three strangers forced Pamela to enter the house and started ransacking the living room and her desk. They gathered up all books, magazines, and videos on the UFO subject and proceeded to tell her not to collect or gather any more information or they would be back and the next time they would not go easy on her. She started to cry and begged them to stop. They actually became angry and shoved Pamela who shoved the dark-haired girl. They became belligerent and warned Pamela that they would not tolerate her actions. Pamela had the distinct impression that she had seen the blonde man before and that these people were with the Air Force. She knew this intuitively, but did not know why she knew. Upon leaving, they had taken 10 out of 25 negatives of the black unmarked helicopters Pamela photographed, as well as her copy of the book, *Intruders* -- an ironic fare the well!

When the three left to get back in their car, the blonde took Pamela to one side out of the hearing range of the other two. He told her that he did not like doing what he had to do, but she had been told previously to remain silent. He said that she knew some things, but others she did not remember, and that she would remember in time. They left, driving off in the direction of the Northrop facility in the mountains. While all of this was happening, her husband Al remained passive and unconcerned. He did not ask the strangers their business or for their identification.

This story was to have an unexpected postscript which I will return to. First, I would like to tell you about another abductee that Pamela and I met who lives in the California desert area. Pamela related a lot to this other whose name is Diane. We met Diane through Joyce. An early abduction occurred when she was eight years old. She was taken out of her home in Ridgecrest by little Greys wearing dark blue jackets with a sash running diagonally from shoulder to waist. An emblem consisting of a coiled snake within an irregular border was displayed on the front of their jackets. They called her name outside of her bedroom and asked her to come out. Pamela also often heard her name called from outside her bedroom window, but she would not go out. Beyond the house was a craft that looked like a toy top. When they asked her to go for a ride, she consented, and they took her to an underground bunker.

At the underground bunker, Diane saw a number of nude children enclosed in glass chambers appearing to be asleep. Pamela's girl friend, Jackie, had a daughter who, at age five, reported that she had a dream where a little man took her up inside the mountains (Tehachapis) and she saw other children in glass chambers. Diane ran away from her captors and came out of a vent that ran from the bunker to the surface. Finding herself in the open desert again, her head seemed to clear (she felt she had been drugged up to that moment) and saw a woman come running after her to grab her by the arm and bring her back. The woman was tall, pretty , and had long dark hair. She wore a dark purple uniform with an insignia on it. She attempted to force Diane to get into one of the glass chambers, but Diane resisted. There were five chambers and the fourth was empty and seemed meant for her. There were black pipes running to the top of each chamber. She could see little black wires were attached to each child's body. On the other side of the room across from the chambers were consoles operated by humans. They seemed to be monitoring the children.

Diane was screaming when a larger Grey entered the chamber and seemed angry at all the screaming going on. The Grey ordered the woman in purple to "to get her in there" referring to Diane. But Diane fought it all the way. The Grey then conceded and said, "OK, take her back. We can't control her." At that time she knew she would return home.

Diane had a fully conscious encounter with a four-and-a-half foot tall Grey around 1972. She went out to her car one night to drive into town and saw someone approaching from the desert. This entity came right up to her car and stared at her from the other side. They came face-to-face. She could see his eyes through the large dark filters that covered them and discerned cat-like pupils. He communicated to her telepathically.

Diane has also encountered a short, dark reptilian or lizard-like entity about the same size as the medium Grey, four-and-half feet tall. These dark reptilians seem to exude hostility toward humans. On one abduction where the Greys took her and her two children aboard a craft, one of the dark lizards was aboard and actually got into an altercation with one of the Greys and swiped the Grey with its claws, ripping open its chest. Green fluid poured out of the Grey as he fell dead! Diane feels there is an interspecies hostility, and so does Pamela. They feel, that this is usually subordinated as they cooperate and work together for a greater purpose.

Diane also remembers being abducted and taken to an underground facility at China Lake. Much of what she describes resembles the Dulce facility. She remembers riding down an elevator that exactly matches the description given by Thomas of elevators used at Dulce. She only saw one Grey, different from others she had seen as he was fully six feet tall. Bear this in mind when you read about our abduction near Dreamland. During this time, she was entirely handled by men in white jackets. She could even remember the name tag on one of the jackets. She saw the little electric carts they use in these underground facilities. The most bizarre sight she saw was that of altered humans in cages. One man seemed to have four arms. A young man with dark wavy hair conducted her on this freakish tour. Have other abductees reported seeing such bizarre sights.

I know that other abductees have reported the bizarre sexual encounters with the big reptoids. Paula Watson from Missouri told Pamela and I of having virtually identical encounters with Reptillians.

Pamela and Diane have shared a similar dream sequence which involves an old multi-story house. Both feel like they have been taken to the same house. Where is this house? It almost sounds like something that only exists in the Twilight Zone, but then again, who is to say where the Twilight Zone really is.

Months after many of the abductions and the visit of military personnel, and the separation of Pamela and Al, I took Pamela to her medical clinic for a check on an infection she had contracted. The nurse had left her medical chart in the room. Dr. K had been treating Pamela for years and was a fatherly figure in his approach to Pamela's health conditions. For the first time she noticed that some of her medical records had been stamped with the instruction to send a copy to a certain flight surgeon (Dr. C. M.) at Edwards Air Force Base. Pamela had never authorized her records to be sent to Edwards. She had never been in the Air Force and had no relatives in the Air Force. Her father had been a Navy man. Why was Dr. K sending her records to Edwards? She asked him and he could not give her an answer. He claimed that he did not know this was happening and told her to check with the medical records department.

Pamela requested copies of her medical records and received only part of them. When she queried the medical records clerk, she was astonished to hear her say that some of her missing records were ordered destroyed! She managed to obtain some copies of records with the Edwards routing on them. Even when she requested that the clinic terminate this routing on her request, the request was ignored and the routing to Edwards continued.

We engaged the help of a Doctor G. who was a member of our MUFON group to give us some data on the mysterious flight surgeon. From the information he gave us, we discovered that he graduated from medical school at the University of San Diego, a prestigious school. While attending a UFO meeting one Sunday, Pamela and I stayed over to visit the university on Monday. When we got to the records office, we requested to see a photograph of the young flight surgeon from his graduating class photos. After Pamela examined the photo with a magnifying glass, she came to the conclusion that the man in the photo, the flight surgeon who was receiving copies of her medical records, and the good-looking blonde man who accompanied the two airman in Khakis on the October 1991 visit were one and the same! She had positively identified someone from the Air Force who monitored abductees. What could we do with this information? No one had any good ideas. So the matter rests.

Pamela is still having encounters. She twice saw a little Grey in our new house in Lancaster. He comes up to her within a few feet and cocks his head to one side with a curious expression, then vanishes into thin air. She once saw a dark cloaked figure in the living room. Soon after we moved in she found, photographed, and drew the outlines of a three-toed footprint on our carpet in the hallway. We have heard strange sounds upstairs while we are both sitting downstairs in the den. And on Christmas night, she photographed a luminous orb that made a sharp-angled turn in front of the Christmas tree. She has caught strange things on film before, including some lights that were glowing in the bushes alongside the road into Long Canyon in Sedona. This was in broad daylight in the afternoon.

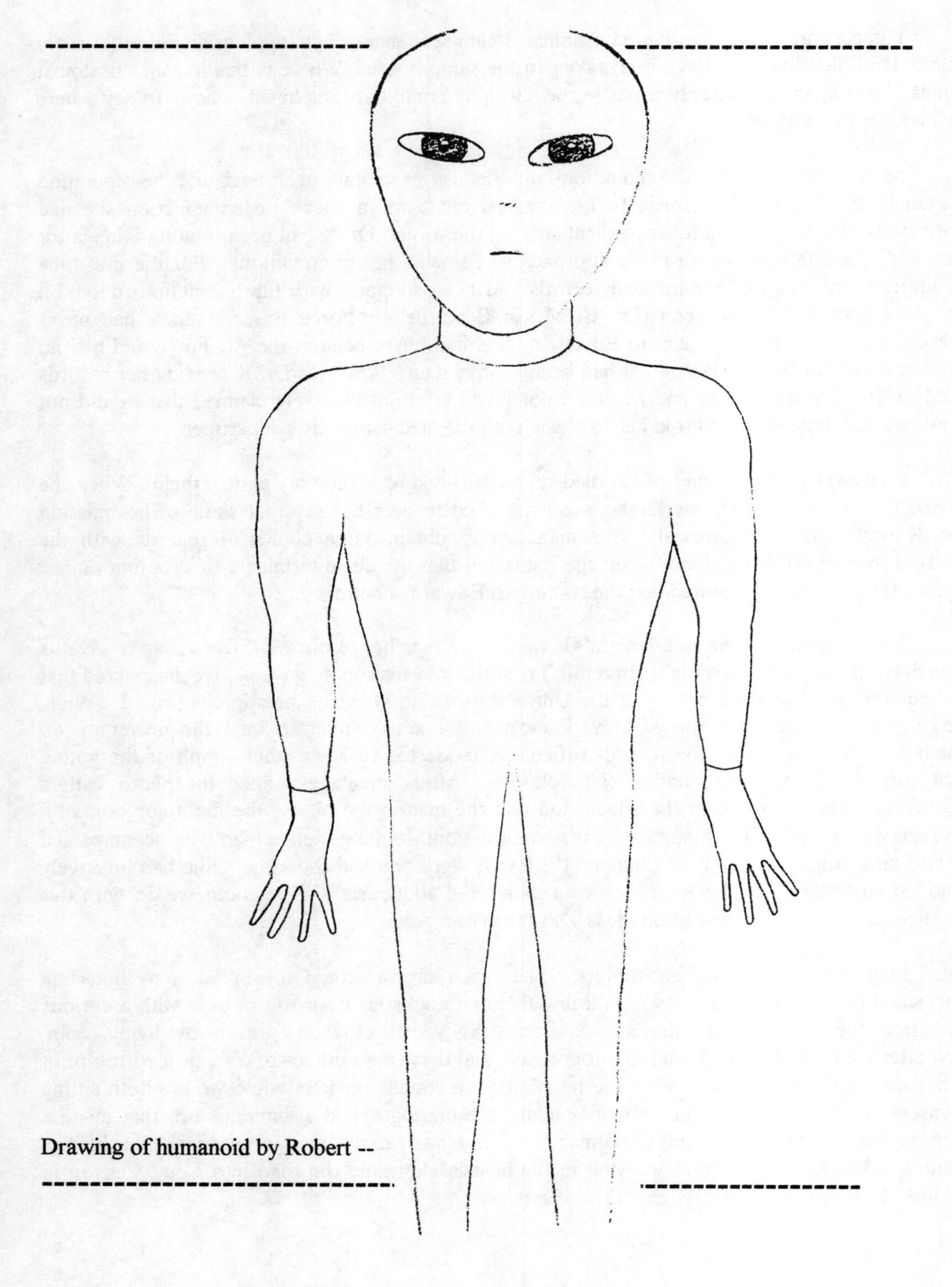

Drawing of humanoid by Robert --

Marks have continued to appear as if overnight on various parts of Pamela's body, and when we see them, we photograph and document them. Her health has deteriorated since some of these later encounters. Pamela knows the world will change. Changes are imminent. She fears the nights when she finds herself paralyzed. It may be a long while yet before the world pays attention to the perils of Pamela or any of the others who have had these encounters. Don't tell Pamela or the others that they merely suffer from sleep disorders. The truth is many of these events have happened in the real world in the waking state.

Pamela and I have now moved to Arizona, yet her sleep is still disturbed and she continues to experience paranormal events during her waking hours. On one occasion in September, 1995 a supporting wall in the house started to mysteriously vibrate. A few seconds later, the wall stopped its vibration and a bookcase near the wall started vibrating. There was no apparent source for the vibrations. Mysterious sounds have also been heard in the house. She seems to be the focus of invisible attention and, wherever she goes, she does not escape its influence.

CHAPTER EIGHT
AEROSPACE VALLEY

Aerospace Valley would be a good nickname for the Antelope Valley of Southern California. On the north side of the valley is sprawling Edwards AFB, site of many interesting UFO encounters. On the south side of the valley is Air Force Plant 42 in Palmdale where they rolled out the B2 Stealth Bomber. Northrop has a plant nearby and Lockheed-Martin skunkworks occupies a large imposing building just east of Sierra Highway. On the extreme east end of the valley is a secret Douglas electromagnetic research facility, and on the west side of the valley is the secret Northrop electromagnetic research facility, the Anthill in the Tehachapi Mountains. Palmdale also houses the FAA facilities for Los Angeles area control. Stealth bombers, stealth fighters, and other advanced technology aircraft in flight testing can be seen flying day or night over various parts of the valley. People are used to looking up when they hear the roar of a jet, but otherwise keep their eyes on the ground just as you might find in any American city.

On May 28, 1991, the night of a full moon, I went to an observation area just west of the city of Lancaster and south of the Northorp facility in the Tehachapi mountain range. Joined by three other observers, we saw our first aerial light emerge at the crest of the mountains in the south. The light was white with an amber tinge. It moved westward above the mountain ridge, reached a certain point, then started strobing fluorescent red and white lights.

As it continued to move west, then northwest, it began to jump and dance in erratic movements. When it reached the far end of the west valley I could see a silhouette against the twilight blue sky. The object appeared to be boomerang-shaped with several strobe lights dancing around its perimeter. The object suddenly and instantaneously vanished. A second and third object appeared above the same mountains and followed roughly the same pattern of activity except that they continued on their course and disappeared in the distance. The wild "jumpers," as I nicknamed them, were sometimes so erratic that normal aircraft could easily be distinquished from them. If normal aircraft moved with such erratic behavior, the structural stresses on airframes would tear them apart.

On the following night, with thirteen other witnesses gathered at our desert observation post, I viewed a spectacular light show that started in the same way as the previous night. We saw between 25 and 30 "jumpers" that night. Several of these danced and zig-zagged at all points of the compass. Two of these also disappeared when in clear view.

In addition to the strobing jumpers, we saw what appeared to be a large craft maneuvering to the east. It appeared to be triangular with a steady fluorescent red light on the right side and an aquamarine-colored light on the left. This object flew forward, backwards, and on its side. It turned and tilted until it came to the south end of the street as if it were peering at us. It then tilted on edge and turned to return to its point of origin. I snapped four photos of the object, but nothing registered on the 1000 ASA Ektar film. Robert Puskus was also present and took photos, but nothing registered on his film either.

I phoned Edwards AFB the next day and discussed the sightings with the PIO at the Public Affairs Office. The PIO was extremely interested in our sightings, but could offer no immediate explanation for them except to say that he was aware that several secret projects involving advanced technology aircraft were conducted in the valley, but he did not have access to that information.

In the early morning hours of July 25th, Pamela and I were watching the valley skies as we have done so often on warm summer nights. At 12:45 AM a string of gold-colored lights approached silently and rapidly from the west, moving east. The golden lights were surrounded by a coronal field that may have been ionized layers of plasma. Some of this plasma was shed from its source and trailing off behind the formation. As the string reached the perimeter of the city of Lancaster, the lights disappeared one by one. At least two other parties had a camcorder and starlight scope and videotaped this procession of lights.

There have been other peculiar activities and light shows reported to me from the east side of the valley. Some of these sightings are near the Douglas facility, or El Mirage Dry Lake and Shadow Mountain. A team of skywatchers from Victorville has seen many strange balls of light and one huge lighted craft near Shadow Mountain. They have also reported seeing an identical string of golden lights similar to the ones we saw.

Other amazing sightings have taken place throughout the Antelope Valley. Some of these were directly over residential areas and close to the flight paths of aircraft and within the zone scanned by radar. None of these UFOs were ever intercepted or challenged by interceptor jets from Edwards or George during the periods of time that I investigated these sightings. If these UFOs were intent on abducting people, they could not be stopped. I started investigating sightings in the area in 1987.

There were three witnesses to the sighting of October 5, 1987. There was 14-year-old Michelle, her 11-year-old sister, Laura, and their dad. They went to bed around 10:30 PM. There was a full moon that night and the sky was clear. Michelle had pulled the curtains of her bedroom windows aside, laid back, and looked up past the roof of the two-story apartment building when she first spotted a perfectly round object encircled with lights, spinning, and moving slowly at low altitude past the edge of the roof. She got excited and fearful at the same time. Laura also caught sight of the object a little after Michelle. Their first thought that it was a plane was quashed when they could see the strange appearance and action of the object. They left the bedroom to call their father to the window. He could sense how frightened the girls were and was afraid they might have seen an intruder in the neighborhood. Reluctantly, he peered out the window, but could offer the girls no explanation for the object. Its silvery form reflected the bright full moon. Michelle said there were lights all around the rim of the ellipsoidal object that spun with the object, but in a digital ticking fashion. The object was large and had a protuberance on its top side. It also had some sort of projecting flange around the rim. They also saw the UFO pass from view beyond the rooftops of the apartment buildings across the way. This object passed through a narrow corridor between Edwards AFB airspace, and that controlled by Palmdale Air Traffic Control. The father did call Edwards AFB as well as the Antelope Valley Sheriff's Department to report the strange sighting.

On July 16, 1988, a woman named Helen reported seeing two dark objects, shaped like ice-cream cones, descend silently near her yard in downtown Lancaster at around dusk. The objects appeared perforated like a fishing net, were larger than kites, but smaller than a private plane. They seemed under power as they ascended after descending. There was a "dead zone" effect when the objects passed overhead.

While living on a ten-acre ranch in the west valley on October 26, 1988, a strange procession passed over my rear property line. My neighbors Ken and Katy saw a large boomerang-shaped craft between 8:35 PM and 8:45 PM that Ken estimated to be more than 660 feet in breadth, traveling low and slow. The first boomerang was joined by a second one. Ten to twenty disc-shaped objects accompanied the boomerangs. The lead boomerang made a humming sound as often described when UFOs are close. The last one in the formation had a light that alternately flashed yellow and red. My attention was distracted by a pick-up truck that was pacing the object on 230th Street west and shining a spotlight to the rear of my property. I could not identify the driver of the truck. The objects rose in altitude to clear the Tehachapi Mountains to the north and flew directly over the Anthill facility. Later I found two additional witnesses who saw the objects from a side view from the vicinity of Avenue J and 110th Street west. These objects were the same ones seen later that night over Fresno by Brian Neel and several other witnesses. Later I learned that a property owner reported 30-foot burn rings on his property. There were an amazing 17 of these. This was in the Three Points area and would have been beneath the flight path of these objects. I attempted to get to the site of the rings shortly after we had rainfall, but never got to the actual site as it was a grueling hike.

On July 9, 1989, a security guard named Archie reported the following sightings. In late May or early June he was working a guard post at Air Force Plant 42 when at approximately 11:15 in the morning he observed a bright silvery object in the vicinity of a B1-B bomber that was doing touch and goes on the field. The object was very high and moved slowly from north to south. The following week on a Friday, the same object reappeared, this time the object appeared to come out of the west, stopped at about 20 degrees off the horizon, maintained its position, then proceeded south across the base. Archie picked up his radio and notified the FAA control tower to ask if something had fallen off the B1. They acknowledged and said that everything was OK. He watched the silver speck until it disappeared, then, from that same spot, saw three round balls appear out of nowhere traveling from north to south, changing color, then disappearing. He contacted the control tower again saying, "I don't know what the hell is happening around here, but I just saw 3 balls fly across the base." The tower replied, "we believe you, we believe you." Shortly after, a large white helicopter with red markings (USAF) flew in from the north and orbited in the vicinity about 10 minutes and left.

On November 18, 1989 Robert Puskus observed a large boomerang-shaped object, describing it as a black mass, moving soundlessly over Avenue J-4 near Sierra Highway at 7:42

PM. He estimated its span between 800 to 900 feet. The black mass had low intensity lights about the brilliance of stars along its edges. Off the left tip of the object was a silvery disc that had no running lights, but reflected ground lights clearly.

On May 21, 1990, Robert witnessed another disc about 50-feet in diameter traveling rapidly on a SW-NE trajectory nearly collide with a KC-135 from Palmdale Airport as it circled over Ave. J-4 in Lancaster. He saw the KC-135 take an evasive maneuver.

Our friend Betty Murray reports stopping for a red light at the corner of Ave K and 12th Street west about 3 P.M. on February 26th, 1991 when she spotted a dark gray metallic disc hovering low just above the traffic signal. The disc was at least as wide as the street (25 - 30 feet). The disc was there for the duration of the signal light.

There have been sightings of black triangles, cigar-shaped craft, discs, and other phenomena throughout the Antelope Valley somehow keeping a peaceful coexistence with all the conventional and experimental aircraft that fly over this valley. In September 1990, AP wire services carried a story about strange aircraft seen over the Antelope Valley. It said that several large, quiet, triangular wing-shaped aircraft of unknown origin have been spotted in the air near Air Force bases in the west. The Air Force declined to confirm or deny that the sightings were of new warplanes. The article reports that Aviation Week magazine said there have been at least 11 sightings of the triangular aircraft near Edwards AFB and one near Fresno. It said that there have been other sightings of similar aircraft in central Nevada near ranges operated by the Air Force and the Energy Department. The speculation was that these triangular craft were secret advanced technology warplanes. Their quiet travel, unusual maneuverability and appearance makes these craft far different from conventional jet planes. Maybe some of these craft are just not airplanes in any sense of the word. One of the most amazing series of sightings was reported by Archie again.

One will rarely read in the annals of UFO reports of a continuing series of sightings that apparently involves the same UFO or its cousins. Such a series has taken place over the Antelope Valley of California, home of many aerospace enterprises. It all began with a sighting made by an ex-Sheriff's deputy named Archie on June 8th. Fortunately, Archie kept a log of his sightings. As I and others started spotting these daylight objects, I further extended the log. The sightings continue up through early November. Some of the entries made in our log will be presented here to demonstrate something unusual is occurring on a regular basis high in our atmosphere, but is virtually ignored by the Air Force or anyone else for that matter.

Archie had his first sighting of the object he dubbed "critter" on June 8, 1993 at 1100 hours. He was sitting on his patio at his home in Rosamond chatting with his lady friend when she asked what kind of birds were circling in the sky. Archie identified the birds as ravens, common to the area. Far beyond the ravens was what appeared to be a dim daytime star. Both of them studied this apparent star with seven and ten power binoculars. It appeared to be round and bright white, and sitting at a stationary point approximately 30 degrees from the horizon and southwest from Rosamond. They watched this mysterious object until 1230 hours when they viewed two slim silver objects fly from the vicinity of the primary object and make a high speed turn from north to west and disappear within a second. When attempts were made to locate the original object, it too had disappeared.

On June 12, Archie spotted the object again from his place of work in Palmdale. Another witness also saw the object. After this second witness left, Archie observed the object move away at high speed. He saw it again on June 13 and again it was moving at very high speed. He made an additional sighting on July 2nd and 3rd. On July 5th he watched the object sit still high in the sky for approximately 45 minutes. Then it moved slowly north. Archie watched it through binoculars. It seemed to accelerate steadily, wobbling as it moved then suddenly stopping and hovering for a moment. Then it moved west and was out of sight within seconds. It had appeared at 11:45 AM and had departed at 12:30. It reappeared in the same spot of the sky at 1:15 PM.

On July 20, 1993 Archie spotted the object again at its usual location in the sky over Rosamond. This time he had his Minolta camera ready mounted with a 300mm lens. When he took his first picture, the object seemed to discharge other objects and he continued snapping pictures at a setting of F8 at 125th of a second with the focus on infinity. The object showed up as a bright spot against the sky.

On July 22nd, Archie's observations convinced him that the object he was viewing was not a natural object and could fly away from its stationary position. Just as he raised his binoculars to watch the object, it began to move north at a steadily increasing speed, changing from white to beige and flattening in shape. It moved with incredible speed, and without slowing, turned a "U" turn to the south and disappeared into the overcast. Archie stated that watching this object maneuver was like watching a fly or a bee. At this time Archie went back into the house to grab his camera. When he came back out, the object was back in position. Archie then snapped 18 pictures!

Shades of Gulf Breeze! Multiple photos of a UFO. For some obscure reason this is cause for instant skepticism by the debunker crowd. One blurred photo is allowable. Perhaps we can arrive at no solid conclusions about one photo. Multiple authenticated photos are more difficult to deal with and the skeptics have to try harder. However, there is no rational reason why an astute observer like Archie could not snap multiple photos of a UFO and he was not the only one to snap photos of this object. On the 25th of July, Archie equipped himself with a Tasco 75x astronomical telescope on a tripod to see if he could determine the mysterious object's shape, but the object appeared no larger that a pinhead, round with a diagonal black line crossing through it. When he changed the eyepiece from a 2.5 mm to a 4mm lens, he could not re-acquire the object. Usually an observer obtains subjective impressions about the target of observation, not just the objective data concerning the object's appearance and behavior. Usually these impressions are ignored by investigators, but I think it is worth mentioning in this case because of other reports Archie has made that indicate very strongly that he is also a CE-IV case and has been contacted or taken by entities associated with UFOs. According to Archie, the object (i.e. the intelligences guiding the object) seem to know when it is being observed as it plays a game of "hyperspace hide and seek." The object possesses a high technology, apparent in its movements and its ability to place itself in alignment between the observer and the sun in some instances.

Sometimes when it takes off slowly, it appears to wobble. Its position in the sky indicates that it would have a clear sweeping view of all military establishments in Southern California, from Vandenburg in the north to Edwards to the Navy station south of Santa Cruz Islands. Archie thinks this object is a "mother ship" of unknown origin or a large unmanned probe. Because of the object's appearance and behavior, he excludes explanations of it being a planet, balloon, satellite, or known aircraft.

On August 9th, Archie spotted the object below the clouds. He obtained four photos of the object in various positions relative to the clouds. This object was also photographed by another skywatcher who attends our UFORUM meetings at Fox Field from another perspective near Palmdale. The other photographer usually uses 300-1000mm telephoto lenses and obtained an excellent shot of this object in the clouds, but he has not given me a copy of the photo. Archie felt the object became spooked around 1220 and darted in and out of view. At 1225 hours, two fuzzy white elongated objects flew from the vicinity of the main object's usual location. These fuzzy objects appeared roughly pointed and cigar-shaped. Archie kept describing a shape that reminded him of a parakeet seed.

On August 13th I had the opportunity of sending my fiance, Pamela, to visit Archie and observe whatever he observed. She reported seeing the object after noon traveling from west to east.

On August 14th Pamela and I visited Archie and it was the first time that I had an opportunity to view the UFO that showed up as if on a train schedule. It was 12:15 in the afternoon. Archie says he sees the critter through his binoculars. There is a crescent moon near zenith. He tells me where to point my 10x50 Bushnells, moving my aim one lens diameter west of the moon (which is about 80-85 degrees of elevation). I spot it. It's sitting stationary and is sharp and clear under magnification. It appears to be round and silvery though I am sure it is also glowing faintly. After hovering for thirty minutes in one position, it begins to move rapidly and chaotically in tight S-curves and loops with the agility of an insect. That is when I nickname this object Skydancer. What appears to be a solid metallic object is moving with total disregard of inertia. Fascinating! Nothing in our inventory (that I know of) can move with such fantastic speed and agility. I could fully understand any motivation to attempt a replication of the technology that can produce this type of performance in an aircraft or spacecraft. We stopped viewing Skydancer at around 1300 hours. I took three photos with my Fuji camera at maximum zoom (115mm) and one photo with my Chinon at maximum zoom (85mm).

On August 21, my two friends, who travel to video tape UFOs, arrived at my home at around 11:30 AM. Mike worked for an aircraft company and brought his Sony 8mm videocam, and his friend, Steve, who works for a cable access station, brought a Panasonic. We stationed ourselves at 30th Street and Avenue B. I spotted Skydancer at 12:05 PM drifting slowly east then returning to a stationary position at about an elevation of 75 degrees and about 250 degrees azimuth. Steve and Mike had a hard time spotting it with binoculars. Mike finally got it in the viewfinder and started taping at 12X magnification. Mike helped Steve point his videocam and Steve started taping at 16X. Later, Mike accomplished the remarkable feat of taping Skydancer at 96X, aiming his camera at an extremely narrow field of view. Skydancer hovered in this position for over an hour. I also managed to see the object through my refracting telescope using a 20mm eyepiece (about 25X). Later after viewing the hour of taping he had accomplished, Steve noticed that he had picked up a second object that was moving in a tumbling fashion past Skydancer. He digitally magnified this portion of the tape at the studio. So we now have video, photos, and multiple eyewitnesses. It couldn't get much better , except for our elusive object to come closer for a better view. On August 23rd, one of our local group, Mario, called to report spotting a disk from the vicinity of his music shop in downtown Lancaster at K and 10th Street West. He had two witnesses with him at the time of the sighting around mid afternoon. The disk appeared at relatively low altitude (perhaps around 5,000'), tipped at an angle, and had a visible dome on its topside. It was bright as polished steel and moving erratically and silently. I have no way of knowing whether this disk was Skydancer or one of it's associates.

On August 28th I alerted another party, Drue, to watch for Dancer. Archie was also watching for it. I first spotted Dancer hovering at about 85 degrees elevation and about 240 degrees southwest at 12:11 PM. I phoned Drue to give him the location. When I went back to locate Dancer again, it was in motion. It moved slowly at first, but seemingly without inertia, it traveled westward to about 35 degrees of elevation, then it seemed to blur against the sky and disappear. Archie called, then Drue. Drue saw something flitting about within the sun's bright glow. From time to time, Archie and I both noted that we could see dragon flies and other insects against the blue sky through binoculars and we could distinguish these from high-flying metallic objects. When I went back out to look in the sunglow, I spotted an object that was Dancer or its twin traversing south of the sun, traveling westward, then reversing direction and moving off southeast. One should be careful attempting to view objects in sunglow. Use sun filters or shield against direct sunlight.

On September 7th, Archie reports seeing two Dancers, a boomerang, and dumbell-shape that hovered. On September 9th, my neighbor Vicki reports seeing a formation of gold-gray objects flipping at different angles in the northern sky at low elevation at around 2:15 PM.

On many sightings of Skydancer, I would spot it hovering motionlessly at a very high altitude. Sometimes it seemed silvery, other times, white. Another viewer asked me if it could be a planet or a very bright star that could be seen in daylight. Of course, I replied that it wasn't a planet or very bright star as only novas have been seen in daylight sky. The brightest, nearest planet is Venus and Venus was seen rising in the early morning hours before the sun. All the planets travel along the plane of the ecliptic and progress at roughly a degree of arc every four minutes. Skydancer did not progress westward with the sun, but maintained its original position for as long as an hour. Another speculation was that it was a balloon. Balloons are at the mercy of high velocity high altitude winds and could not maintain the same position as long as Skydancer. Other aircraft and conventional artifacts are ruled out when Skydancer goes into motion and accelerates at high speeds without gradually gaining speed, or executes swift turns that would place severe G-stresses on its structure. When all datapoints of observation are taken into account, the evaluation is that Skydancer is a UFO and exhibits classic UFO behavior.

On Sept 18th Archie observed Skydancer a few degrees from the sun. It was stationary at first then began to drift to the east. By this time the object was so consistent in its schedule that Archie recorded observations for Sept 28th, Sept 29th, Oct 1st, Oct 4th, Oct 7th, Oct 18th, and Oct 22nd. Most of these appearances occurred between 1200 hours and 1250. On several of these occasions Archie reports that the object did its "bee's dance."

Skydancer returned to the Antelope Valley skies as early as April 1994. In July, Pamela kept a vigil during the week and spotted the object six days in a row. She then called the PIO at Edwards AFB and reported the sighting to him. He was very interested in finding out the details. He did not give the standard line that the Air Force was no longer interested in pursuing investigations of UFOs as it had gotten out of the UFO business in 1969 with the Colorado study. When Pamela informed the PIO that we had videotaped the object, he became even more interested. When she volunteered to point out Skydance for him, he said that it would not be necessary for her to do so as they had their own team assembled for these purposes. It is difficult to escape speculation on the purpose of Dancer's visits over the Southern California desert on a repetitive schedule. It seems like something of interest was monitored, perhaps on a daily basis, but I doubt if we will ever know what that something was. Recently I have heard two reports of the silent dark triangles traversing the twilight skies over the valley. The mysterious UFOs will not go away, but neither are they making themselves any less of a mystery.

CHAPTER NINE
DREAMLAND

BACKGROUND - AREA 51

They call it the Ranch, Watertown, or Dreamland. It is part of a vast military reserve in central Nevada. Spy planes have been tested, taking-off and landing on the long runway at Groom Lake. Since 1989 and the release of Robert Lazar's story of having worked at S-4, a few miles south of Groom Lake at the base of the Papoose Mountains on back-engineering alien spacecraft, hundreds of visitors have come to the Little Ale'Inn in Rachel, Nevada and what is called the Mailbox Road to look for the glowing lights of UFOs that appear beyond the Jumbled Hills. Indeed, many witnesses claim to have seen classic UFOs and dozens of photos and videos support their claims. Critics have proposed that witnesses are seeing advanced experimental aircraft near Groom Lake as this has long been a testing site for advanced technology aircraft. However, interviewing several witnesses along with written testimony reveals that witnesses are describing classic disc-shaped aeroforms that move in zig-zag manuevers, fly silently, and are surrounded by glowing plasma. One enterprising photographer filmed one of these craft using a movie camera with a telescopic lens. The film distinctly shows the seething changing shape of a plasma field.

Not all experiences along the so-called *Extraterrestrial Alien Highway*, Highway 375 have been skywatcher sightings. Unsuspecting curiousity seekers have experienced encounters with bright lights and missing time. Before I detail my own experience along the Alien Highway as Nevadans call it, I would like to recall some insightful statements made by a Nevada abductee by the name of Gina. Gina claims that her abductions started when she was only 16 months of age.

Gina reported abductions by two groups of aliens, Greys and Reptilians. She says the Greys have been used by the Reptilians as middlemen, doing their work and exposing themselves to us on behalf of and instead of the Reptilians. The Greys are engaged in abduction and related activity, as they tell it, in order to survive. They use biological substances from humans (such as glandular secretions) in a manner we can compare with eating (they absorb nutrients through their skin). As a species they are using material from us to recreate themselves, by creating their next generation with hybrids. Most of them can no longer individually produce offspring.

Gina has stated that she has had conversations with Greys, but not Reptilians. Often the Reptilians were present during her abductions, but standing off to the side. She is under the impression that the Reptilians have little regard for humans as living beings. However, they consider some humans as valuable property.

Gina says that a significant part of the abduction experience is the government factor, for abductees that have no direct involvement as well as those that do. According to her, the American government knew of the abductee situation in the 1960s. She says that "handlers" were assigned to some of the abductee children at that time. These handlers were human agents and their job was to keep an eye on the abductee and observe abductions.

Gina remembers one of her first experiences with a "handler." She says she was seven years old and lying on an examination table in an underground base. The Greys had finished with her and left the room, leaving her on a table, fully conscious but paralyzed. She could see, feel, and hear, but could not speak or move. She could hear a man in the room tell another that he could have her. She recalls that a young man in a khaki-colored uniform came into the room and raped her. After awhile, a second man, the "handler", came into the room and pulled the first one off her and appeared to beat him up. This was done purposely to forge a bond between her and the agent. She was told not to talk about these events.

A few years ago, Gina's story sounded bizarre and like something she invented to attract attention. Since she only allowed her story to be told using a pseudonym, such a motive is doubted. I had a unique opportunity to interview Gina in 1991 and ask her some questions concerning the Nevada Test Site. I found her to be a sincere and intelligent young woman who had a number of insights on aliens and abductions. She has been abducted by the large, independently-acting Greys and the smaller clone-like Greys. She described the appearance of the Reptoids, including one that appeared to be an honored leader. The Reptoid with rank was different from the others in its albino appearance. She also claims to have met individuals of the Orange race.

Gina says that she is used as a breeder. The Greys are harvesters and experimentalists. They cross-breed and produce variations in many different species, not just humans, for their own particular purposes. They instruct the breeder by training them on many tasks. Gina has had weapon training, flight training, training in using ESP, and other training exercises designed to imprint the training pattern onto the genetic pattern. I gathered that the Greys were trying to alter the morphogenetic field in order to pass on desired traits to their progeny. The bred hybrid will then have a predisposition for learning a training pattern in a more efficient way.

She told me that she had been abducted and taken to an underground base that she knew to be located within the Nevada Test Site. I asked her if she could describe the security forces she had seen at this site. She said they were known as ASI (Advanced Security Intelligence) and they all wore black jump suits and black hats. She also stated without hesitation that they were a branch of the NSA (National Security Agency). Consider this information when reading about Pamela's encounter with men that fit this description. I had not told Pamela about this.

Gina went on to say that the Greys used a little black box to locate the abductees they singled out of populations. She did not elaborate on this point further. She knew of a black box that used to control abductees, producing a field that caused headaches, nausea, numbness, and a quick loss of energy.

I asked her for a description of the Reptoids that she had seen in the underground areas and she described them as tall and strong. They have a quiltwork pattern of squares on their skin and have green eyes. They take charge of the situations she has found herself in. Others have described Reptoids with charcoal skin and yellow eyes.

Gina was trained on a weapon that might be described as a nerve-triggered beam weapon. The weapon fits on the hand and arm with a wire embedded underneath the skin. The weapon generates a minature hologram that teaches the user how to aim and fire the weapon on impulse.

She claims that she was taken to several underground bases. One was located at Dreamland, another inside Sandia Mountain in Albuquerque, and another time she was taken to the Dulce facility. She saw aquatic animal biotech experiments at the base inside Sandia. These animals were also being trained by aliens.

She also learned the alien symbol language and described how she sat at screens and was taught to read the symbols.

There are an ever-increasing number of abductees who report being taken to underground facilities or have interaction with human agents in company with the alien abductors. Granted we can feel comfortable dismissing these stories as fantasy and going on living our lives under the illusion that we are the lords of earth, the highest form of life in creation. To come to the realization that other intelligent species inhabit the earth, from some other location in space and time, that they may be controlling our lives and destiny from hidden enclaves, is a shock to all that we have come to think of ourselves. In this, we cannot forget, that witnesses have described a variety of encounters, and not all such encounters were as menacing as Gina's.

PRELUDE TO MISSING TIME

I met Pamela in 1991. She had several encounters with alien life forms at her house near Rosamond, California at the base of the Tehachapi Mountains. She remembers having an encounter in June 1990 with a small cardboard-colored entity that resembled a Grey. This entity was wearing a form-fitting one-piece black suit. She was standing on the stairs of the summer deck arguing with this entity into the early hours of the morning. It was neither her first nor last encounter. I have detailed some of her experiences in Chapter 7.

I have had one or two encounters of my own. The most distinctive took place on May 8, 1981 in Arizona. I remember three little white-skinned beings appearing at the foot of my bed. I was in a hypnogogic state. When they departed suddenly, a pungent odor of ozone permeated the air of the bedroom.

I have been investigating abductions since 1976 and am familiar with many types of experiences with various entities. However, never did I dream that Pamela and I would experience missing time together.

I am well aware that abduction reports have generated a backlash from the public sector from authorities such as Carl Sagan and Dr. Robert Baker. They would like dismissing these encounters as hypnopompic hallucinations or some other reasonable psychological category in order to avoid dealing with the possibility of physical events that carry more profound implications. I am aware of the fact that witness exposure to UFO material tends to "contaminate" the individual's recounting of events and lessens the value of witness testimony. In that case, one may consider that my testimony is hyper contaminated by a background of 40 years researching this subject. On the other hand one might hold the consideration that I have had 40 years to observe, reflect, and evaluate UFO experiences. Bearing this all in mind, here is our story.

BRIGHT LIGHTS OVER THE DESERT

Pamela and I headed for Rachel, Nevada on Tuesday, March 16, 1993. After stopping in Las Vegas to pick up Ektar 1000 high-speed film for my camera from the Camera Center on Eastern, we headed north on highway 93, also known as the Great Basin Highway. I estimated our arrival at the Little Ale' Inn at around 6 p.m. We actually arrived at around 5:45 p.m.

While traveling on highway 93 we decided to snap pictures of some of the scenery to use up the slow speed film in my Chinon ZoomCam. Some of the higher mountains around the Parahnagat Valley were capped with white blankets of snow. Yellow flowers were Spring blooming along the roadside. We were in a good mood.

We stopped at Mail Box Road near mile marker 29 on highway 375 to snap additional pictures. The surrounding mountains had already hidden the sun for the day. A little further up the road just before mile marker 26 I noticed a large dirt pull-out. I was determined to return to this pull-out later in the evening.

We arrived at the Little Ale'Inn and greeted Pat and Joe Travis. Pat recognized me instantly, and both of them were happy to see us since our last visit. Copies of my book, ***Cosmic Top Secret***, were stacked on the shelf and offered for sale. I picked up a new book, ***Area 51 Viewing Guide***, written by Glenn Campbell, an itinerant geographer who had settled in Rachel to study the strange stories of this region and map out the area. Later, we were introduced to Glenn, an affable young man. We were eager to swap information, but food was also a priority. We ordered dinner and talked. I also booked a room in a trailer for the night so we could take an early morning trip out to the viewing site and would not have to drive far to get some additional rest.

We placed our suitcases in the trailer and left Rachel sometime after 7:45 that evening and headed east on 375. I decided to travel no faster than 50 mph as this was open range and cows still wandered onto the road in the early evening. When we got to mile marker 17 up on Coyote summit at about 8:13, we spotted a security vehicle, a large green Bronco, parked off the other side of the road facing Rachel. Its amber front lights were on. We continued slowly until we reached mile marker 26. Passing this, I started to look for the dirt pull-out on the right and when I spotted it, pulled off the highway about fifteen to twenty feet with my truck facing the skyglow of Las Vegas due south.

ALIEN MAGIC by William Hamilton

I switched off the lights of my pickup truck and as soon as my eyes adjusted to the darkness that enveloped the Tikaboo Valley, I got out to look at the stars. Though it was partly cloudy, I could clearly make out the Big Dipper, Orion, Sirius, the Pleiades, and Arcturus. I could also see the craggy outlines of the Jumbled Hills and the Groom Mountains against the faint skyglow. It wasn't as cold as I expected and I only wore a pull-over sweater. As soon as I saw the lights of a vehicle appear coming down Coyote Summit, I got back in the truck. The first object I spotted in the sky was an aircraft with its positional lights and strobe blinking as it moved away from Groom Lake toward the southeast. Nothing exciting there. Pamela commented that the vehicle from the west was getting closer and she wanted to see if it was the security vehicle we had seen earlier at mile marker 17. We had first spotted its lights coming down from the summit at about 8:21.

When the vehicle passed us at 8:30, we were certain it was the same one we had seen on the summit. It was now heading east on 375. I was looking at my watch at 8:31 and asked Pamela how long she wanted to stay and skywatch since we wanted to return in the early morning hours to see "Old Faithful." Glenn had told us that he had thought that "Old Faithful" was just a 737 from Las Vegas McCarron airport that ferried in workers to Groom at the same time each morning, but we wanted to come out and see for ourselves if that was the case or whether it was something else.

We talked for about five minutes when we spotted a light about ten or fifteen degrees to the left of our heading. We both had 10X50 Bushnell binoculars. I looked at the light through my binoculars and saw a small round white light above a small round amber light. At this time, I speculated that we might be looking at a security vehicle that was anywhere from 3 to 6 miles from our position, but I could not think of a road that was located where this light was emanating. We talked for additional minutes. Pamela was relating this story about a healer who had come from Sedona, Arizona to find a man named "Jim" in Rachel. Jim was Pat Travis' grandson and he had been in an accident. We talked for another five or six minutes when we spotted another ground light to our right. I looked at it through binoculars and it seemed to be on or near the Groom Road and casting a beam on the ground. We decided that I should keep an eye on the light on the right while Pamela kept an eye on the original light which now appeared to be below our line of sight and was casting a fan-shaped glow into the air. We talked another three to five minutes when Pamela said, "Something is happening. Look back at the first light."

Events started happening fast. The first light appeared to be an object the size of a bus with square light panels lifting off from the ground! The panels appeared to glow amber and blue-white. The object was tilting to the right. Then the lights rapidly resolved into two glowing orbs or discs of brilliant blue-white light that steadily increased in brilliance. These lights became so bright they hurt my eyes and were still getting more brilliant with time. I had to put down my binoculars, but Pamela kept her binoculars trained on these baby suns as they started to move toward us. My heart started to palpitate and my adrenalin was rushing as this lighted object appeared to be on a collision course for my truck. These bright orbs were clearly flying over the desert. The lights did not bounce over the mounds of sand and sagebrush. I reached for my camera behind the seat and felt it snag so I diverted my eyes to free it. Pamela said that at this point the orbs transformed again into a ring of multi-colored lights that moved in a "digital" counter-clockwise revolution around what now appeared to be a disc. When I looked back and raised my camera to snap a picture of this oncoming object, it had again transformed into two or three bright orbs and was closing distance rapidly.

I remember saying that they were coming to get us and Pamela asking why I was so scared. I had to snap a picture fast so I snapped it before exiting the truck. The automatic flash went off with light bouncing against the windows, but I felt that the object's brightness could not fail to register on my Kodak Ektar 1000 film.

Then confusion reigned. As I finished snapping the picture and exiting the truck at the same time as Pamela, I had not removed my eyes from the orbs which now appeared east of us as automobile headlights traveling west on 375. That was clearly impossible! I had not seen these lights move from a south bearing to an east bearing and neither had Pamela. This car made a gentle whooshing sound as it passed by us, but made no motor sounds or tire sounds on the pavement. We watched its tail lights change in intensity as it whisked away toward Coyote Summit. This was no ordinary car. Pamela saw gold-speckled paint and white-walls on an older long American car. I glanced at my watch. It was 9:15. No way! It should have only been about 8:50 at the latest. What happened?

I was angry. I told Pamela that the vehicle we saw could not possibly be driving across the desert to our south, then appear abruptly as if coming from the east. And a ring of lights does not transform itself into a car in normal reality. We discussed this all the way back to the Little Ale'Inn. We went into the bar for a drink, talked with Pat for a few moments, then went to our trailer.

I tried to get to sleep around 11:30 that night. At 1:46 the next morning I awoke with a yelp. I had dreamed that a dark human-like form was examining me and had a hold of my left ankle. Pamela had already awakened asking how long we would be gone. She sometimes talks in her sleep, but this time it also had awakened her. I wanted to go back to the site even though it was a little too early for "Old Faithful." We eventually went back to mile marker 26 arriving by 3:30 the morning of March 17th (St. Patrick's Day). We slept for awhile, then my watch alarm awoke me at 4:30 to start looking at the southern sky for "Old Faithful." At precisely 4:50, we spotted it. It was a glowing amber-gold light without strobes, rotating beacons or other conventional aircraft lighting. It was in view for about five minutes and seemed to descend on Groom Lake. It did not appear to be a 737 or other conventional aircraft, but it did not execute any extraordinary aerodynamic maneuvers.

REGRESSION SESSIONS

After more rest back at the trailer, we left Rachel around 12:30 in the afternoon and returned to Las Vegas to find a room. We checked in at a Super 8 Motel on Koval Lane and after dinner, I called John Lear. He seemed insistent that we come up to see him for awhile so we did. When we got there, we told him our story. He asked if he could regress me under hypnosis as he thought I looked a little stressed-out from the previous night's adventure.

John was only attempting to hypnotize me for thirty-five minutes to help relax me and decided not to tape record the session. The session lasted one hour and thirty-five minutes and Pamela ended up taking twenty-four pages of notes. I recalled the period of disorientation we had in the incident and as it unfolded I saw the craft stop above us, brightly illuminating the ground, the truck, and us in its glare. Then I seemed to have ascended through the bottom of this craft and was met by a being walking out of the bright interior light. Actually, he had just stepped through a brilliantly-lighted interior wall of the craft.

This being was grey in color and about six feet tall. His eyes had what appeared to be black plastic shields slanting in insect fashion around his egg-shaped head. He had on a two-tone gray suit, lighter gray V in the front, and a black belt with a black tube on his right side. There was a triangular symbol (actually giving the impression of a tetrahedron) enclosing a helical coil on the left breast of the suit. His long arms ended in four long fingers. His face was a mask of non-expression, yet he communicated with me in blunt, concise phrases. I was concerned about Pamela, but he showed me her frozen form on the ground. Off to her left side was a small gray creature as if posted on station. I was confused. She was the abductee so why was he taking me inside this craft? He indicated it was my turn and I needed an adjustment and I would learn some things. He took one arm and escorted me gently inside a dome-like room that was evenly and brightly illuminated in all directions. In the center of this room was a tilting metal table which he placed me against. It tilted back about thirty degrees from the vertical. In front of me, projecting out from the curving wall, were what appeared to be a row of small computer screens. I knew that this table was a sophisticated sensor and was registering my thoughts, emotions, and physiology which were displayed on these screens. This being identified himself as Quaylar. Quaylar had replaced my leg at the ankle back onto the tilt table's surface at one point. This process lasted about five minutes. The telepathic or mind-sharing process allowed me access to a great deal of information that wasn't simply communicated. Quaylar returned me to the exit and I jump-floated to the ground about fifteen or twenty feet below. When I re-synched, I saw the phantom car lights. Was this a signal to my sub-conscious that something odd intervened in the missing-time period?

Another idea that impressed me strongly under hypnosis was that the missing-time or missing-memory state was caused by a phase shift in time. The time frequency in the field of this object was not in synch with our normal earth time frequency, giving us a conscious gap in memory.

I did not wait to follow scientific procedures and have Pamela and I hypnotized separately on different occasions though we did do this later. We tried to document all that we could. I took a daytime photo of the pull-out from the same truck angle as the night shot of the object to show the view from our angle of bearing and the desert scrub the object was traveling over.

When I hypnotized Pamela Thursday night, March 18, more details emerged. Pamela remembered being frozen outside of the craft and the little gray standing at her side. She also reports a painful buzzing in her left ear. Up to this point of separation, our description of events agrees completely except for the brief period of time when I went to snatch my camera from

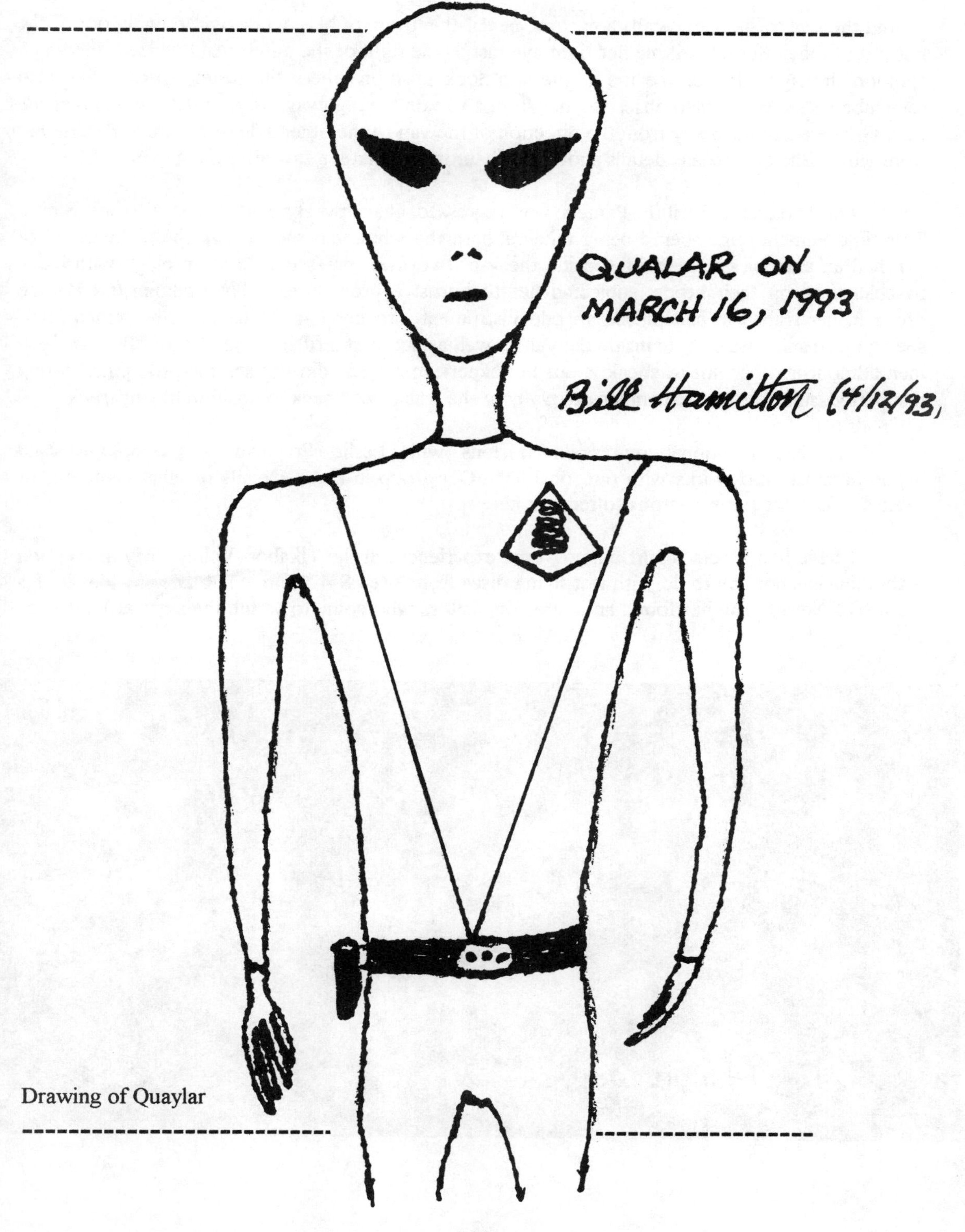

Drawing of Quaylar

behind the seat. She then recalls a narrow, pencil-thin beam of blue-white light coming out of the bottom of the craft and striking her right eye just to the right of the pupil. And, indeed, there is a spot on the right side of the iris at the 9 o'clock position where the beam struck. She also remembers seeing two men observing her from a van on the highway. She actually states that the little Gray walked her away from the direction of the van to the other side of the truck to hide her from view. She also recalls details about the phantom car that we saw after the gap in time.

On Thursday, April 1, Pamela was regressed again by Hypnotherapist Yvonne Smith. This time Pamela remembered being taken aboard the white van she saw on the highway. The van had an antenna on the roof. Inside the van, two men, dressed entirely in black with black baseball caps on their heads, subjected her to intrusive procedures. They administered some drops in her right eye and placed an odd instrument into her left ear canal. She remembered seeing electronic instruments inside the van as well as automatic rifles. She also recalls that these men admonished her not to speak about her experiences. She did not see the little Gray during this period, nor does she remember exactly how she was placed back in position by our truck.

We had additional regression sessions with Leslie Freeman, a psychologist and hypnotherapist who works with our local MUFON group in L.A. Details of what came out of these sessions are too numerous to recount here.

I have had others report missing-time experiences in the Tikaboo Valley. My impression is that this has nothing to do with test flying discs from Area S-4. Something alien resides in this section of Nevada and has found an interest in visitors who come to watch the skies around Area 51.

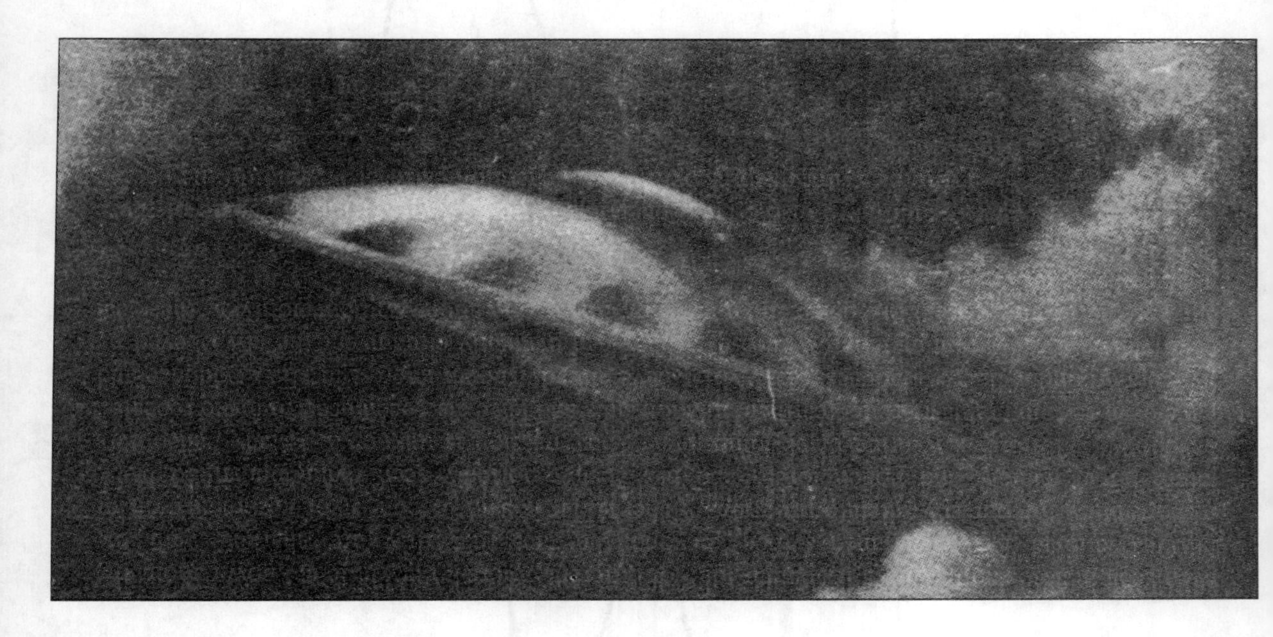

CHAPTER TEN
UNDERWATER MAGIC

What secrets lurk in ocean depths? Are there alien forms of intelligent life that occupy the vast volumes of water that constitute our oceans, seas, and lakes? The largest of our oceans, the Pacific, covers 64,000,000 square miles and reaches a depth of 36,198 feet, a depth that no ray of sunlight ever reaches. Could these depths hide alien submarine bases?

Underwater UFOs have been sighted on many occasions lifting out of their submerged depths and taking to the air. In an article entitled "UFOs - at 450 Fathoms," UFO Reporter Ed Hyde told of the sighting made by Dr. R. J. Villela, a Brazilian scientist, who saw a UFO smash through an estimated 40 feet of ice at the South Pole and soar into the sky at amazing speed.

It was author and researcher Dr. Ivan T. Sanderson who suggested that aliens could remain undetected by building their bases beneath the world's oceans. Dr. Sanderson found that by actual count, over 50 percent of the UFO sightings had occurred over, coming from, or plunging into or coming out of water. This includes oceans, seas, lakes, and reservoirs. Of the oceanic UFOs (some term them USOs or Unidentified Submersible Objects), one was tracked by the U.S. Navy near Puerto Rico in 1963. Of course many of these objects have been tracked over Puerto Rico since that time. On a training manuever, a sonar operator detected a subaqueous object traveling at over 150 knots! The technicians tracked this object for four days and it manuevered down to the incredible depth of 27,000 feet. Submarines of 1963 could not dive further than a fraction over a mile into the ocean deeps. What kind of submersible could withstand the tremendous ocean pressures? And how could it overcome the tremendous resistance of water moving at such incredible speeds?

Many witnesses have reported huge cigar-shaped vehicles emerging from the oceanic hydrospaces of earth to take to the sky. In 1965, such an event was logged in the records of the Norwegian ship T.T. Jawesta on the 6th of July and in the log of an Argentinian ship, the Naviero off the coast of Brazil on July 20, 1967. The officers and crew could see a shining object in the sea no more that 50 feet away from the Starboard side. It was cigar-shaped and about 110 feet in length and emitted a powerfule blue and white glow. It ran silently and without wake through the water. There was no periscope or conning tower or any protruding parts to this mysterious submarine. It paced the Naviero for 15 minutes, then suddenly dived and passed beneath the ship and vanished rapidly into the great depths.

For years witnesses have seen many types of UFOs cruising off the Palos Verdes Peninsula in Southern California. UFOs have actually been seen to come out of the water in the San Pedro Channel. In the early seventies, my friend Jim was on the boat returning from Santa

Catalina Island to San Pedro Harbor when he spotted a low, flying disk cruise silently over the channel boat. The craft was so close he could make out every detail of its structure including the four hemispherical pods on its underside.

Strange blue-green lights have been seen in the water since 1989. In 1989, and again in 1990, witnesses have seen as many as 20 events an hour. One large light appeared to be as much as 100 feet in diameter. This large light spawned babies no larger than 10 to 12 feet in length. These lights were seen to move swiftly under the ocean's surface some 500 to 1,000 feet from the coastline in Abalone Cove. The hypothesis that these may be luminescent fish is discounted by a local marine biologist. These lights were too large and too swift to be fish. One of the lights was reported to have emerged from the water.

In 1992 a sea kayaker viewed an amazing sight off the Palos Verdes Peninsula. He was four or five miles off the Peninsula when a waterspout suddenly formed some hundreds of yards ahead of his kayak. As he observed this spout, the forward motion of the funnel stopped, the curtain of light mist surrounding the waterspout disappeared and a rotating column of what seemed to be solid ice appeared. As the sun reflected off the rotating mass of ice crystals, it appeared to be a sight of extraordinary beauty. The height of the ice column was estimated at 100 to 150 feet. When the ice column collapsed back into the ocean, it created a whirlpool. After this amazing event, the kayaker paddled over to examine floating fragments of ice and found specimens of fish embedded in the frozen pieces.

The site of these phenomenal occurences is near the old Marineland Park which closed in 1987. Snoopers believe that the Park is now a Naval Experimental Marine Biology Lab. Access to the Park is now restricted and many "no trespassing" signs are posted around fenced areas.

Planes and boats have disappeared or had mysterious accidents in this area. On Thanksgiving of 1990, Robert Reid and his wife took their 34-foot cabin cruiser, the Lucky-R on a holiday jaunt to Catalina. The wreckage of their boat was found about 10 miles off Catalina on November 23rd. According to a newspaper article, Robert and his wife were found dead of drowning despite the fact that the hull of the vessel was destroyed by a mysterious explosion. The Navy put forth the explanation that the explosion was caused by a fuel leak in the gas line but the family of the couple has raised doubts about this explanation.

Another mysterious drowning took place in April, 1993. Seven men disappeared off the coast of Santa Cruz Island after their fishing trawler sank. Although rescue crews searched over 1,400 square miles surrounding the Channel Islands, they still found no trace of the missing men.

In the exact area where the strange blue lights are seen, two helicopter pilots escaped injury after their new copter lost power forcing them to land in ocean waters off Rancho Palos Verdes. The copter was up about 700 feet when it suffered drive system failure and lost power, sending it into auto-rotation. The cause of the power failure was unknown. Is it possible that this copter encountered an UFO force field or energy source that interrupted its drive system similar to the electromagnetic effect produced on automotive engines? If there was a UFO in the water during the daylight hours (the accident occurred at 1:15 PM in July, 1990 off Seacove Drive in Abalone Cove), then the pilots might not have seen it.

The most mysterious set of circumstances occured in the Sea Cove starting in February 1994. Coast Guard and Navy ships have been seen cruising the Channel where the strange lights had been seen. Black helicopters have also been spotted circling the old Marineland Tower. Then the lights returned on the morning of February 28th at 1:30.

A company security guard was making the rounds near Vanderlip Park. This park is a small grassy area off Sea Cove Drive that is fenced off from the steeply-dropping sea wall below. Its always pleasent to take an evening stroll over to the fence and view the sweeping grandeur of the world's largest ocean. One doesn't expect to see more than the breakers or hear the sound of the surf and night birds which call out from the cliff wall. This morning, the guard Mike J., saw five blue-green glowing objects moving through the water just west of Abalone Cove and east of the Marineland tower. One of the five appeared to be a fat disk surmounted with a dome of a size he estimated to be 30 to 40 feet in diameter. The other four objects appeared to be orbs around 6 to 10 feet in diameter. At this point Mike decided to try to signal these objects with his flashlight and, as he did so, the objects responded with an equal number of pulses. Then, the big disk emitted a beam of light that illuminated the seawall cliff below him. Mike then went back to his car parked on Sea Cove Drive and connected a mega-candle-powered light on a long cord and turned it on and toward the objects. In response, the disk rose out of the water, and the whole entourage flew off toward Catalina Island. The orbs, still in the water, left a wake in their trail. Earlier, Mike said, he had observed a black helicopter cruising the channel area with its running lights off.

Mike was back on his midnight to dawn patrol again on March 2nd when, around 2:30 that morning, he saw the five objects back in the water , one fat disk and four orbs. One of the orbs came out of the water. One was observed to come down from the sky over the Marineland tower leaving a white trail in its wake. The sightings lasted until 3:15 that morning.

On March 23rd, Mike saw a boat in the water that had USAF and a star marked on the side. He thought it was peculiar to see a boat with Air Force markings. Another boat belonging to the Coast Guard seemed to ignore the USAF boat. The USAF boat threw a spotlight on Mike. He also observed a small plane going back and forth over the area. What could they be looking for?

On April 13th, a bizzare series of events were observed by Mike. This is when the MIBs arrived at about 3:30 in the wee hours of the morning. Mike saw three strange cars pull up at the east end of Sea Cove Drive and went to a phone booth to call TAL, a veteran UFO researcher who works as a security guard on night shift. TAL advised Mike to take a close look at the cars and call him back. Mike told him that two of the cars were solid black and one was a solid white. One driver was seen stepping out of each car. All three men were dressed in solid black. They had flashlights and walkie-talkies. They headed off toward the trail to the beach in the cove. When Mike sees the drivers head off, he approaches the cars for a closer look. None of the cars have license plates, front or back. Inside each car, Mike sees a computer with the words "DIAL

TONE" glowing on the computer screens with a flashing cursor. Mounted in the doors of each car were two sawed-off shotguns. The security alarm in each car was beeping indicating that they were armed. Mike then went to the fenceline overlooking Abalone Cove. Leaning over the fence, Mike could see two of the men carrying flashlights walking along the beach toward something that carried a pulsing red light. The third MIB was at some position in the west holding a pulsing blue light in his hand. Mike started to climb over the fence to go down the trail to get a better look when two black helicopters came around, one from the east and one from the west. Already frightened out of his wits, he retreated away from the fence and watched the helos land on the Marineland landing pad. He then made another phone call for advice. TAL was burning with curiousity at this point and told Mike that he should go down to the beach and confront these MIBs. Mike was on security patrol for the area and should find out what these men were doing in the area. TAL told Mike to call him back as soon as he had anything new to report. The third call never came that morning. As soon as TAL's shift was over, he headed over to Sea Cove Drive, but all had vanished in the dawn mist and Mike was nowhere to be found.

I talked with TAL over the phone the next day and asked him to find out more details concerning Mike's sighting. He would attempt to reach Mike at home. He told me that Mike was an ex-Green Beret and should not have had trouble handling himself if he had gotten in trouble.

The next day TAL called me to tell me the rest of the story. Mike had gone back to the fence line and ran smack into one of the MIBs who asked him where he thought he was going. The MIB spoke in a very commanding voice and told Mike, "You had better leave this area now." However, Mike did not leave immediately and took another peek at the events going on below on the beach. He could hear the clamor of seals on the rocks. Then he saw a group of men who seemed to have come out of nowhere approach the seals trying to snag some soft, pliable object away from the mouth of one of the seals. He could not identify what this object was. Mike then returned to his car and waited until the MIBs returned to their cars and watched them depart around 5 AM. He went on to say that these men were wearing black coveralls (no turtle necks), and no insignia or name tags. The red light he had seen on the beach was attached to a small boat. There is an old underground Nike missle site in the hills behind Marineland that is now active for other purposes and he had wondered if the parade of men on the beach had come from that installation. An antenna has been seen to emerge from the concrete structure behind the fence and point at the sky. It is unknown whether this underground activity in the area, or the new uses of the Marineland facility is directly connected in some way with the frequent sightings of these underwater lights.

The friendly underwater disks returned again on July 19th at about 1 AM, but by this time Mike had been fired and TAL was walking the rounds. TAL saw 4 objects in the water that appeared to be "puffy disks" (oblate spheroids?) about 10 feet in diameter. They glowed with a blue-green light and pulsed intensely every 10 or 15 seconds, each with a different period. When first seen, one was on the left and three were on the right. The three on the right had assumed a perfect triangular formation as seen from the Bay Club. They moved slowly, then formed a straight line. After that, they moved randomly and were gone after an hour.

I have been to the park site, but have not seen the lights. The night I was there, I could hear the sound of seals on the rocky beach below. The Marineland Tower is an imposing sight. The visiblity from the cliff was excellent and clear for miles. I could only wonder about the meaning of all the events that had transpired below me beyond the pounding surf.

Three-quarters of the surface of this planet lies underwater and this constitutes a volume of some 280 million cubic miles. That is a lot of volume to hide in. Our futurists have conceived of building habitats underwater on the sea shelfs off our coasts. Perhaps the Navy is already operating a number of these habitats for its own operations. Further, entire resort cities have been planned in order to further our occupation of the planet. Certainly, we could extend our food-growing fields into vast underwater farming lands and mine the immense reserve of minerals to be found in the ocean and under the ocean.

It seems entirely possible that any space-traveling race would immediately recognize the potential for exploration and occupation that our hydrosphere offers. Perhaps alien lifeforms have taken up residence, not only in underground bases, but also in underwater cities and bases of operation. I found an intriguing article by Paul Stonehill on Soviet Underwater Mysteries in which he mentions underwater encounters in a deep water lake where frogmen had seen very large (about nine feet in height) swimmers that were clad in silvery suits. He also goes on to mention a bulletin that has references to giant luminescent disks and spheres seen descending and emerging from deep water lakes. Disks have been seen coming out of Pyramid Lake in Nevada and Clear Lake in California. Indeed, the population of our planet may be much greater than recorded in our census.

The second great mystery here is the Men-In-Black. In the early days of MIB reports, these mysterious and threatening individuals had a menacing and alien appearance and behavior. The modern MIB is human and is a member of some covert operations force. They have been linked to black military ops, NSA, NRO, and more recently the MJTF (Multi-Jurisdictional Task Force). It is even likely that they may be a combination of these or other. Sometimes they have been seen in association with a triangular logo of different colors. Very little is known about the NRO (National Reconnaissance Office) beyond the fact that they are charged with the responsibility for our spy satellite programs. The MJTF is said to consist of a combination of international military and police forces and has been reportedly seen flying unmarked black helicopters with crews wearing black jumpsuits. Their mission is unknown. Black helicopters have been seen in the past around cattle mutilation sites and have also been used to make repeated flyovers around abductee's houses. The MIBs have already shown interest in UFO evidence and have played a role in intimidating witnesses. They can evidently circumvent the law obeyed by citizens (no license plates) or appear in an area for covert operations without notifying the local police authorities.

As we see more and more of the UFO phenomena, the mystery deepens Some of these UFOs have emerged from the watery depths below us. Where on earth or beyond do they come from and what are they doing?

ALIEN MAGIC by William Hamilton

A late breaking story from the Palos Verdes Peninsula News of August 27, 1994 says that helicopters are buzzing the skies over the Palos Verdes Estates area. Sharon Burke says that her family home has been inundated with increasing helicopter traffic and has had this complaint added to the City Council's agenda. Her sister had a near miss with a hovering helicopter. Burke's parents have logged the fly-overs and say that an average of eight helos per hour fly over their residence. This is an interesting figure considering that the Coast Guard only admits flying two or three per day in the area. These helos have been spotted flying below 500 feet. Who owns and operates all these helicopters? The police chief has explained that in the past, it has been virtually impossible to obtain the number off the side of the helicopters in order to report them to the FAA. Are any of these helicopter crews looking for strange underwater lights?

CHAPTER ELEVEN
SECRETS OF THE SAUCER SCIENTISTS

In all probability the first saucer scientists were rocket scientists. Without a doubt one of these great men was the pioneering rocket scientist, Professor Hermann Oberth.

Oberth was a writer, scientist, and visionary from Rumania whose paper, *The Rocket Into Interplanetary Space*, was published in 1923 and served as an inspiration to the rocket designers that followed. Werner von Braun read Oberth's work in 1925 and joined him in rocket experiments in 1930.

In letters to Donald Keyhoe (1), Oberth mentions his belief that saucers are spaceships manned by superior beings. He says that the marvelous aerodynamics of the saucers is accomplished by generating an artificial gravity field. This is the famous G-field theory. The saucers create their own gravitational fields which enables them to hover motionless above the earth, accelerate at tremendous speeds, or execute violent turns that would cause ordinary aircraft to disintegrate. Even with swift changes of speed and direction, the passengers would feel no effect. It would also explain the silence of UFOs in flight as the artificial G-field would drag the surrounding air along with it. And, because the air is not flowing pass the hull, it would eliminate heating caused by friction.

Statements have been made that saucer behavior defies the laws of physics. It seemed impossible that a manned craft could execute such tremendous accelerations from a hovering position to a high-speed linear velocity or in high-speed acute-angled turns. Inertial forces caused by such accelerations would tear apart an aircraft frame. And, often, the picture came to mind of a human pilot ending up flat as a pancake against the cabin wall. Gerald Heard, in his book *Is Another World Watching*?, hypothesized that the saucers were being flown by insects because only insects could survive those wrenching turns. All of these concerns evaporate when one considers the physics of G-field propulsion.

In a revealing document published in Status Report VII by the late pioneering researcher Leonard Stringfield, a preliminary report refers to a recovered flying disc. The report does not specifically mention Roswell, but states that the data in the report was provided by the engineering staff of T-2 at the Air Material Command at Wright Field. One of the scientist examining the evidence is Dr. Theodore von Karmen, founder of Aerojet, and then head of the Army Air Forces Scientific Advisory Group. Dr. von Karmen was a leading authority on aerodynamics and had authored papers, both in English and German on the subject. Another renowned scientist mentioned in the report is Dr. Robert Oppenheimer, Director of the Manhattan Project and a leading physicist of his day.

In the opinion of these two famous scientists the interior of the craft contained a compartment with an atomic engine. The device was a donut-shaped tube approximately thirty-five feet in diameter, made of what appeared to be plastic material around a central core. A large rod centered inside the tube was wrapped in a coil and the investigators believed it to be the source of electrical potential which ionized the surrounding air around the craft.(2)

There will be questions and doubts about this document, but the recurring theme behind the exotic propulsion found in these craft is found again and again. The relation between high electrical potentials and gravity was the object of scientific research and classified studies conducted by aircraft companies in the fifties. In fact, the coming age of anti-gravity was mentioned in popular magazines of the fifties, and yet little is known about what developed from this research.

An experimenter by the name of George S. Piggot conducted some amazing experiments in 1904. He made use of an apparatus that had a rotating spherical electrode mounted on a stand. He was able to suspend, against gravity, small metal balls by means of a strong electric field. Extending for about .5 cm. around the perimeter of the objects there was a mysterious dark band. Such dark bands and dark spots have been observed on UFOs. He also succeeded in suspending nonmetallic objects such as cork and wood. These objects would oscillate up and down around the center of the field. An improved Wimshurst generator supplied the spherical electrode with approximately 500, 000 volts of potential.

Dr. Francis Nipher, once professor of physics at Washington University, St. Louis performed a modification of the Cavendish experiment in 1916. Nipher used a one-inch lead ball suspended with an untwisted silk thread approximately 180 cm. long and centered inside a 5-inch-square box or Faraday Shield. He placed an insulated 10-inch-diameter lead sphere next to the iron box. A copper wire connected the large sphere to the metal box to keep them at the same potential. When the large sphere was electrified using a high-voltage influence generator, the normal attraction of gravity between the two spheres was reversed and the small suspended sphere was repelled from the larger by about twice the deflection caused by gravity. Reversing the polarity did not alter the effect. Nipher thought that the gravitation force was reduced by the electrical potential applied to a mass.

In a letter to researcher William Steinman, Dr. Robert I. Sarbacher who was with the Washington Institute of Technology, confirms that some of the scientists involved in the study of recovered flying discs were Dr. Vannever Bush, John von Neumann, and Dr. Robert Oppenheimer. (3) Steinman also discovered that one of the scientists working on saucer technology from the early days was Dr. Eric Henry Wang who became Director of the Department of Special Studies, within the Structures Division, of the old Wright Air Development Center, near Dayton, Ohio.

Another significant scientist and UFO researcher from the early era was T. Townsend Brown who conducted experiments with suspended charged capacitors which exhibited anti-gravity effects. When the capacitor was charged, it exhibited a forward thrust towards the

---

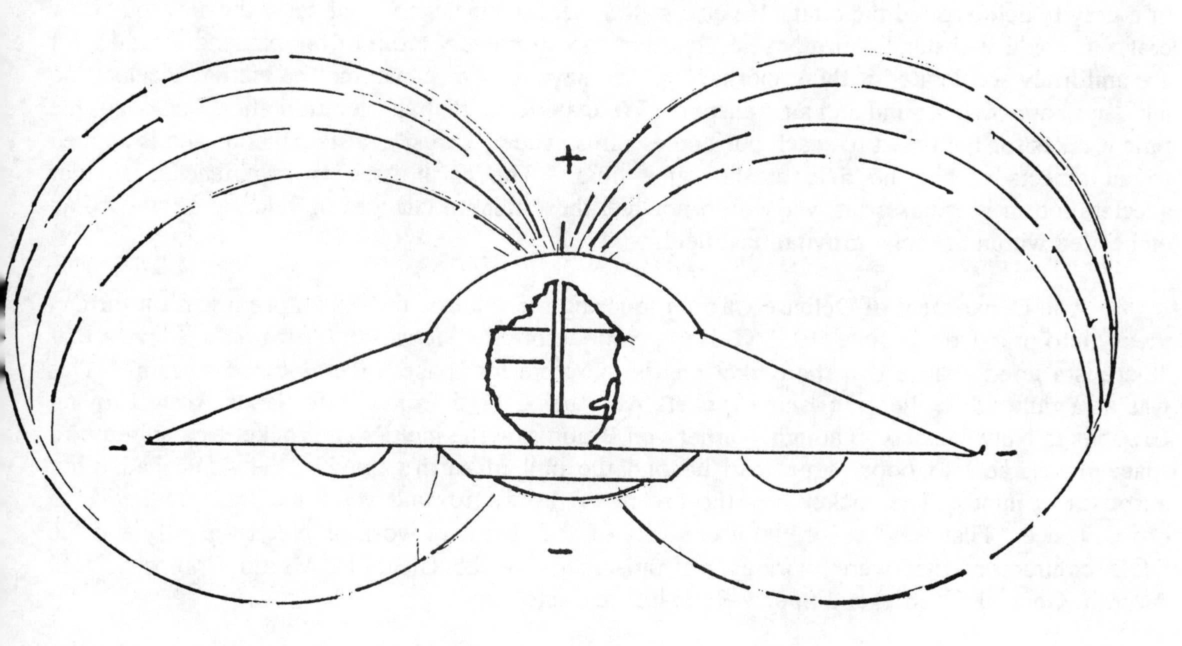

Drawing showing the magnetic field around saucer

---

positive pole. When the capacitor was mounted vertically on a beam balance, the positive-pole vectored thrust lifted the capacitor. This did not involve the expulsion of charged particles to produce thrust as in an ion rocket. Brown felt he discovered the principle of electro-gravitation.

Agnew H. Banson Jr. was another inventor who studied saucers and experimented with electro-gravitation. He patented an electrical thrust-producing device in 1966.

Lieutenant Plantier of the French Air Force was another scientist who theorized about saucer technology in the early era. Like Oberth, he attributed saucer dynamics to the generation of a gravity field around the craft. He also stated that the machine would carry the air around the craft. It could withstand enormous accelerations because every atom of the passengers and craft are uniformly accelerated without inertial lag. We have grown accustomed to inertial acceleration and lag in our own ground and air transport. We experience that acceleration after a time lag, the time it takes for the thrust to reach our bodies. In a saucer, thrust is instantaneous and is applied to all objects within the field at the same time. The earth itself is experiencing angular acceleration in its solar orbit, yet we do not feel these minute changes in velocity as we are all embedded within the solar gravitational field.

The Department of Defense was not ignoring these ideas, but was more intent on turning theory into practice. In June, 1957 G. Harry Stine wrote for *Mechanix Illustrated* magazine that "there is a good chance that the rocket will be obsolete for space travel within 50 years". This was at a time when the multi-stage rockets were being fired from White Sands Army Proving Grounds in New Mexico. Though Werner von Braun saw the multi-stage rocket as a solution to space travel, able to boost a payload beyond the pull of earth's gravity, the DOD had other purposes in mind. The rocket was the dream of the future, and yet Stine was predicting its obsolescence. That was because he was aware of T.T. Brown's work on electro-gravity and the DOD contractors that were working on anti-gravity -- the Glenn L. Martin Company, Bell Aircraft, General Electric, and Sperry-Rand just to name a few.

In July, 1957 another article appeared in the same magazine. This one written by Michael Gladych. He begins by describing the following: "The spherical craft squatting on a concrete strip emitted a faint hum. A ghostly glow surrounded its shell. The strange craft rose and hovered momentarily while its landing gear retracted. Then the hum increased and the craft shot eastward and vanished beyond the horizon before the witnessing scientists could click their stop watches." Sounds like a typical UFO sighting, but he goes on to say that the Canadian government's Project Magnet had been working on a gravity-defying vehicle powered by electromagnetic forces. He also states that at least 14 United States universities and other research centers were hard at work cracking the gravity barrier and also mentions the Glen L. Martin Company and Bell Aircraft as well as others. Even the late Lawrence D. Bell said that they were on the threshold of amazing new concepts (beyond the Bell research rocket planes) . Bell said, "We are already working with nuclear fuels and equipment to cancel out gravity instead of fighting it." This article concludes by saying, "Make no mistake about it, anti-gravity motors and G-ships are coming."

And, we are still waiting! Or, have we developed anti-gravity spacecraft in secret?

April 13, 1965 V. GRADECAK **3,177,654**

ELECTRIC AEROSPACE PROPULSION SYSTEM

Filed Sept. 26, 1961 3 Sheets–Sheet 3

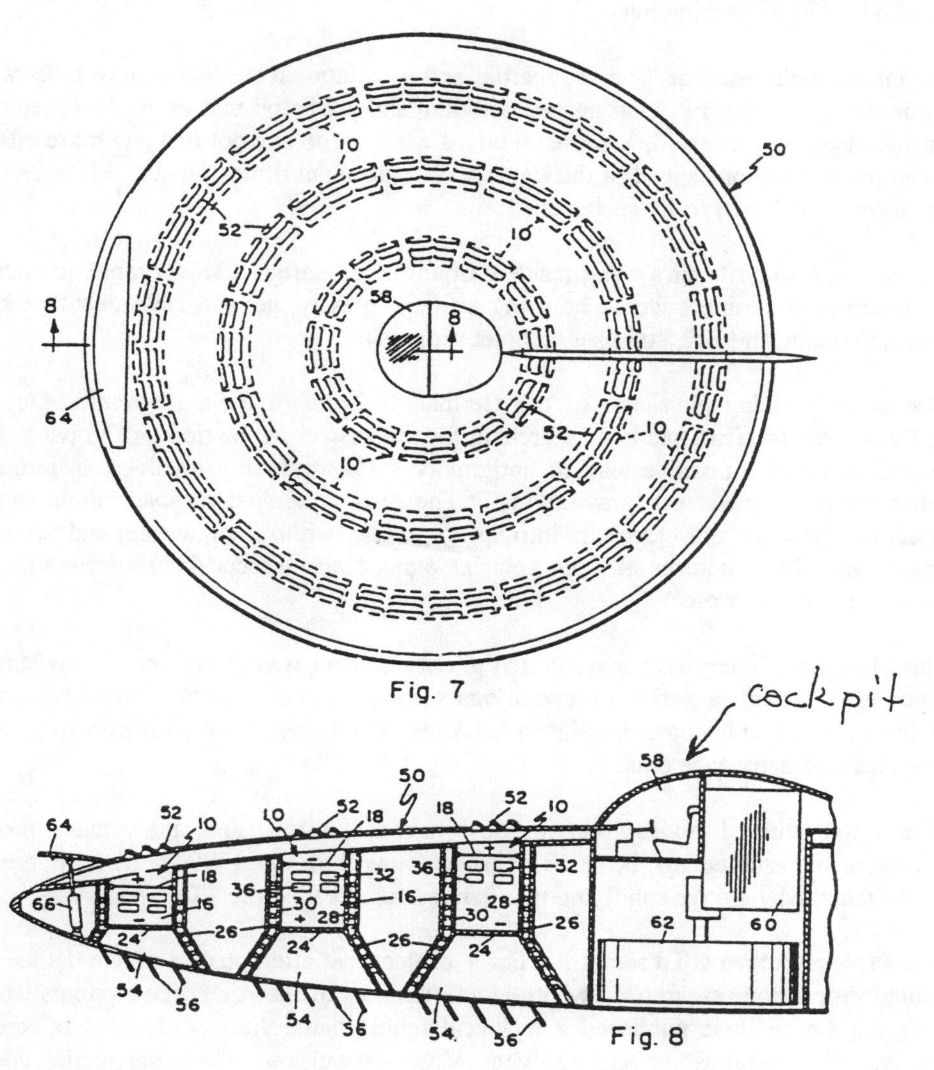

INVENTOR
VJEKOSLAV GRADECAK
BY *Knox & Knox*

Patent drawing of Electric Aerospace Propulsion system

Donald Keyhoe looked into this possibility and found that our government had set up 46 different research projects on various aspects of gravity control. The Air Force ran 33 of those projects. Experiments and research were conducted at two Air Force laboratories: Flight Dynamics and General Physics Research. Other labs involved were RCA, MIT and several engineering centers. A large number of corporations were involved in gravity research of the fifties: Bell Aerospace, General Electric, Hughes Aircraft, Boeing, Douglas and others. There were at least 65 to 70 projects going on.

Dr. Oberth believed that "energy, inertia, and gravitational fields are only aspects of one and the same thing". William P. Lear agreed with him and predicted that future U.S. vehicles will also use artificial gravity. He said, "people on board would probably not feel any more effect than they do from the tremendous speed of the Earth as it rotates and orbits the sun." It is certain that Lear's son, John, is prepared to fly such a craft.

Years ago, Glenn Martin's vice-president of advanced design, G.S. Trimble, predicted that by 1985 practically all airliners would be using artificial gravity, yet the 1995 debut of Boeing's most advanced jetliner, the 777, still uses turbojet propulsion.

One of the leading physicists of the German Institute of Field Physics at Goettingen, Germany, Dr. Burkhard Heim had been searching for the answer to the riddle of gravity. He said that he had discovered a positive lead to antigravity. The discovery involved an intermediate field, neither electromagnetic nor gravitational. The results, applied to space flight, would be direct levitation, conversion of electricity into kinetic energy without any waste, and "immunizing the occupants and the structures of such vehicles against any effects from acceleration of the vehicle, however great or violent."

The Martin subsidiary that investigated gravity control was RIAS Inc. Now, the Glenn Martin Company through a series of evolutionary mergers has absorbed GE Aerospace and merged with Lockheed to become the Martin-Lockheed Company, a company known to be in the forefront of classifed aerospace craft.

In a book entitled *Spacepower* (1958), fusion, photon, and anti-gravity propulsion techniques were considered to be accomplished facts beyond 1990. If they are secret accomplished facts, why are we still flying that flaming torch called the STS?

Was Project Outgrowth a secret Air Force project that attempted to utilize the knowledge gained in field propulsion research? Twenty-eight members of the Air Force Systems Command at Edward's Air Force Base published a technical report dated June, 1972 that covered such categories as: electrostatics effects, Alfven wave propulsion, electromagnetic spacecraft propulsion, superconducting particle accelerators, and anti-gravity propulsion. The Air Force Systems Command also has a presence at Groom Lake in Area 51. I asked a colleague, Randy Koppang, to see if he could get a hold of this document. He contacted the Edwards AFB library. The librarian informed Randy that the report was removed from the library and was not available to the public.

ALIEN MAGIC by William Hamilton

According to Bill Jenkins who hosted the Open Mind talk-radio show a few years ago, there was a secret showing of our own antigravity aircraft at Norton AFB on November 12, 1988. Norton was also home to the Air Force's Audio-Visual Division for the investigation of crashed aircraft (or UFOs). A flying saucer was put on display in a guarded hangar. The electro-gravity engine in the craft was built by GE Aerospace and the composite skin structure supposedly made by AMOCO. Was this craft a result of back-engineering of alien spacecraft?

By now most Ufologists have heard the story told by the controversial Bob Lazar concerning his work at S4 on the Sports Model. He described a high voltage glow around the craft and the use of gravity waves to propel it. It almost sounds like a reprise of the *Mechanix Illustrated* article from 1957. Skeptical scientists do not think Lazar is a physicists as he professes, but stop short of saying that he has fabricated his detailed story of S4. In actual fact, others have talked about the S4 site in hushed tones.

I have now talked with two other saucer scientists who have worked on alien technology and have confirmed the S4 site and the Sports Model. Some will say that they are fabricating based on previous revelations and that all of it is nonsense. There are still researchers who believe that witnesses have only seen advanced technology aircraft, remote-controlled vehicles, lifting bodies, hoaxes by engineers having fun, and other such paraphanelia at the borders of Dreamland in the Nevada desert. Yet, witnesses describe classic UFO phenomena with all the fantastic aerobatics attributed to them.

A friend of mine met Charlie in a photocopy shop in the summer of 94. Charlie was contacting *OMNI* magazine about their article on the UFO coverup. I met Charlie later after writing a letter to him that he never received. Instead, I received a reply from a veteran's organization that warned me not to contact Charlie anymore. According to the letter of reply the subject of UFOs was classified permanently. It also stated that UFOs and aliens should be the responsibility of the military and that civilians had no business delving into military secrets. Nevertheless, Charlie contacted me later through our local MUFON group.

Charlie had been in the Marines and aboard the U.S.S. Oriskany aircraft carrier in 1958 during the early Vietnam era. His father was a commander in the navy and was stationed with the Pentagon's Research and Development Board. His father had been with President Eisenhower at Edwards AFB in 1954 when an extraterrestrial spacecraft had landed. The base had already been renamed Edwards at the time of the occurrence and was no longer known as Muroc (Corum spelled backwards after one of the early families who settled in the Mojave Desert). Charlie said the aliens at Edwards were human types with flaxen hair and pale blue eyes. Charlie's first experience occurred when he was assigned to a special operations team that retrieved a crashed disk in Vietnam and stowed aboard the aircraft carrier.

According to Charlie, this disk was 10 meters in diameter and lighter than a Volkswagon. It had a crew of two aliens. The recovery team transported the disc back to the Oriskany where it was stored on the flight deck between mattresses that were used to cushion the craft on deck. A tarpaulin was thrown over the disc and when the Oriskany put into port in San Francisco, the cover story told by the Captain was that a special water tank was being brought in for maintenance and the tarpaulin was used to protect it from storms at sea. Charlie referred to this disc as the IRC-10. IRC is an abbreviation for Instellar Reconnaissance Craft. Charlie refers to the Sports Model as an IRC-16 because it is 16 meters in diameter. It is not known whether these metrics are exact.

Charlie explains that not all UFOs or discs are from another planet. Some are from a parallel world. These parallel worlds exist in another time dimension. It's as if our universe runs on the beat on one clock and another on the beat of another clock. Normally, the two are out of phase and there is no interaction between universes, but, occasionally, there are locations where the two universes synchro-phase and a portal opens up between the two allowing passage from one to another. Many discs originate from another dimension and use a transpatial field resonator to bridge the gap between their universe and ours.

The aliens project their thoughts into a thought amplifier plate that carries signals to the avionics controls via optical fibers. Another saucer scientist, Bill Uhouse of Las Vegas, says that he designed flight simulators for our pilots because our pilots had difficulty controlling the aliens' avionics. Bill worked at Los Alamos in conjunction with an alien scientist on designing a simulator using our own avionics technology. Bill said that General Electric built the antigravity engines for U.S. discs and Westinghouse provided the nuclear reactors to power the engines. I asked him if he knew any reason why U.S. discs could not fly in space and he replied that he thought they could. Bill was a Mechanical Design Engineer when he was recruited for this highly secure position. Today, he is retired and talking about his work openly with the permission of his security guardians. Perhaps they would like some of the story told.

In 1993 I met an electronics engineer by the name of Vince. Vince and his wife were having alien encounters. Vince felt like he was receiving technical information from the aliens. I gave him some material to read on the Brown effect. Soon he started to build a rig to test the concept of electrogravity. I assisted him as much as I could. Our idea was to provide external power to light-weight aluminum models. Vince designed a high-voltage power supply that he described as a variable-parameter that consisted of a current pulse-modulated by bi-polar transistors and variable-switched capacitor banks for tuning. This pulse-modulated 12-volt current is fed into an auto ignition coil to raise it to a high voltage. Leads connected the power supply to a dielectric aluminum levitator for testing the effects of varying the voltage and frequency parameters. An oscilloscope was connected to the rig. Vince claimed that he turned on the unit one night in his garage and the levitator jumped off the workbench and wobbled in the air at which point he reached out to grab it, burning his hand, and shorting out the coil. He planned to rebuild it when the Northridge quake came along and destroyed most of his equipment. He never returned to this project, but we obtained some interesting insights from these experiments and may continue them at some future date.

An English inventor named John R. Searl built levity discs as early as 1951. The Searl Effect Generator consists of a number of magnetic rollers in the form of cylinders that rotate around a magnetic annulus. These rollers generate extremely high voltages which decouples the whole assembly from gravitational and inertial forces. Each roller is a composite of 4 components: titanium; iron; nylon; and neodymium. He also uses aluminum, silicon, and sulphur in the magnetic rings and rollers. Searl is now in the United States working with a man named John A. Thomas in New York to rebuild the levity discs.

Contactee Howard Menger claims to have built a craft with an electro-dynamic propulsion system in 1951 called the HMX1 by experimenting with information given to him by space visitors. Today, in Florida, he is constructing small models with specially designed coils and capacitors that demonstrate electrogravitic effects.

Even some Aerospace engineers have presented papers on anti-gravitic propulsion devices and some have gone so far as to patent some of their ideas. F. E. Alzofon presented a paper on anti-gravity with present technology to a Joint Propulsion Conference in Colorado Springs in 1981. The abstract from his paper says that he proposes a method for decreasing (or increasing) the gravitational force on a vehicle, using presently-known technology and various ways of utilizing this effect for vehicle propulsion.

An earlier report on Electrohydrodynamics was given on June 30, 1967 which describes the use of electrostatic fields creating hydrostatic pressure in a dielectric medium. This form of electrohydrodynamics proposes an aero-marine vehicle that generates toroidal vortices for lift.

For those who wish to become diehard experimentalists I recommend the *Electric Spacecraft Journal* published from 73 Sunlight Drive, Leicester, N.C. 28748 by Charles Yost. The publishers of this journal have access and publish all the known data on electrogravitics. Members performing relevant experiments publish articles in the journal. Not all the work in this important field of research is being conducted in government labs.

We must re-examine the physical properties of space itself if we are to understand the relation between electromagnetic and gravitational forces. We must also re-examine our concept of time. It is possible that time is more than one-dimensional. This also will be cause for us to contemplate wondrous possibilities. Can different moments of time be revisited?

The announcement that two physicists, Ed Witten, and Nathan Seiberg have simplified the study of the fourth dimension deserves plaudits and admiration. However, there is little recognition for scientific viewpoints that differ from the reigning paradigm.

It is generally acknowledged that space seems to curve into an unseen fourth dimension according to Einstein's General Theory. This curvature is a kind of macro curvature impressed on space by physical bodies. Thus, it is argued that the gravity force we sense is actually our tendency to follow a curved path in space-time. However, geometry does not explain how how acceleration and gravity causes bodies to accelerate. Perhaps curvature could explain the path an object traces through space, but how does it explain increasing acceleration as when rocks fall on earth?

There are alternative theories of gravity and perhaps one day a more rational theory of gravity will be considered which may explain the so-called missing matter in the universe as well as why high-voltage potentials reduce gravity.

And what of the aliens? We have only discussed the physical technology of UFOs up to this point. What of the alien biology and anthropology? Charlie says that some of the Grays are synthetic lifeforms and undergo transdermal osmotic dyalsis on a regular schedule. In other words, they undergo a process whereby the excrete effluents and absorb nutrients through their skin in a pressure chamber. If these Grays are synthetics, then what beings synthesized them?

The existence of alien discs in our possession or the revelation that we are constructing similar craft is going to raise a lot of eyebrows. Today, we are not only constructing secret aircraft, but secret spacecraft, or even secret timecraft. Our technology may actually be leapfrogging us into the undiscovered country, the future. That future may already exist in some variation on some distant worlds in space.

References: (1) *The Flying Saucer Conspiracy* (1955) by Donald E. Keyhoe
(2) *UFO Crash/Retrievals: Search for Proof in a Hall of Mirrors Status Report VII* (1994) by Leonard H. Stringfield
(3) *UFO Crash at Aztec* (1986) by William S. Steinman and Wendelle C. Stevens

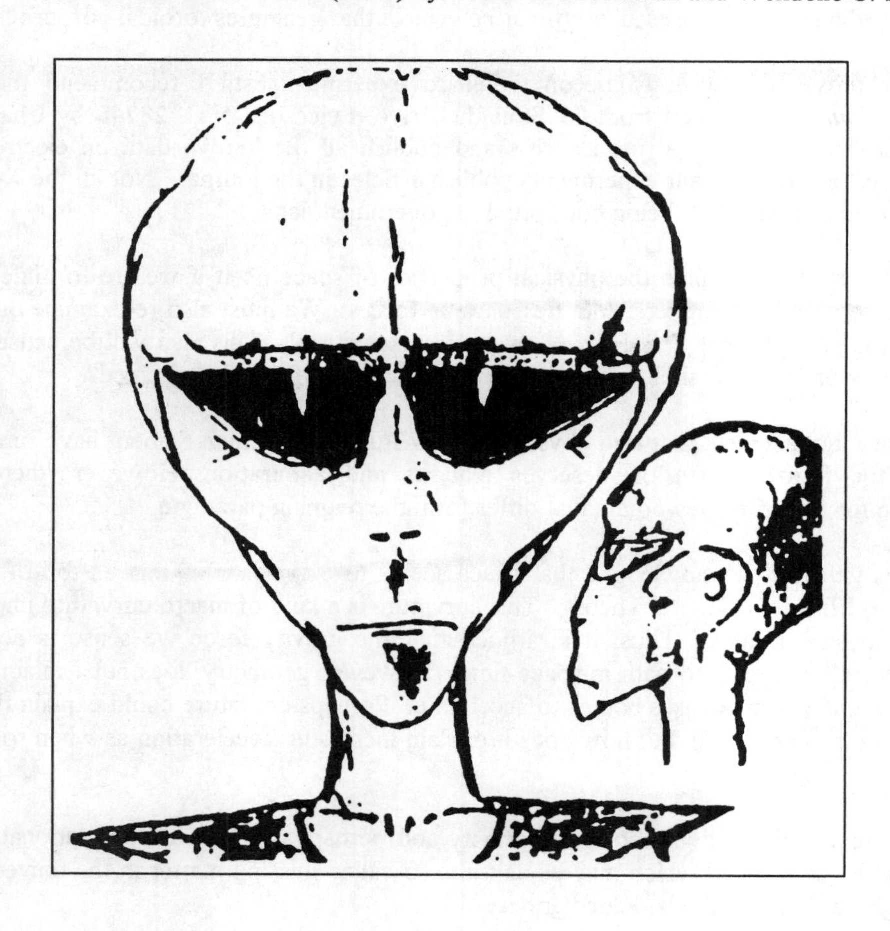

CHAPTER TWELVE
MYSTERIOUS UNIVERSE

"It would of course be a great step forward if we succeeded in combining the gravitational field and the electro-magnetic field into a single structure."

- Albert Einstein

Einstein's dream was to build a Unified Field Theory, a theory that could unify the forces of nature into one comprehensive whole. Einstein stunned the world of physics in 1905 when he wrote his paper "On the Electrodynamics of Moving Bodies." At the time he held the post of a Swiss Patent Examiner. There were no references to previous papers in this seminal work on physics. The foundation he gave birth to became known as the Special Theory of Relativity. In this paper he postulated the Principle of Relativity and established the constancy of the velocity of light in a vacuum and further stated that the concept of a luminiferous ether would prove to be superfluous inasmuch as the view he developed did not require the absoluteness of a stationary space with special properties, nor assign a velocity-vector to a point of the *empty space* in which the electromagnetic processes took place.

In 1916, Einstein further expanded on his theory of relativity with the introduction of the equivalency of inertia and gravity in his General Theory of Relativity. The General Theory postulated the curvature of empty space, then endowing empty space with physical properties. It was further postulated that the path bodies followed in gravitational fields were paths that followed the curvature of space. This space curvature was produced in varying degrees by the mass-density of bodies in space. The greater the mass-density, the greater the curvature.

Today, Einstein's theories are accepted facts of physics. Experiments have been constructed to test various predictions of his theories, and mathematical analysis of the results of these tests have tended to verify the predictions extrapolated from Einstein's theories within experimental margins of error. Or so we are told.

Today physics has escaped its earth-bound experimental basis and has soared into realms of exotic mathematical theories. One of these mathematical theories has become known as String theory. Essentially, String theory postulates that particles can be described as more than zero-dimensional points; they can be conceived as one-dimensional strings that vibrate in a number of modes. These modes determine the mass and characteristics of the particle under study. String theory is not a theory that experimentalists can rush in and test in order to falsify or verify predictions. In fact, String theory has its skeptics and is not as widely accepted as a Theory of Everything.

ALIEN MAGIC by William Hamilton

There have been many Theories of Everything proposed in the last decade of theoretical physics. One theory was called Supergravity. It, too, is a highly complex mathematical theory. Many of these Unified theories invoke mathematical constructs involving from 5, 10, and 21 dimensions. In String theory, some of the dimensions, beyond the three known dimensions of space, are said to be rolled up, or compactified, into dimensions below the Planck length, an inconceivably small and immeasurable length. In other words, we could never detect or perceive these other dimensions in our universe because they never expanded into the real world. Such a hypothesis goes beyond testability. Have we somehow gotten off the right track in physics and gone into an ever-increasing black hole of ignorance?

Theoretical physicists tend to be vain folks who believe that they can evolve answers for everything. Of course, not all of them fit this trait. They will expound at length on speculative fantasies such as rotating worm holes and time travel, but shun the real world physics of flying saucers. Amazing!

Only recently, and outside the world of academically approved physics, have physicists postulated the existence of something beyond the material world. If we cannot sense it, measure it, or experience it, then it does not exist. One of the characteristics of the world discovered by science is its measurability. But, how do we measure the breadth and sweep of an idea? How do you measure the power of love? There are experiences that humans have in the material world that transcend the limits imposed by material spaces and masses. What space do we occupy in a dream? How fast is a speeding thought?

When we take into account the existence and presence of real aliens and how they operate in our world, then the boundaries of our science seem too narrow to accommodate the expanded view of an alien reality.

There are many scientific mysteries to contemplate when contemplating the alien presence in our world. First, there is the mystery of their origin. Are aliens extraterrestrial beings who travel from another planet in another solar system across the vast uncrossable gulf of space to our planet? If so, how do they cross such vast distances and arrive in the numbers accounted for by sightings and encounters? Or, are aliens visitors from another dimension of space and time, a dimension as close as the next room, but invisible and intangible and undetectable by our normal senses and instruments? If so, how do they cross over the dimensional barriers or gulfs that separate them from our world? Is there a third possibility for the origin of aliens, one which we have not yet conceived of?

First, let us address the problem of alien origin.

From the averaging of voluminous pages of reports concerning aliens, we can arrive at the tentative conclusion that most aliens are biological entities, especially those who have been retrieved from saucer crashes. Although the Roswell craft was not a conventional saucer-shaped craft, we mean to include other categories under the generic term "saucer." The reports indicate that these beings have appendages similar, but not identical to our own. Long fingers that curl and bend to grasp instruments is definitely a function of biological creatures. The most prominent feature of aliens are their eyes. In many cases, the true alien eye seems to be shielded by a filter or covering that is black and almond-shaped. When irises have been seen, they are described as cat-like except in the case of the human-like alien. Nose and ears seem like vestiges of those organs. It is even possible that some of the Grey aliens do not employ sexual, but asexual reproduction.

Biological entities are known to arise from biologically-conducive environments. Since these entities arrive in metallic craft, it is perfectly deducible that these entities are probably extraterrestrial and originate from an extraterrestrial environment. The type of biologically-conducive conditions that may exist in a region or zone in a solar system is known as the ecosphere or ecozone. Astronomers have determined that the ecozone for our own solar system is confined to a narrow band that only includes Earth and Mars. In the search for extraterrestrial life, we are confined to searching for ecozones around sun-like stars. Our sun is classed as a G-type star in the stellar spectral classification system. Out of a survey of 166 G-type stars in the sun's neighborhood, only 18 percent are non-binary stars with possible planetary systems. If the binaries are separated by enough distance, it might not be a hindrance to the formation of a planetary orbit within an ecozone.

Not only have protoplanetary discs been discovered around other stars, at least 7 since 1983, but evidence of a planetary system has been discovered around a pulsar, an extremely unlikely find. A pulsar is a burned out neutron star. Previous thinking envisioned the exploding shell of the neutron star blowing away any orbiting planets. If planets do surround neutron stars, it makes the existence of planetary systems more probable than previously thought.

It is even considered possible that satellites revolving around massive planets could favor the development of life on the satellite.

Even when life is possible on a planet, various conditions involving the sun's stability, the planet's stability and climate make it possible for higher forms of life to arise. The unique hypothesis offered by some Ufologists is that life is cultivated and tended by higher life forms that preceded the development of higher forms of life on a planet. In other words, humans did not just evolve on earth as a consequence of natural selection, but by intervention and cultivation. If this happens elsewhere, then it can accelerate the seeding of life and its subsequent cultivation on many worlds throughout the universe. The Extraterrestrial Cultivation Hypothesis changes our view of developing life in the universe.

Planets orbiting on the edge of solar ecozones may not have the right climatic, geological, and biological balance for the development of intelligent species. However, with the aid of terraforming, planetary engineering, advanced biological technology, and other factors, a race of cultivators could alter the conditions of a planet to favor the development of life and intelligent species. It could instruct the fledgling species on hunting and agriculture. It could teach it the basics, then let its development take a natural course, only to intervene when the survival of the new species is threatened.

As we consider this scenario, we must also consider that other alien races may come into conflict with one race of cultivators, having different intentions, and may try to interfere with the watchers of one race to impose their own designs on that race. Such a situation may be what has arisen on Earth today. This would also account for the covert and secretive activities of these visitors.

Since the cultivators would have traveled from their own home world a long time ago, then it is also conceivable that they would set up bases of operation in order to carry out their long range plans. They could set up such bases of operation on the moon, under the earth, and underwater. Most of the craft seen out on midnight cruises could emanate from these bases of operation. These entities would have actually lived on Earth for millennia, watching over our development with a minimum of interference except where they deemed it necessary. Their purpose would be to insure the long-term survival of the most able and adaptive intelligent races for purposes that go beyond our immediate knowledge. Species who do not clash in purpose may form alliances and societies that encompass large areas of space.

Taking into account the wide range of types of encounters, there is an additional dimension that can be added to our hypothesis. Some of these entities seem to emanate from different dimensions of existence than our familiar world. They have found a way to cross over from their level of existence to ours. It is as if the universe had hundreds of television channels. The life we are familiar with is playing out on one particular channel and we are unaware of the drama and comedy that plays out on other channels.

UFO and alien behavior such as their sudden appearances and disappearances or passing through solid barriers has provoked thinking about a multidimensional universe. Our universe as we know it could be embedded within a larger invisible structure that we could term the Hyperuniverse which could have the configuration of a Hypersphere. Another possibility, one often discussed by spiritualists, is the hypothesis that universes exist in different bands or frequencies of vibration. Neither one of these concepts has been clarified and reduced to a mathematical theory capable of predictions. In order to comprehend the existence of such mysterious universes, we need to return to the concepts of a Unified Field Theory.

The Hyperuniverse model could be a model developed from standard theory. If we looked at a cross-section of the hypersphere, it would reveal 3-dimensional spheres nested within a 4-dimensional space. The fourth dimension could be extended as it is in relativity or compactified as it is in String theory. The thickness of our universe in the fourth dimension would not exceed the Planck length (L=Gh/C3)/2. Another spherical universe would be separated from ours at a length greater than the Planck length and would not share any points of intersection with our own universe.

It is interesting to note that a fourth dimension of space can be transformed into a dimension having the property of a negative time vector. For instance, an electron can be transformed into a positron by time reversal. The positron then exhibits mirror symmetry with the electron. The same transformation of an electron into a positron can be accomplished by rotating the electron around a fourth dimensional axis.

The properties of each of the universes in a Hyperuniverse are dependent on the values of the specific physical constants in that universe, such as the Gravitational constant, or the speed of light. It has been noted by others that the universe-specific time frequency may be altered by the Gravitational constant or Planck's constant. We could have a time spectrum across universes.

Perhaps Einstein's theories contain flaws that have lead us to construct pseudo-universes based on the principles and mathematics of relativity. It is the physical interpretation of the mathematics that is uncertain in the theories of relativity, rather than the mathematical formulations. Perhaps the Hyperuniverse is a set of universes separated by time domains instead of spatial vectors.

The fourth dimension has been used to explain paranormal phenomena. It is supposed that an apparition appears by temporarily moving through our three dimensions along a fourth-dimensional axis. If a three-dimensional ball passed through a two-dimensional plane, it would be seen, if examined from all sides, as an expanding and contracting circle.

In order to comprehend an alternative theory, let us re-examine some of the postulates of relativity that may need revision.

For many years now scientists have rejected the idea of material speeds greater than the measured velocity of light. This rejection has been used as the basis for ruling out the possibility of faster-than-light (FTL) space travel and has been used to negate theories concerning visiting extraterrestrial spacecraft. The light velocity barrier is derived from ideas presented by Einstein in his Special Theory of Relativity (STR). It is herein proposed that there is a fundamental error in the analysis of this theory that has led to the an erroneous conclusion; that the velocity of light is fixed and invariant with respect to any frame of reference. With respect to the measuring platform, light appears to travel at a constant velocity, but not with respect to other moving frames or an absolute frame such as the Cosmic Background Radiation.

Einstein assigns Cartesian coordinate systems to rigid bodies. The rigid body then becomes useful as a measuring rod. Einstein postulates that all physical measurements depend on physical measuring rods. Marks on rigid measuring rods will not alter their position with respect to each other. In later considering this postulate, Einstein concludes that no ideal rigid measuring rod exists. For instance, a rod could expand or contract depending on temperature. Instead of Einstein's rigid rod, we could substitute a specific wavelength of laser light as a reliable means of measuring length.

Imagine coordinate system K fixed to some position on the moving Earth. The length x in coordinate system K is measured to be 100 meters. Some distance from coordinate system K is coordinate system K' fixed to a moving spacecraft which has a velocity of .9C (90% of the speed of light in vacuo). Spacecraft K' has a length x' = x. In accordance with the STR, if x' is parallel to the direction of motion of K', then x' is contracted in its length by the Lorentz transform:

$$x' = x - vt2/ /1-v/c2$$

which is computed to have contracted to a length of 56.41123 meters from the frame of reference of rod K in which the translational velocity (vt) has been subtracted from x, the length of our measuring rod. Since Einstein's principle of relativity allows us to occupy either frame, K or K', then the contraction is an illusion dependent on the occupied frame.

The Michaelson-Morley experiment was designed to measure the absolute motion of the Earth through a stationary ether. The M-M experiment made use of an interferometer, a device that measures the amount of interference between two beams of light. The interferometer has four critical points. A beam of light from some suitable source (S) is split into two beams by a partially silvered mirror (A) with one beam deflected at 90 degrees to a second mirror (B) and the other beam directed at 0 degrees to a third mirror (C). The beam from mirror B is now reflected through A to a detector (D) and the beam from mirror C is deflected 90 degrees by mirror A and is also sent to the detector D.

The distances of paths within the interferometer are such that AB = AC = AD = SA, or SC = BD. Thus, it is reasoned that if a beam of light of a specific color is emitted at S and travels along equal path lengths and arrives at D in phase, then it is concluded that the beam has traveled at the same identical velocity along the paths SC-CD and SB-BD. Something that travels equal distances in equal times is equal in velocity.

If the whole rig were a car traveling down a freeway, and a gun were fired from the car to a reflecting target set at 90 degrees to the motion of the car, and one set at an equal distance ahead of the car, we could say that the bullets have equal velocities as they arrived back at a detector on the car at the same time. The bullet aimed at the wind would be retarded in its forward velocity to the reflector, but advanced in its velocity on its return to the detector. Relative to a coordinate system on the ground, the bullets would not have traveled equal distances. Relative to the ether, the light beams would not have traveled equal distances.

In other words, the velocity of light is not a limiting velocity as it is a velocity that can never be approached by a moving system. The velocity of light is a medium-dependent velocity. The Michaelson_morley experiment did not rule out the existence of a non-material medium suffusing all of space.

Physicists Walter Greiner and Joseph Hamilton asked if the vacuum is really empty, and concluded that the vacuum has the properties of a polarizable medium. Rene Descartes (1596-1650) used the term "aether" to name the elementary substance that filled all space, the one substance from which all substances are composed as stated in the ancient tradition of the hermetic sciences. It was the universal medium for the transmission of force.

Einstein discarded the notion of an ether after the Michaelson-Morley experiment. Since that time scientists have been filling empty space with everything from a neutrino sea to a sea of electrons and anti-electrons.

Einstein's theory of gravity invokes the curvature of space. The bending of starlight by the sun's gravity at a specific angle is said to verify Einstein's theory that light is influenced by gravity and is bent out of line by following the curvature of space caused by the sun's mass. Physicists have concluded that space must be extremely rigid, millions of times more rigid than steel. Rigidity is a property of solids. Dense solids are extremely rigid and difficult to bend. On the other hand, quantum physicist envision space as a foam of energetic quantum events, bubbling and frothing with energy. These two concepts seem to be in conflict.

If we attempt a thought experiment, similar to models that are supposed to depict the action of gravity, we can uncover a basic flaw in the curvature idea. Say that we placed a bowling ball on a rubber sheet and it causes a dimple to appear on the sheet. This dimple represents a gravitational field. A real gravitational field would supposedly be dimpled in 4-space. We roll a golf ball so that it will pass around the bowling ball on the rubber sheet. The golf ball will be deflected by the dimple in the same way that a meteor could be deflected from its path by the gravitational field of a planet. The golf ball will follow a curved path. So far, so good. However, in our demonstration, we have attributed the dimple or depression in the rubber sheet to an invisible force that presses the bowling ball against the rubber. The golf ball seems to accelerate because of this force. We have removed the curvature by one dimension, and yet attribute gravitational acceleration to curvature. Curvature may define a path, but it cannot exert a force! This is apparently a hard concept to grasp. One of the attributes of gravity is the production of acceleration. Even if we roll a ball down an incline, it is not the incline that accelerates the ball. The incline could be placed in free-fall, and the ball on the incline would not move. There must be a force that moves the ball.

An alternative theory is that the Universe is filled with an energy-medium and that this energy-medium produces the elementary forces due to various states of the medium. If the medium increases its pressure and density when in contact with mass, then that pressure is experienced as gravity. The change in density of the medium could refract a ray of light. The medium could have a fundamental vibration that we call time. Different rates of vibration could produce different density variations in the Universe. Life might exist at a different frequency level.

Indian physicist Paramhamsa Tewari postulates the existence of the substantial space medium and postulates that the medium does not contain the properties of mass, inertia, density, discreteness, compressibility or viscosity. He further postulates that voids can be produced when the medium, moving like a fluid, forms vortices and that such vortices are the basis of our elementary particles.

My view is that the etheric medium behaves in a manner similar to a superfluid and forms quantum vortices, solitons, and waves that give rise to the material forces and particles. The static pressurized state of the medium is what is interpreted as gravity in this view, while a dynamic state such as a vortex gives rise to electromagnetic fields. Space-time craft could tunnel through the universal medium at virtually unlimited rates of travel and vary their vibratory rates of time.

That our three-dimensional space may contain a superfluid does not preclude the idea that it may extend into a hyperspatial fourth dimension.

This chapter offers alternative hypotheses to account for space travel, time travel, and the appearance of alien life forms in our world. Thus we could postulate that some of the alien life forms coming to earth come from hyperdimensional spaces. They pass into and out of our world like the mysterious balls that pass through a plane surface and are seen as changing circles. There may be much more living space than we have accounted for in our survey of the universe. We live on the brink of a new world of discovery.

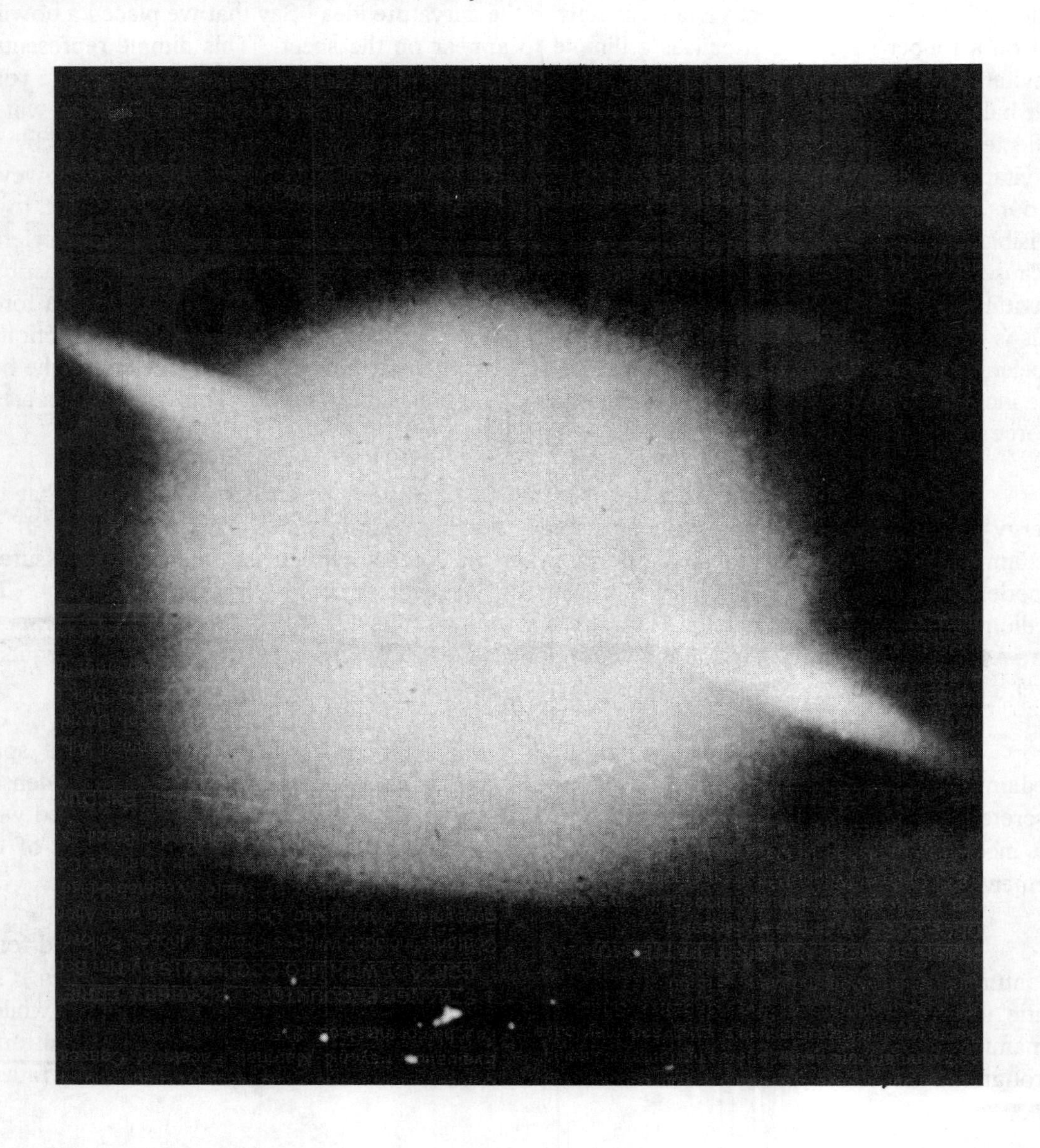

CHAPTER THIRTEEN
ALIEN AGENDAS

"Our universe is vastly more mysterious than science has grasped. There are no accidents in the universe. I believe there is a cosmic plan for us and this belief is based on facts not on faith."
- Allen Spraggett

If one reviews the literature on UFOs going back forty-five years, a number of alien forms have been described by witnesses. It seems amazing that the majority of these forms are humanoid in appearance. A few monsters have been reported such as the Flatwoods, West Virginia monster encountered in 1952. Most of the aliens fall roughly into three categories: Dwarves; Normals; and Giants.

Dwarf-like entities are the most frequently reported usually between .7 and 1.3 meters in height. They are usually reported to have large craniums and large eyes. Their skin is of various colors. Grey or Grey-blue is just one of the common hues reported.

Normals are human in appearance. Sometimes they are referred to as Nordic. They may range from 1.5 to 2.5 meters (around 8 feet tall). Their skin is described as white, tan, brown, or fair. Some have been seen with white hair. Others have golden-blonde hair. There are some with sandy, brown, or black hair. At least 83 witnesses (perhaps more) have described a class of human that looked like the classic Adamski-type between 1952 and 1968. Since 1968, many abductees have reported seeing Nordic-like humans in flight suits that are reminiscent of the earlier types.

Giants have ranged to heights above ten feet. Most of these are also human looking.

Greys and Tans fit into the dwarf category, but are not similar to the early dwarf-like beings that were seen. Some of the smaller types had hair and human-like features. Greys have been described ranging from 3 feet to 6 feet in height with oversized heads and large elliptical eyes. The eyes usually have a black covering. Their limbs are long and gangly. Their skin has been described as smooth to scaly. Most of these have hands that terminate in four digits with no thumb. Sometimes webbing spans the digits or the digits end in suction cups. There are no ear lobes. There are nostrils, but no nose. The mouth is described as a small slit. A grey type has white skin and five digits on the hands. There are apparently many variations of these types.

The Nordics fall into the Normal and Giant category. The early Nordics had extremely fine features, symmetrical faces, and penetrating eyes. ~~They use speech and telepathy.~~ Some can articulate their fingers backward. Eye colors vary and may be blue, green, or grey with silver or gold flecking. There seems to be an irresistible kinship with these types as they mostly resemble Earth humans and can converse with us on a more comprehensible basis.

Reptilians range from 5 feet to 8 feet in height and are rather imposing. Their scale color seems to be dark grey or black, but some are green. The large reptilian is described as massively built with a large chest cavity. Their irises usually appear to be amber with rose-colored pupils that seem to glow in the dark. Their mouth is large and they have teeth. The communicate using telepathy, but have been heard to make a hissing sound. Despite their dreadful appearance, little is known about their motives. Female abductees have reported having sexual encounters with the Reptilian which usually dominates the human female.

Insectoids have been witnessed. The most common is the Praying Mantis. Their agenda is unknown. They have appeared in company with Greys.

A few robots have been described. They appear to have mechanical movements.

Alien life forms associated with UFO contact are many and varied, but all have a recognizable anatomical structure that resembles, but does not match those seen as native Earth life - two eyes, two arms, and two legs with a large brain case. The evolutionary trend of intelligent, artifact-making life forms seems to follow a similar pattern. The variety of alien life forms contain features that are not commonly found among the Earth's fauna, but are similar enough that we can relate to them. Their motivations and activities are mysterious. Some of these life forms may have attributes that are superior to homo sapiens. Some may have greater strength or intelligence or a greater range of sensory responses and sensitivity.

Often UFO researchers are asked: Why are they here? Since UFO researchers are not aliens and have to infer alien purposes from the communication and behavior, it is almost impossible to answer the question without breaking it down further. Why is who here? Why are the Greys here? Why are the Reptilians here? Why are the Nordics here? Or maybe, sub-groups of these groupings have different purposes and agendas.

Based on human-alien interaction for nearly a half-century now, we can speculate about why the aliens are here. Not all alien types behave in the same way, and our knowledge of their real motives is rather limited.

Researcher Forest Crawford conducted a study of alien-abductee communications to determine whether these correlated from abductee to abductee. Debbie Jordan repeats some of these questions and the answers she received in her book, "Abducted." In response to the question on how the aliens use light, they replied, "We travel by means of light fusion. We are able to travel great distances using this power." On questions concerning the nature of God, the aliens replied that God is life, that God is spirit, and that God is the life essence of the universe.

The Greys have not communicated at length with individual abductees during the abduction procedure, but they seem to pick another time to communicate thoughts to their abductees. The Greys have shown abductees scenes of future catastrophes. They seem to be warning the abductees that great changes will be coming to the Earth. Some researchers are puzzled by these warnings and feel that the Greys are only testing the emotional responses of humans to scenes of destruction, but why?

The Agenda of the abducting entities seems to be revealed in the procedures they use with abductees. They have taken hair samples, skin samples, sperm samples, blood samples, and ovum from females. One hypothesis is that they are attempting to cross-breed with humans, and, indeed, abductees report seeing hybrid creatures that could be the product of such cross-breeding. This would be a long-term genetic program to produce a variation in species. Critics have brought up the fact that there is a lack of evidence for abductee hybrid pregnancies, and that an extraterrestrial race would most likely differ enough in its DNA to prohibit cross-breeding. While this is a possibility, we lack enough information on alien DNA or alien biotechnology to make a decisive determination.

It has always been assumed by scientists that if we were to make contact with extraterrestrials through radio waves that they would send us messages encoded in the language of mathematics. In the movie Close Encounters, communication with ETs utilized another universal language, that of music. All of these hypothetical communications are based on certain naive assumptions, not the least of which is that no prior contact with or study of earth humans has occurred.

If we make a study of reported contacts with UFO entities, the actual situation is quite different. They do not seem to experience the slightest trouble in communicating with the contactee. Betty Hill could hear the thoughts of the leader as if spoken out loud when he asked her questions about Barney's teeth. She, in turn, could understand him when he replied to her question as to their origin and then showed her a star chart.

Some of the early contactee messages from ETs should be re-examined in light of the messages received by today's abductees. The contactees were also told of future catastrophes by the ETs. In fact, there is a remarkable similarity in the content of these messages.

For instance, an ET known as Alan told Daniel Fry, "You have a personal duty and responsibility to cooperate in the efforts our people are making to help your people on earth to alter their present flow of events, and avert the holocaust which is otherwise inevitable."

Alan also said, "If we were to appear as members of a superior race...tens of millions of your people...would go to any conceivable length to disprove or deny our existence. About thirty percent of these people would consider us as gods and would attempt to place upon us all responsibility for their own welfare...the remaining seventy percent would consider us potential tyrants who were planning to enslave the world, and many would begin to seek to destroy us."

."..you must realize that any information which your government might acquire concerning us, our craft, or our knowledge, would be considered the most vital 'military' secret they had ever possessed."

Alan also said, "unless some means are found to stimulate the growth of the spiritual and social sciences on your earth, a time will inevitably come when your emphasis on those matters which are material instead of spiritual will cause your civilization to collapse. Ruin and destruction will then be brought to both the spiritual and social side of your civilization. This collapse has occurred before on your planet and your civilization has now entered the stage where it is likely to occur again."

The infamous George Adamski repeated this message from the Nordic travelers he encountered, "we could tell you much about the control of gravity, knowledge that is necessary for safe leaving or approaching another planet...if we revealed this power to you or to any Earth man and it became public knowledge, some of your people would quickly build ships for space traveling, mount guns upon them and go on a shooting spree in an attempt to conquer and take possession of other worlds." They further stated, ."..our purpose in coming to you at this time is to warn you of the grave danger which threatens men of Earth today...the exploding of bombs on Earth was of interest to us...even though the power and radiation from the test explosions have not yet gone out beyond your Earth's sphere of influence, these radiations are endangering the life of men on Earth.

Contactee Orfeo Angelucci was told, "Among the countless worlds in the cosmos, Orfeo, the children of Earth are as babes, although many of them believe they are close to the ultimate of knowledge. Among the worlds of the universe are many types of spiritual and physical evolutions. Each form of intelligent life adapts itself to the physical conditions prevalent upon its home planet. Most of these evolutions exist in *more highly attenuated forms of matter than upon Earth.* But the majority are rather similar to man in appearance. There is a definite reason for this being so." Neptune also told Orfeo, "the days that are to come to Earth are known to me, but they are as yet mercifully veiled from you and from your fellows. This I can tell you: the hour of tragedy is close on Earth...wide devastation, suffering and the death of many will result from it...there is still a chance to avert the War of Desolation for in the Time Dimension nothing is absolute."

Lest you think that the messages of the contactees were confabulations, even though they foreshadowed those being received by today's abductees, then compare the following message received by abductee Bill Hermann of South Carolina who was contacted by little humanoids from Zeta Reticuli-2. This message was received on January 27, 1982 and says in part:
"the ages of years needed to render the civilizations productive and passive in the strata of universal comity are therefore insured to become manifest...those in upper level membership continue to abdicate hostility and self-aggressive inherent attitudes of warishness. Technology must serve to advance the race, not be the means of terminating the race. Knowledge and information attained through the area of research must be ingrained within the whole society, and not hidden within those who would seek to usurp the levels of power away from those given position through the spectrum of the civilization and society involved." They also said further, "It is hoped, though improbable, that radical change will come in time to save the planet from its own death at the hands of its own inhabitants...in retrospect, it was decided by the Network to select various individuals from among the sociological spectrum, inculcate the existence of the Network, and give the masses the ability to attempt to influence the radical change needed to avoid the

eventual *holocaust.* This selective process and change is currently underway. It is hoped that time will not run out before change occurs."

Are we seeing that change now? Are the events in Eastern Europe and the Soviet Union in the year of 1990 now headed in a direction that has been guided by extraterrestrial visitors?

ETs have stated to many of their contactees that they are aligned in groups, networks, organizations, alliances, and confederations that encompass thousands of planetary civilizations that share knowledge and technology.

LYA, a beautiful Nordic extraterrestrial contacted Professor Hernandez of Mexico in 1972 and told him of a cosmic community of civilizations. She said, "you still have a place in the Galaxy. The civilizations that survive acquire a place by right...too many wars, professor, have filled the fields of battle with blood...the first universal law is knowledge...you are destroying your own habitat...but you, yourselves, are the only ones capable of changing this."

These friendly extraterrestrials have warned us that other extraterrestrials travel space and come to Earth for selfish and evil purposes, yet they have continued to point out that our greatest threat is from ourselves, that we must learn how to control our minds and emotions, increase our understanding of each other, and evolve into a peaceful and more spiritually evolved society before we can join the galactic community. We have learned to distrust such messages, yet if we consider our own fateful actions, then it becomes a logical necessity that we act on our own behalf to make positive changes in our world. Our path is clear. The responsibility for the future of our planet is in our hands.

CHAPTER FOURTEEN
ALIEN MAGIC

"A Sufficiently advanced technology is indistinguishable from magic" - Arthur C. Clark

The Alien technology seems miraculous. The aliens can appear and disappear at will. Abductees have reported seeing the aliens come through closed doors, windows, and walls. They read minds and instill thoughts in the minds of humans. Their craft perform incredible maneuvers, levitate, hover, pass through solid barriers, change shape, and other magical feats.

One of the strangest abductions on record happened to Corporal Armando Valdes on April 25, 1977 when an oval-shaped UFO descended and hovered near a secret Chilean Army post at Pampa Lluscoma, close to the Bolivian border. Corporal Valdes went to investigate a violet light that suddenly appeared at 3:50 A.M. When the corporal returned in 15 minutes, his mind was blank, his calendar watch had advanced by 5 days and he had a sudden, five-day growth of beard on his face! What happened? Could Corporal Valdes have literally moved five days ahead in time while the rest of the world only passed through 15 minutes? Corporal Valdes appears to have aged faster than his fellow soldiers. His biological clock was advanced over that of his compatriots.

If the oscillators we call clocks measure local time based on some standard periodic oscillator, such as the vibration of a cesium atom, or the circuit of the Earth around the sun, then these oscillators may be restricted by the density of the spatial medium. If strong gravity fields are indicative of denser spatial mediums, then we would expect to find clocks, pendulums, and oscillators to be retarded by denser mediums. Protons accelerated by synchrotrons are retarded as their velocity increases, experiencing a form of "drag" in high-speed motion. The same sort of drag would be experienced in strong gravity fields. If oscillators are moving at higher than normal rates of speed, then it could indicate an attenuation of the local medium. Inside the field of a saucer, nullification of gravity and attenuation of the local medium could lead to faster rates of time. Instead of time dilation, we would have a condition that can be described as time compression. Yet, Corporal Valdes may have experienced five days of missing time from his point of view.

Orbs have been reported by many abductees. These orbs can appear as very bright light sources. Pamela saw them move through closed screen doors and walls in her house. They made no sound as they passed. The light from the orbs does not seem to reflect off surrounding surfaces. Brian Scott said he could not see a reflection of an orb in the mirror that it passed.

ALIEN MAGIC by William Hamilton

An article in *Science Digest* relates an experiment that scientists conducted with a monoatomic gas. The scientists used a laser of a fixed frequency to inhibit the processes of photon absorption in the gas. Another laser pierced the gas completely without being absorbed. The gas had become completely transparent to the laser. Scientists saw no reason why they could not escalate this process and shine light through a solid barrier.

The orbs must be using a process of light emission that negates absorption or reflection. Either all of the rays that emanate from the orb are absorbed, and none reflected, or they bypass all molecular barriers. Light beams from UFOs have been seen to bend along the path of the beam. This bend could be caused by a boundary layer that surrounds the UFO, a boundary that is created by its gravity field, that causes a change in atmospheric density causing the light to refract at the boundary layer interface. In one particular case the beam from a UFO penetrated the hood of a car, and the witness could see the engine of the car through the otherwise opaque hood. This suggests that they are able to cause light to pass through solids or change the frequency of light at interfaces. The light would upshift to the X-ray band and downshift to the light band.

An abductee by the name of Janet awoke at four in the morning to see tall entities with bright lights pass through the locked sliding glass doors of the second-floor balcony of her apartment. They announced that what they had to do would not take long; then she blacked out and awoke two hours and forty-five minutes later. She found marks on her body and her finger nails clipped.

Ozzie mentioned that he had seen an alien pass through a wall at the early Groom Lake complex. The alien carried a little black box that he referred to as an "augmenter." Could this box have been a device that assisted the alien to pass through the wall? If so, it must have changed the material density of the alien, or the wall! It is possible that the aliens use a device that can change the material properties of the barrier they are passing through.

Another possibility is that when changing their rate of vibration, they are changing the density of atomic structure. A solid wall may appear as dense as fog. It is interesting to note that some of the phenomena noted here has been noted by parapsychologists in reference to apparitions that appear and disappear or pass through doors and walls. People who report out-of-body experiences also report passing through walls in a tenuous replica of the human body. Do the aliens have knowledge of this and have they learned to control it?

Carol reported the "materialization" of books in the craft. Later she saw a ghost car. How do the aliens perform this feat of magic? The books were not just an image as we see in a hologram, but had the real feel of books. It was as if she were on the holodeck of the Starship Enterprise in the Next Generation. Holodeck matter is projected within a certain area and has the appearance and feel of the real thing, but is transitory and dissolves back into its matrix.

Pamela once saw the shadow of a Grey against the wall of her dining room. This was fascinating. She could not see its body, but only its shadow. I surmised that if the entity were bending the path of light rays around his body, then the rays did not have the space to converge again, leaving a shadow projected against the wall.

In theory, the aliens' magic is compounded of at least two factors: their advanced consciousness, and their advanced knowledge of the physics of the universe. We, ourselves, have experimented with psychotronic devices that enhance the latent powers of our mind to move objects or see events at remote points. With the alien's knowledge of telepathy and precognition, it is likely that they have made great advances in psychotronic technology. Psychotronics is the linking of mind with machine. It provides us with a model of the universe, a great machine housing an even greater mind. This linking together extends the power of the mind beyond the body. The mind senses messages from beyond the normal ranges of the senses, then extends its control over a greater part of the environment beyond the perimeter of a body. When primitive people witnessed this kind of control, they called it **magic.**

There is little doubt that the aliens have demonstrated their control over gravity and electromagnetic forces. They could bring this technology to bear on destructive purposes and render us helpless if they chose to do so. In the few cases where the aliens have nullified our electrical devices or caused airplanes to disintegrate, we have seen little in the way of weaponry or weapon use otherwise. The aliens just do not fit the Hollywood mold. They have not come to earth with blazing rays to level our cities and take the land. Instead, they have quietly invaded our homes and examined our people. Their motives are mysterious and their actions like magic.

It is important to remember that someday, we may be the aliens and travel to other worlds in space and time for purposes beyond our present ken. To the natives, our technology will appear to be magical. For now, the future is close at hand. Tomorrow, the aliens will seem common place. Our culture is changing. We are changing. We are simultaneously heading toward crisis and transformation.

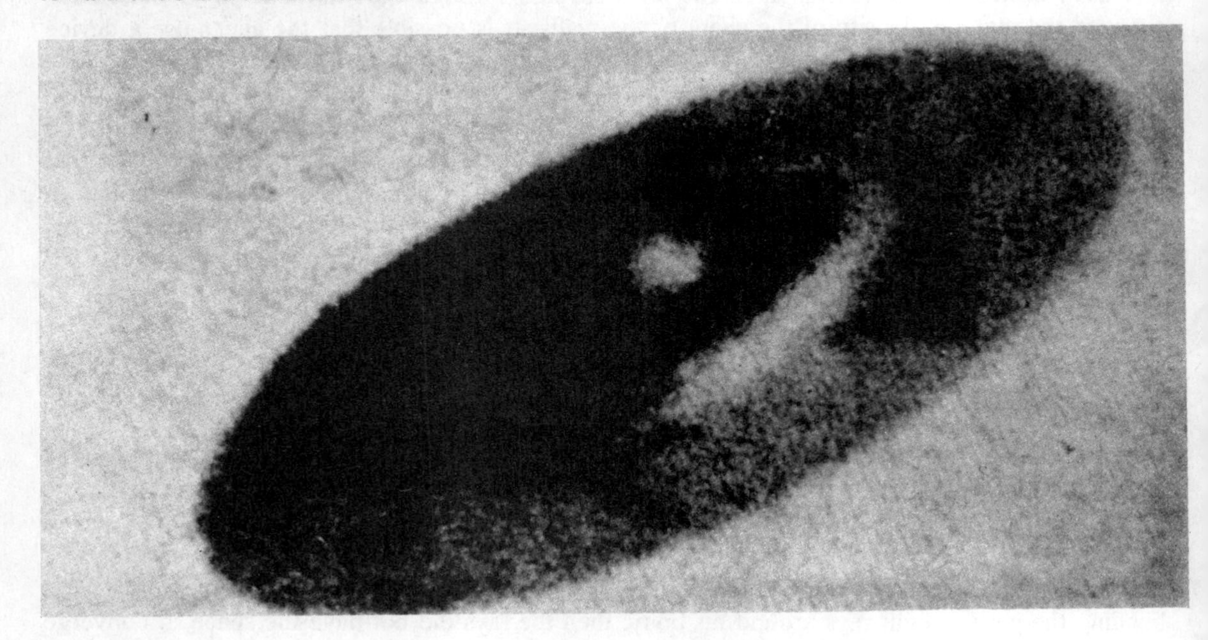

EPILOGUE

The quest for aliens continues. We have come a long way from the early sightings and stories of contact to a new era of abductions and Cosmic Watergates. We are waiting for the cover-up on the Roswell crash to end. Some think it will come to an end and we will receive official word from our government that the aliens and their ships are real and it has been kept as a high level secret for years.

Recently, the Santilli alien autopsy film was shown on Fox television. This caused quite a stir. The presentation called upon experts to judge the authenticity of the film. Experts in one particular area would disagree about some element in the film. Special effects experts believe that if the film was hoaxed, it was a quality job. Some believe that the alien in the film is a specially fabricated dummy. Others believe that it is a deformed human corpse. Still others are willing to call the being non-human. According to the pathologists called upon to render an opinion, the organs viewed in the film are not human, but they will not speculate on what type of being the six-fingered, six-toed creature represents.

Early reports represented the film footage as associated with the famous Roswell incident. Statements given later by the cameraman who took the footage indicate that the crash site was near Socorro, New Mexico on June 1, 1947, more than a month before the Roswell crash. Roswell researchers have almost been uniform in their rejection of this film as authentic evidence of an alien crash-retrieval event. One researcher objected because the creatures resembled humans so closely, and biologists believe that human-like life will only be found on earth because of the unique conditions found on earth that resulted in the evolution of the human life form. We have seen that contactees and abductees have reported encounters with varieties of human-like life forms contrary to apriori beliefs.

The judgment on the alien autopsy film is not final. It may never be final. Researchers and scientists ask for proof when evidence that contradicts their paradigm is offered in favor of a competing paradigm. The alien autopsy film has raised public interest. Will the public's interest be raised enough to demand the truth from their government?

Laurence Rockefeller has held meetings with Ufologists. The 85-year-old philanthropist attended Bill Clinton's 49th birthday party. Rockfeller has been pushing for the Clinton administration to put an end to the government secrecy on the subject of UFOs, and especially the crash of an extraterrestrial vehicle at Roswell in 1947.

Perhaps the aliens want to come out in the open. Perhaps there is a secret war going on. There is a lot of speculation in the absence of knowledge. People are wary of misinformation and disinformation. All we want is the plain truth. Are we ready for the truth? I think we are.

ALIEN MAGIC by William Hamilton

We have been exposed to almost five decades of science fiction. The Star Trek generation has reached its adult years. Our troubles on earth have not vanished or lessened, but have shifted from one focus to another. We are now prepared to accept extraterrestrial beings. Many of us who have spent years making a study of UFOs have long passed the acceptance point.

We must repair the damage that we have done to the Earth. We must also repair the damage we have done to our economy and society. We must solve our earthly problems if we are to survive as a successful species and we must bring new life to our space program knowing that others are out there. We have seen the evidence that our moon and the planet Mars contain features that appear to be ancient alien artifacts. That will eventually prove that aliens have been here for a long time. Now it is time for us to acknowledge their presence and openly meet with them.

Perhaps many have not stopped to think of the knowledge that we would gain from open communication with other intelligent species in the cosmos. We all want to know more about the origin of life. Have other races of beings come to earth with seeds of our beginnings? How are we related to these others? How did the universe begin? With a big bang? Are there other universes beside the one we feel is visible and tangible? Are there gateways to these other places?

There is also technical knowledge to be gained. We know the military has learned that lesson, but has the general public? There are those, like the Unabomber, that feel that technology has contributed to the degeneration of our society and has caused us untold grief. Others see technology as a savior, the way we might perceive a new miracle drug. The truth is that technology is usually designed to accomplish some purpose, whether that purpose is for the public good or not. When that technology goes into wide use, it can also be abused. An example of this in this day and age, is the computer. The computer was designed as a tool for the mind, to amplify the way we perform data-processing tasks. It has been abused by hackers and marketers to invade our private lives. It has the potential for great abuse by powerful governments. This is the stuff of science-fiction nightmares. In the seventies, research had begun on a mind-reading computer. A helmet with electrodes is attached to the head to pick up brain waves. The brain waves take on certain patterns dictated by the phonemes (parts of speech) which, in turn, are interpreted by a special-purpose computer. Such a helmet has been developed and used in the laboratories of Wright-Patterson AFB to enable a pilot to send mental commands to a jet airplane. Disabled people could use this system to pilot and navigate wheel chairs. Early articles on these mind-reading computers mentioned neurocybernetic loops. Information could not only be sent to the computer by a human mind, but received from a computer by the human mind. The mind-reading computers are not science fiction. They have been used in laboratory experiments.

Some experiencers have reported seeing the aliens guide their ships by mental commands. The aliens have developed mind-reading computers long ago. The aliens are not hindered by language considerations. They have communicated with contactees in the contactee's own language. It is possible that all sorts of inter-species communication is possible through the use of telepathy and instrumentally-augmented telepathy.

An integral part of the alien's magic are their wonderful craft. I have recounted developments in electrogravitics and the insightful thinkers who have dared to dream of plans for advanced space propulsion systems. The September, 1995 issue of *Popular Mechanics* reveals a craft dreamt up by mechanical engineer Leik Myrabo. Science editor Gregory Pope details how Myrabo's craft would be guided by a beam of microwaves. The beam would create a plasma from the atmosphere around the craft, and powerful magnetic fields generated by the craft would cause the plasma to flow around the periphery of the craft generating thrust. The craft itself has the shape of a fat saucer. Part of the microwave beam is focused ahead of the craft forming an air spike. The cone formed ahead of the leading surface reduces atmospheric drag. The engine concept employed by Myrabo's craft is known as an magnetohydrodynamic (MHD) fanjet. In effect, Myrabo's craft in flight would look like a glowing disc-shaped craft, a typical flying saucer. These kind of developments hint that we are in the process of imitating the alien technology, at least on a primitive level.

Carl Krafft wrote treatises on an ether-vortex theory of matter and seems to have foreseen Myrabo's craft when he considered the antigravitic possibilities of supermatter (a form of plasma) for spaceship propulsion. He wrote, "Its disintegration would liberate large numbers of positive ions which would not only give the entire spaceship a positive charge, but would also propel the spaceship by repulsion from the liberated ions if they are all sent out in one direction." Krafft felt that such a positively charged spaceship would also have an antigravitic action by virtue of the Biefield-Brown effect. He felt that the high potential of the spaceship would reduce the ether pressure on the upper side of the spaceship which would result in a lifting force in direct opposition to the force of gravity. By controlling the field around the craft, it would be possible to keep the spaceship hovering in mid-air or have it move vertically upwards. Such a spacecraft could be moved straight up to orbital altitude, then hover, then vector into an elliptical orbit around the earth.

We have seen that the flying saucer not only gave us inspiration for science fiction, but has given our scientists and engineers inspiration for new designs for spacecraft of the future.

What else could we learn from the aliens? They might know more about the nature of mind and consciousness and whether mind and consciousness survive the transition from life to death. Their very existence challenges the beliefs of our western religions. Science has left the door open for the existence of extraterrestrial life. Likewise, religion has left its door open. All sorts of extraordinary life inhabits the pages of our sacred texts. There are angels and demons. There are classes of angels and demons. They are found in the sacred books of the east and west. Other heavenly worlds are mentioned. Angelic visitors are always pictured as descending from the sky to the earth. Our religious tales may be challenged by the truth of alien visitation if the truth is revealed, but our religions will eventually accommodate this truth. God will only be seen as more wonderful for creating all these diverse life forms and filling the universe or universes with life. Indeed, God would be omnipresent.

Will our daily lives change? When the alien cultures begin to mix openly with our own earth-bound cultures, life will change. The way we work and the way we play may be as different from our modes today as our modes today are different from those just one hundred years ago.

We do a lot of talking and a lot of traveling from place to place. Alien modes of communication and travel may someday become common place to us. It will change us. The one constant in life is change. And we must change for the better. Our survival depends on it.

Can we survive as a species? Can we give birth to a new civilization? Will we someday go where the aliens go? Will we continue to reach for the stars? If anything, the presence of the aliens has stimulated our imagination and has given us hope. We can reach the stars. We can survive. We will live in the future.